PUBLICATIONS IN LI

MW01503720

TRAINING LIBRARY INSTRUCTORS:

VOLUME TWO

A Guide to Training Librarians

Edited by
Matthew Weirick Johnson

Association of College and Research Libraries
A division of the American Library Association

Chicago, Illinois 2024

Contents

VOL 2: A GUIDE TO TRAINING LIBRARIANS

Acknowledgements

These books would quite literally not be possible without the contributions of all of the authors. I'm immensely grateful to all of them for trusting me with their work and for joining me in this journey to publication. Similarly, Erin Nevius from ACRL has been instrumental from the start and a wonderful collaborator and guide. Dawn Mueller has made this book (and so many things at ACRL) beautiful. Thanks to the Publications in Librarianship Editorial Board for their feedback on my initial proposal and the final books.

To me, this is ultimately a book about how librarians build community to help each other succeed. I'm grateful to all of my colleagues at UCLA and the University of South Florida who have helped me succeed. I'm particularly grateful to my biggest supporters, in life and librarianship: Sylvia Page, Salma Abumeeiz, and Hannah Sutherland. There is no one I would rather watch a Christmas movie with than Sylvia, no one I would rather get unicorn lattes with than Salma, and no one I would rather dance all night with than Hannah. I'm grateful to them and to the community of friends and colleagues that we built together in LA.

Finally, I first wrote the proposals for these books in the loft above my parents' house, which I think is the equivalent of starting in their basement or garage since they live in a flood zone. I'm grateful for their perpetual support and feigned interest.

Introduction

Matthew Weirick Johnson

Training Library Instructors, Vol 2: A Guide to Training Librarians continues the work of the first volume, recognizing the value of lifelong learning and the limitations of what can be taught in a two-year master's program. So many librarians value lifelong learning and the opportunity to learn from each other. In this volume, authors share various approaches to learning together, exploring library instruction for the first time, or expanding existing knowledge through continued education.

Librarians share their knowledge about teaching, learning, and pedagogy through a variety of activities, including formal and informal training programs taking the form of workshops, courses, communities of practice, peer observation, and more. Programs involve mock instruction, nano-teaching, and other feedback and homework mechanisms. Programs may provide certificates or be seeking accreditation, may happen at the level of the individual, institution, or consortium, and may involve collaborations across library or university departments.

The case studies in this volume are organized into three categories: continuing training for library instructors, training for new librarians, and training for both new and experienced librarians. These cases provide various approaches to training library instructors from libraries and librarians in China, the United Kingdom, Italy, Canada, and the United States of America.

Chapters on continuing training for library instructors include Caplan and colleagues' discussion of a consortial approach to providing professional development for library instructors, Preest and Sewell's consideration of the development of the Teaching and Learning for Librarians course at the University of Cambridge, and Melissa A. Wong and Laura Saunders' overview of LIS Pedagogy Chat, an online community of practice.

Chapters on training for new librarians include Beem and colleagues' program for training, mentoring, and supporting new library instructors individually and holistically at the University of North Carolina at Charlotte, and Kubicki and colleagues' reflection on their experience changing their library instruction model in response to planned and unplanned changes, such as leadership transitions and a global pandemic.

Chapters that discuss training both new and experienced librarians include Piotto's discussion of the development of their learning outcomes and training program for instruction librarians, Munro and colleagues' chapter about their libraries' collaboration with their Learning and Teaching Support Innovation team to provide professional development for librarians, and Lemmons and colleagues' discussion of a training program for new and experienced library instructors at George Mason University.

All of these cases provide detailed overviews of the learning outcomes and objectives, learning activities, materials used, and the specific conditions and contexts that made the programs possible. There are endless opportunities to mix and match components of each of these programs to develop training that works for different audiences, different contexts, and different institutions.

The volume closes with six reflections from current library instructors about how they developed into their roles. Ginelle Baskin discusses how being introverted impacts her teaching. Mitchell considers the possibilities and opportunities provided by learning together in libraries primarily through peer observation. Russel Peterson also considers peer observation but uses autotheory as a method to inform his reflection. Nicole Westerdahl discusses the value of learning about instructional design for her work as an instructional librarian. Sam Mandani and Fannie Ouyang reflect on an unconference-style workshop they organized to share experiences and build community around doing library instruction. Closing out the primary content for both of these books, Jamia Williams discusses her multiple and varied experiences of receiving mentorship as a library school student and librarian. She discusses the value of mentorship, encourages others to seek out mentorship, and provides strategies for finding mentors.

Training Library Instructors, Vol 2: A Guide to Training Librarians provides a starting point for readers considering their own programs. These chapters present detailed cases with useful appendices, careful reflections, and clearly outlined approaches to training library instructors. The cases presented provide everything that readers need to implement or adapt the training programs discussed, and the reflections provide critical considerations for how we train library instructors.

PART V

CASE STUDIES:
CONTINUING TRAINING FOR LIBRARY INSTRUCTORS

CHAPTER 15

Developing Library Instructors Together:
A Case Study from the Hong Kong JULAC Consortium

Victoria F. Caplan, Christopher Chan, Lisa Janicke Hinchliffe, and Eunice S. P. Wong

LEARNING OUTCOMES

Readers will be able to

- recognize the potential of libraries partnering together in order to arrange and carry out professional development and foster a community of practice;
- build on the "lessons learned" and tips for sharing with their colleagues in-house or with professional colleagues in partnering libraries in order to identify a strategy for developing a training program; and
- adapt activities from this case study to create a meaningful professional development program that supports library instructors.

Introduction

Many university libraries devote considerable effort and resources to the professional development of their staff. This commonly includes supporting conference attendance and training opportunities outside their libraries (for example, sponsored by professional associations) or

185

developing in-house programs, such as Munoo described in Singapore in 2018.[1] However, they may not be taking advantage of the potential power of their local or regional consortia in professional development and capacity-building among academic library staff. In a survey of selected US academic library consortia, Al Bidiri found that only 57 percent offered regular training to their members.[2] Robinson provides an example of consortia-provided training for librarians, but the program described focused on technology skills rather than instructional training.[3] There are relatively few studies focused on the potential role of local or regional consortia in the provision of continuing professional development for teaching librarians.

This chapter is a case study describing how a consortium in Hong Kong has worked together to deliver continuing professional development (CPD) for its instruction librarians. It focuses on delivery and assessment of this CPD in 2016–18 and a "refresher," held in 2022 and 2023. It describes a model for working collaboratively across several institutions in library instructor CPD and developing related communities of practice at a city/regional level. Emphasis is placed on enhancing librarians' skills and knowledge as well as their ability to identify and partner with faculty members in delivering relevant and useful information literacy teaching and learning embedded in the curriculum. The CPD also served to build up a community of practice among the consortium's instruction librarians, supporting the transformation of their practice at member libraries.

We hope this chapter will inform and inspire other consortia and communities of practice to band together for city-wide or region-wide staff development for information literacy teaching, learning, and assessment.

Context and History of the Consortium and Its Work in Professional Development

Since its establishment in 1967, the Joint University Librarians Advisory Committee (JULAC) consortium has provided a forum for publicly funded university libraries in Hong Kong to discuss, coordinate, and collaborate on library information resources and services. It is comprised of the libraries of each of the eight government-funded universities in Hong Kong: The Chinese University of Hong Kong (CUHK), City University of Hong Kong (CityU), The Education University of Hong Kong (EdUHK), Hong Kong Baptist University (HKBU), Hong Kong Polytechnic University (HKPolyU), The Hong Kong University of Science & Technology (HKUST), Lingnan University (LU), and The University of Hong Kong (HKU).

Major JULAC initiatives include resource-sharing efforts. One example is Hong Kong Academic Library Link, a service that allows eligible users at JULAC institutions to cross-search the collection of over five million print monographs held by the participating libraries and request them for delivery to their home library. Another important offering of the consortium is the JULAC Library Card, allowing holders physical access to all member libraries.

JULAC's collaborative efforts extend beyond resource sharing. Under the auspices of its Learning Strategies Committee (LSC), the consortium has sponsored and organized CPD opportunities for instruction librarians. These learning interventions have been designed to help both early-career librarians and more established professionals in their teaching and assessment practices. These efforts form the substance of this chapter.

The timeline summarizes the events that are detailed in the sections that follow.

First Steps – ACRL Immersion comes to Hong Kong: June 2013

In 2012, the JULAC directors decided to bring the ACRL Immersion program to Hong Kong. Held in June 2013, this was the first time the program was delivered outside of North America. ACRL Immersion faculty provided instruction, training, and inspiration to sixty-six librarians, mainly from JULAC member libraries but also from Singapore, Taiwan, and mainland China.[4] The instruction included common (plenary) sessions as well as two tracks: teacher and program.

The program worked in several ways. First, it focused attendees on what information literacy is or should be. Second, Immersion provided new knowledge in a variety of domains: "learning theories, learning styles, teaching methods, assessment, presentation skills, and leadership."[5] Third, it

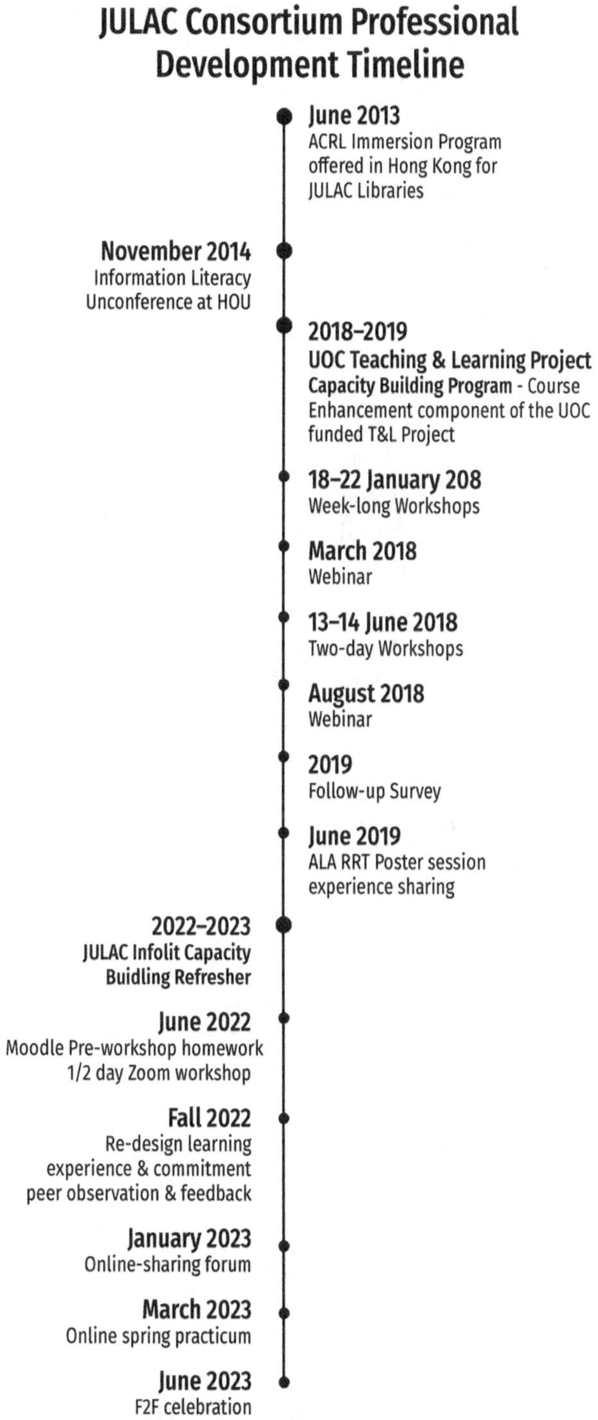

JULAC Consortium Professional Development Timeline

June 2013
ACRL Immersion Program offered in Hong Kong for JULAC Libraries

November 2014
Information Literacy Unconference at HOU

2018–2019
UOC Teaching & Learning Project Capacity Building Program - Course Enhancement component of the UOC funded T&L Project

18–22 January 208
Week-long Workshops

March 2018
Webinar

13–14 June 2018
Two-day Workshops

August 2018
Webinar

2019
Follow-up Survey

June 2019
ALA RRT Poster session experience sharing

2022–2023
JULAC Infolit Capacity Buidling Refresher

June 2022
Moodle Pre-workshop homework 1/2 day Zoom workshop

Fall 2022
Re-design learning experience & commitment peer observation & feedback

January 2023
Online-sharing forum

March 2023
Online spring practicum

June 2023
F2F celebration

Figure 15.1
The timeline outlining the steps in the development of the JULAC Professional Development program.

encouraged the adoption of effective dispositions—for example, by "being intentional"[6] about all aspects of instruction, from individual sessions to entire programs. The five points that Nichols shared in her 2008 article about Immersion experience describe our main takeaways from Immersion: "Create a shared vision … shift focus from teaching to learning … tackle assessment … lead the way … and take action."[7]

The running of ACRL Immersion Hong Kong in 2013 was crucial for two reasons. First, it created a common language and understanding among academic librarians about information literacy teaching, learning, assessment, and programs. Second, it helped build connections between librarians at the same institutions and beyond their institutions within the region (Hong Kong, Taiwan, Singapore, and mainland China), especially among JULAC librarians. For many of us, it was the first time we heard the term "community of practice." Proposed in 1991, this concept was fully expanded upon by Etienne Wenger in his seminal book published in 1998. The theory emphasizes the social aspects of learning, highlighting the importance of the informal communities that naturally emerge as individuals pursue shared enterprises.[8] Since then, librarians have explored the concept of using communities of practice in various ways, including professional development of librarians—for example, via in-house single library programs,[9,10] via an online library school course for school librarians,[11] and via ongoing virtual communities of practice, such as described by Qutab et al.;[12] but no research appears to have been done on consortia as communities of practice for CPD.

So, equipped with the insight of being intentional, academic librarians in JULAC began to consciously develop a community of practice centered around information literacy instruction at their institutions and between institutions. From this beginning, future developments flowed.

Information Literacy Unconference (November 2014) held at HKBU

Inspired by reading about the experience of other libraries, HKBU Library staged an Information Literacy Unconference in late 2014. This type of event is characterised by a purposeful lack of structure.[13] As part of their preparation, attendees were asked to submit what questions they had about information literacy in Hong Kong higher education. These responses helped guide the discussion at the beginning of the event, where participants were asked to create the agenda for the unconference. The photo below shows the result:

This was followed by two lively breakout sessions that were a marked contrast with the traditional "sage on the stage" style of conference to which Hong Kong librarians are generally accustomed.

Participants provided positive feedback afterward and highlighted the social aspect (community-building) as being of particular value. The lack of formal structure allowed for the sharing of views and experiences that mattered most to attendees. There was also a clear desire for future similar events, but unfortunately this did not materialise. To open the event to non-JULAC members, HKBU Library organized the Unconference independently. In hindsight, leveraging the collective resources of JULAC may have made

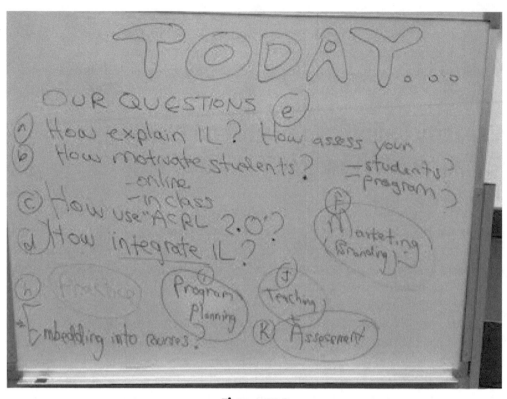

Figure 15.2
Whiteboard displays questions posed by attendees at the 2014 HKBU
Information Literacy Unconference.

it more likely that the momentum generated would have led to future similar events. However, the Unconference helped to continue to build our community of practice by bringing us together to experiment and play. It also reinforced the idea that we could try and do things in Hong Kong, with members of our community of practice.

ACRL Immersion Inspires a Cross-Institutional Teaching & Learning Grant (2014–15)

Following the success of Immersion, librarians at HKUST and HKBU were encouraged by their senior management to submit a grant proposal to support capacity-building and course enhancement funds for information literacy initiatives. At the same time, other JULAC libraries had created a separate proposal on information literacy development seeking funding support. At the UGC's suggestion, both proposals were combined into one multi-component three-year grant project (2015–18) awarded to JULAC libraries to develop information literacy in higher education across Hong Kong. The overall project consisted of five sub-components:

- Assessment of information educational needs of undergraduate students
- Research Readiness Self-Assessment (RRSA-HK) questionnaire instrument

- Shared online IL courseware
- Capacity Building Program for librarians of JULAC libraries
- Course Enhancement Funds

This case study focuses on the Capacity Building and Course Enhancement Fund components, as the other pieces are less relevant to the development of library instructors.

Capacity Building Program and Course Enhancement Funds (CEF) – 2016–2018

The Capacity Building in January–August 2016 combined with the actual work of the CEFs exemplify deeply embedded praxis (uniting theory and practice) in professional development. Just as information literacy teaching and learning is made more relevant to students when they have a research need, designing the CPD to be directly applied to participants' work (with an expectation of assessment and reporting back) created conditions for deeper learning and transformation.

The Capacity Building Programme series was conducted by Ms. Lisa Janicke Hinchliffe, professor and coordinator for Information Literacy Services and Instruction, University of Illinois at Urbana-Champaign to thirty-nine librarians from across the eight JULAC libraries. Its main aim was to develop the ability of instruction librarians to teach and assess information literacy, especially via deep collaboration with faculty members. A secondary goal was to facilitate the creation of communities of practice both within and among university libraries in Hong Kong. It combined two multi-day face-to-face sessions with webinars and online work (both individual and group).

Key concepts covered included communities of practice, expert/novice mindset, organizational cultures in higher education, collaboration and partnership, informed learning, information literacy, logic models, instructional design, curricular structures, program planning and evaluation, assignments and assessments, rubrics, innovation adoption, and communication for advocacy.

TABLE 15.1

Events for the 2016 capacity-building program

Date	Format	Purpose
18–22 January 2016	Face-to-face weeklong workshop	Capacity-building; creation of action plan based around CEFs to put knowledge gained into practice
21 March 2016	Webinar	Progress check-in
13–14 June 2016	Two-day face-to-face workshop	Capacity-building with a focus on learning assessment
9 August 2016	Webinar	Capacity-building with a focus on faculty collaboration; CEF capstone

The program was designed for continuous learning. Before the January face-to-face workshops, a course website was created on HKPolyU's Blackboard learning management system. There, the facilitator posted readings and discussion questions for the participants to prepare themselves for the subsequent learning experiences. The January curriculum took as its focus information literacy program design and development in the higher education context. Exploration of academic cultures and theories of collaboration established a foundation for a deep analysis of curricular structures and how information literacy instruction might fit within those programs and frameworks. A deep dive into different models of information literacy curricula informed the development of institutional action plans.

Immediately following the January 2016 week-long workshop, the facilitator and organizers did a feedback survey. Thirty-two people responded (88 percent response rate). Overall, the results were positive, with 93 percent of the participants satisfied or very satisfied with the program. Over 80 percent agreed they were better prepared to build collaborative relationships with faculty members, and more than 90 percent agreed they had a better understanding of action planning and logic model development because of the workshop. There was also evidence that participants consciously recognized the benefits of embedding praxis in professional development, with one commenting, "To connect knowledge with application, more real-life practice is required."

Apart from specifically building up these capacities, the workshop also proved to be a good catalyst for information sharing and action on the overall UGC-Teaching & Learning project.

Among the important learning outcomes of the January 2016 workshop, the participants created an action plan for themselves to put what they learned into action with the CEFs. This was then linked to the webinar held two months later in March. Before the webinar, participants had to submit "homework" on the progress of their CEFs and other initiatives. This webinar, which the facilitator led from Illinois with the Hong Kong participants gathered at HKUST, served as a useful check-in and prepared the participants for the next face-to-face workshop in June.

The June workshop focused on different aspects of instructional design with particular attention to assessment of learning. Participants explored a continuum of assessments, from formative to summative, using a range of methodologies, including observation, student reflection, and performance. The goal was to understand both how assessment can be used to guide the learning process and progress as well as evaluate student achievement and program success.

The post-workshop participant survey indicated that the content was relevant, practical, and useful but also challenging. As such, participants particularly appreciated the community of practice approach, enabling "an excellent learning and sharing atmosphere."

The final component, again delivered as a webinar, had as its theme "Building and Sustaining Faculty Relationships" and helped provide a capstone to our preparation and work for the CEFs. Below is a poster about the capacity-building program presented in spring 2018 at the official launch of the shared online courseware (a big component of the overall project), where JULAC librarians also shared information about their CEF partnerships.

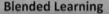

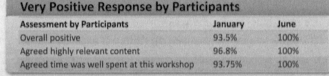

Figure 15.3
Poster for the spring 2018 Capacity Building Programme outlining its
profile, learning sessions, schedule, and participant response statistics.

Information Literacy Teaching and Learning Enhanced – Results of Capacity Building and CEFs

The Capacity Building had as one of its central aims to prepare the librarians for the CEFs. So, although a fulsome description of the planning and implementation falls outside of the scope of this chapter, a brief comment on the success achieved is warranted. All eight institutions used their CEFs to embed information literacy more completely into their programs and curricula at their institutions. Typically, funding was used to support the development of learning objects. For example, librarians at CUHK used a CEF grant to develop a video called *Getting Data for Journalism* for a postgraduate course on applied communication research. Funding could also be used to provide access to software tools. In one HKBU project for final-year public relations and advertising undergraduates, librarians introduced concepts around information visualization and led a workshop on best practices for infographics. A classroom subscription to a web-based design platform called Piktochart gave students access to a tool to help them put what they learned into practice. In total there were forty-two projects across the eight universities, reaching 5,200 undergraduates across a wide variety of disciplines, as can be seen in figure 15.4.[14]

Many of these partnerships in embedded information literacy have continued at JULAC libraries since 2018 without the extra funding provided by project grants. For example, at HKUST, the Chemistry department values the several workshops, research coaching, and mini-conference components to the extent that every semester they continue with the partnership, footing the bill with its own departmental funds.

Disciplines	Number of Students	%
Language	1,782	33.9%
Health Sciences	752	14.3%
Business	510	9.7%
Social Sciences	376	7.2%
Engineering	305	5.8%
Fashion	234	4.5%
Building and Real Estate	211	4.0%
Journalism	171	3.3%
Design	151	2.9%
Creative Media	130	2.5%
Hotel Management	90	1.7%
Science	88	1.7%
Education (inclusive education)	88	1.7%
Education	60	1.1%
Communication studies	57	1.1%
Humanities	50	1.0%
Education (ECE)	45	0.9%
Education (IT in education)	40	0.8%
Law	38	0.7%
Architecture	35	0.7%
Music	22	0.4%
Chinese Studies	9	0.2%
General Education	9	0.2%
Total	**5,253**	**100.00%**

Figure 15.4

Students used Piktochart to create projects in several disciplines that reached more than 5,200 undergraduates.

Follow-up Survey with 2016 Capacity Building Participants – How It Has Impacted Their Work (18 Months After the End of the Program)

In 2018, in thinking about the unique experience of Capacity Building as a consortium-wide training activity in information literacy teaching and learning, participants of the 2016 program were asked to reflect on what they learned through it and how they had applied it, eighteen months afterward. The response rate was rather low (nine respondents, 23 percent) but still provides useful perspectives.

The first question asked participants to look back and reflect upon "what you have found to be most useful from the program and why?" Several respondents highlighted the advice on how to make their instruction more interactive, suggesting that this was an area they had been struggling with before the program. One specifically referenced the example set by the facilitator, stating that they were impressed by Hinchliffe's ability to lead the workshop without presentation slides and instead convey her ideas through well-designed activities. Another participant noted that the program was the first time that they had received formal training in information literacy instruction. This underlines the importance of the program in filling in the gaps new librarians might have in their training.

The survey also asked the extent to which they had achieved the learning outcomes of the capacity-building. Respondents agreed or strongly agreed that they were able to design lessons and learning experiences to develop student information literacy as well as design assessments for information literacy. However, some respondents were neutral or even negative about their ability to build collaborative relationships with faculty or advocate for information literacy in the curriculum. These results suggest that future training may focus on developing these specific areas of practice.

The Capacity Building experience and results were shared at the IRRT Poster session at ALA in 2019.[15]

JULAC Information Literacy Capacity Building Refresher – 2022

> "Time blunts the keenest knife and changes the meaning of words and the thoughts in human minds, so that finally the firmest knot must be retied, and the sincerest word spoken once again." - Ursula K. Le Guin[16]

Time marched on. The COVID-19 pandemic brought new challenges to Hong Kong and the world in how to deliver useful and relevant information literacy teaching and learning to university students. At the same time, demographic and societal upheavals in Hong Kong also resulted in a large turnover in information literacy librarians. In several libraries, at least half the teaching librarians had not participated in ACRL Immersion in 2013 or the Capacity Building in 2016. Even among those who had, some felt that a "refresher" would help reinforce or build up our skills and help us mentor our early-career colleagues. Thus, two HKUST librarians (Victoria Caplan and Eunice Wong) and one at HKBU (Chris Chan) decided to seek the backing of the JULAC LSC and the JULAC directors to create a refresher session.

Brainstorming and planning ensued and a proposal was created and then endorsed by LSC in November 2021 and then endorsed by the JULAC directors in December 2021. While these may seem like minor bureaucratic details, this signalling of support from library leadership was critical to the development and success of the consortia-wide program. It indicated that the program developers (Chris, Eunice, and Victoria) had created a solid proposal that would get buy-in from the instruction librarians and their departments. The endorsement by the JULAC directors also meant that both program developers and participants were granted time and approval from their own library admin-istration to work on the initiative as part of their duties. This helped lay the groundwork for success because lack of administrative support can be a real "de-motivator" for CPD.[17]

The ACRL Immersion documents allowed re-use among JULAC libraries, and Prof. Hinchliffe also allowed some re-use of her materials from 2016. At the same time, we also wanted to build upon some of our skills with newer technologies, particularly audience engagement platforms like Mentimeter. Bringing all of this together meant that planning the refresher took several months. We considered what we wanted to accomplish and then what elements we had found especially useful from our experiences with outside trainers at the 2013 ACRL Immersion in Hong Kong and the 2016 Capacity Building, as well as lessons learned from the 2014 Unconference, and built from there.

We first considered "What problems we are trying to solve?" and decided there were four main ones:
- Scattershot IL instruction (non-programmatic)
- Mechanical "training," "click here" by-rote instruction or demonstration
- Some instructors may never have had the chance to develop their IL teaching capacity.
- Some experienced instructors may want to share about and address any issues with burnout they have encountered.

From there, we settled upon three intended learning outcomes (ILOs) for the program:
- Create useful ILOs for individual library workshops and programs to improve infor-mation literacy learning at their institutions.
- Use "backward design" (a form of instructional design) or the USER method to create more effective workshops and online learning objects or modules with effective assessment in order to improve information literacy learning at their institutions.
- Strengthen the community of practice in information literacy teaching and learn-ing at JULAC libraries in order to benefit from each other's ideas and practice and perhaps explore opportunities to scale up collaborative efforts in this area.

Among the useful practices from the past, we found that both the 2013 and 2016 programs had "homework": reading, reflecting, and online engagement, and the 2016 program had it on an LMS. We also thought the 2016 approach of expecting participants to apply what they had learned in their practice and then report back on it would be vital to success. In the same way that students find information literacy instruction more relevant when it is linked to an assignment, instruction librarians will find CPD more compelling when explicitly linked to their professional practice. Thus, we planned and held the following program.

TABLE 15.2

JULAC capacity-building for information literacy teaching and learning 2022–23.

June 2022
• June 13–24: Prepare for workshop – Read, Watch, Reflect, Write.
• June 30: Workshop – Reflect, Practice, Learn, and form peer-mentor groups.
Summer and fall 2022
• Groups form and list on Moodle.
• Use "backward design" to design or re-design a learning experience (workshop, tutorial, or e-learning object).
• As a peer mentor: share your own plan and comment on those of your groupmates.
• Deliver the learning experience and observe your groupmates delivering theirs.
• Assess (self-reflect) on the learning experience (what worked, how it felt, etc.).
• Share constructive observations on your groupmates' learning experiences.
Winter 2022–23
• Meet to share what we learned and how it went. Celebrate our achievements!
• Plan the way forward.
Spring 2023
• Groups reformed for the spring semester.
• Followed the same methods (used backward design, peer mentoring, delivered learning, assessed learning experience).
• Groups worked together to share with and support each other.
• 2 mid-semester online check-ins with all groups.
• Final meet-up and celebration – Face-to-face at last, after COVID-19 restrictions lifted!

Librarians at HKBU set up the infrastructure for the online component on Moodle. We worked on creating six modules for participants to read, think, reflect, and respond before the first "live" program, a two-hour and thirty-minute webinar delivered via Zoom. The bulk of the materials were open access on the web or self-created, with a few links to licensed or fair-dealing material. We created the online material collaboratively, writing and giving each other feedback and refining the look and feel. We worked hard to try and create it at the right level: not so demanding as to alienate nor so simple that participants would find it worthless. We also tried to model what we understand to be good pedagogy in our teaching about teaching. It got rather "meta" at times.

We estimated that it would take participants about three to four hours to go through the materials and respond to the polls and forum questions. The material was released on June 13 and participants were asked to finish working through it by June 24 (eleven days) to then give the facilitators (Victoria, Chris, and Eunice) time to provide feedback on the participants' responses.

TABLE 15.3

Summary of self-learning materials prepared for capacity-building refresher.

Module	What it covered	Materials used	Self-reflection questions/ forum activities
• Information Literacy	• What we are trying to teach: information literacy • What we want the students to learn to become: information literate	• Definitions and goals of information literacy from some JULAC organizations and overseas organizations • Models of information literacy	• How do you define information literacy? • Which of the 6 models do you match your personal views?
• Librarians as Teachers	• What makes a good teacher?	• Self-written material on qualities of good pedagogy and teachers	• Learning from our previous teachers: describe one of your best teachers: what they taught, how they taught, how it felt to you. • Describe one of your worst teachers: what they taught, how they taught, how it felt to you.
• Learning	• What is learning? • 7 principles of learning	• Material adapted from HKUST's Center for Education Innovation (CEI)	• Which of the 7 principles of learning did you like the most and why?
• Instructional Design	• Outcome-based education[18] and intended learning outcomes (ILOs)	• Material adapted from HKUST's CEI and two short YouTube videos on backward design	• N/A
• Writing Effective Learning Outcomes and Mapping Them onto Bloom's Taxonomy	• What are ILOs and what is Bloom's Taxonomy, why care and how to use	• Material adapted from HKUST's CEI, College of Wooster's and Bronx Community College's LibGuides on Bloom's Taxonomy, a short video on YouTube, and material (including two videos) from Iowa State's Center for Excellence in Teaching and Learning	• 3 polls: • How often do we make ILOs for our teaching? • How do we create the ILOs for our library instruction? • Where on Bloom's Taxonomy do I usually set my ILOs?
• Assessments: The Way We Check for Learning	• What learning assessment is and how it differs from workshop evaluation	• Self-written material, adapted from many resources; example rubrics from HKUST and the AACU Value Rubric for Information Literacy	• Poll on present practice of assessment • Forum posting of our own understanding of assessment vs. workshop evaluation • General comments or questions before the webinar

1. We conducted the webinar via Zoom held on June 30, 2022, with forty-two people joining. Below is an outline of the workshop. First, we went over what we had learned online and how we responded, sharing from the forum postings and polls. Second, we practiced creating ILOs. Finally, Chris shared about active and engaging teaching. He conducted this completely via Menti (which HKBU and several other Hong Kong universities subscribe to), presenting (as we joked) "the Full Menti."

TABLE 15.4

Outline of June 30, 2022, webinar session.

Time	Content
09:30–10:20	Goals and information literacy teaching • Reminder of what we are trying to do here • Information literacy, teaching and learning, Bloom's Taxonomy
10:20–10:30	Break
10:30–11:05	Writing ILOs, assessments, and instructional design
11:05–11:15	Break
11:15–12:00	Active and engaging teaching
12:00–12:30	Wrap-up and fall teaching • Applying what we have learned and will learn together • "Homework" [heart of the program] • Q&A

2. After the workshop, we asked the participants to give feedback via an online survey. Twenty-three people responded (a 54 percent response rate). Like the 2016 Capacity Building, it was well received. The main problem discovered was that only 52 percent agreed that they could cope with the workload. In planning the continuation of this training and future training, we need to reduce the workload, lengthen the time we give participants to do it, or manage their expectations better.

3. The "homework" phase of the training started in July 2022 and was originally expected to last through the fall semester of 2022. However, as the participants went through the practical application (homework) and its challenges, the planned learning grew and evolved.

4. Forming groups was the first challenge. We planned to have participants create cross-institutional groups, to help achieve the third ILO of the overall program by encouraging the development of our community of practice. Rather than self-forming as we had hoped, we needed to take an active role to ensure the peer groups had representatives from more than one library. Ultimately, eight groups were formed. Members enjoyed coming up with creative names for their group, sometimes based on their initials (e.g., N&N) or on the number of people (e.g., High Five). The cross-university peer group structure was vital

to the capacity-building and as such attention was paid to their composition. Apart from connecting colleagues from different institutions, we consciously partnered more experienced librarians with those with less experience. This did not just benefit new librarians. The more experienced librarians got to learn novel insights (technologies, attitudes, etc.) from the newer ones or those whose prior experience was outside of information literacy instruction.

5. Once in the groups, the following would take place:
    - Each participant was expected to use the backward design template to develop a "learning intervention" (a workshop, a class, a learning video, etc.). They would then share with their group mates.
    - Groupmates would give constructive feedback on their work to each other (peer evaluation).
    - Participants would then incorporate this advice and deliver the learning intervention, with groupmates observing (if possible).
    - Groupmates would give further feedback on what they observed.

The group was then expected to reflect individually and together on what they learned through the practical (homework) part of this staff development. All groups would then share their reflections at another online meeting, which was held on January 11, 2023.

During this session, participants revealed that the cross-university aspect of peer grouping was more challenging than expected. With COVID-19 restrictions resulting in difficulty/reluctance in meeting face-to-face, most groups communicated by email and Zoom. Some also formed WhatsApp groups, and one even met off campus for dinner and chat.

Despite the lack of in-person communication, many groups shared that they found the experience of trying to use backward design and sharing their plans and lessons to be useful. Encouragingly, participants shared specific insights on how what they had learned improved their praxis. Some representative examples from the presentations include:

- "Useful: The way of teaching is changed from providing a lot of content to what users can learn, it will be more focused."
- "Learnt how to set-up interactive activities with concrete details in the plan."
- "Backward design helps us design the curriculum by setting goals before choosing instructional methods and forms of assessment."

The January 2023 meet-up was where we originally thought we would end this effort. Our expectation was that the participants would express the view that this cross-institutional capacity building was "kind of" useful but rather onerous to maintain given their institutional responsibilities, and they were glad it was over.

Instead, the facilitators were pleased (if slightly surprised) by all the positive feedback the groups expressed about the practicum, and in the discussion of "the way forward," most participants said they wanted to continue in their group learning for another semester. There was a genuine eagerness among the librarians to continue to learn together in groups beyond their own universities and become better library instructors.

In addition to agreeing to continue building our capacity together in spring 2023, our online meeting discussion revealed that despite forging bonds within their groups (as described above) some groups felt a little lost in the summer–fall 2023 practicum without a re-connect with all the groups joining. To remedy this, the facilitators proposed two online check-ins during the spring 2023 semester (March 24 and April 28), but not all group members would have to attend. This combination of structure and flexibility proved useful: groups were spurred on by the expectation that they would need to share with their peers but without the pressure that everyone needed to show up for the multi-group meetings. In both online check-ins (March 24 and April 28) participants shared similar results to the January 11, 2023, session: looking over each other's plans to give and receive feedback, and that observing each other's teaching (whether in-person or online) was useful.

In March 2023, Hong Kong's COVID-19 restrictions were finally completely lifted, and we began to plan for a face-to-face sharing and celebration of our common work. We set it to be held on June 2, 2023, (a Friday) and timed it for the afternoon to give participants a more relaxed celebratory feel and provide opportunities for face-to-face networking. The facilitators decided to keep the group presentations very short. This provided another opportunity to learn new things. In the April 28 sharing session, we explained the rationale behind the presentation time limits, how this would be enforced (in a humorous way), and then provided some guidance and ideas on different ways to present effectively within a short time: PechaKucha, Lightning Talks, Say It in Six, etc. The idea was to give the groups freedom to choose how to communicate their experiences but also provide tools for them to select from, use, combine, or choose different methods.

In terms of content, the facilitators urged that it not be "show and tell" (we did X number of classes in Y format and Z ILOs…) but instead to be a reflection on the learning experience. These were some suggestions on what the groups could share on: expectations before the program; most important things applied from learning; things we are still not sure about; biggest take-away; what could have been better in the program, what we want to do in future; what the overall experience meant to us.

At the June 2, 2023, Round-up and Celebration, six groups presented in less than an hour. In addition to most of the participants, three of the eight JULAC directors were present to see the accomplishments and show support for staff development efforts.

Perhaps the most frequently cited "biggest takeaway" was to avoid being too ambitious with the amount of content and number of ILOs. This suggests that many librarians were previously trying to cram too much into their teaching. Typical reflections from the presentations included: "Trimming contents is essential, and divide a course into several modules if necessary" and "Always keep ILOs and assessing them in mind and when in doubt, REDUCE the ILOs."

For the facilitators, one of the most gratifying reflections was from a participant who stated that they went into the training expecting a repeat of their 2015 experience, which they described as: "Attend -> Do the Homework -> Forget." Instead, their experience in 2023 was: "Learn -> Apply -> Share & Feedback" (which they also described as one of two major takeaways, along with networking).

After the presentations, some quick feedback from participants was solicited using online polling. When asked how best to increase interaction among JULAC instruction librarians, respondents indicated that Microsoft Teams (or a similar online tool) and more face-to-face events would be welcome. We then moved on to the vital in-person socializing and snacks. The facilitators were delighted to see that toward the end of the official tea time (around 5:00 p.m.) several participants were still talking eagerly and had drawn their chairs up in a large circle.

Overall, the 2022–23 Capacity Building program was successful in connecting JULAC librarians. Participants will be encouraged to maintain the momentum of the program by continuing to communicate and share advice and/or materials, probably through an online platform.

Conclusion, Lessons Learned, and Tips for Others

Use the power of local consortia. A single library may have difficulty sourcing and paying for expert trainers from outside their home city or region. By combining budgets, skills, and staffing, a group can achieve higher-level training and economies of scale than a single library could have done. At the same time, having consortium members and library directors give a stamp of approval and release staff time greatly facilitates such group action.

Combine theory and practice (praxis). Having something concrete that we must show our colleagues and bosses incentivizes us to apply what we have learned. By requiring participants to apply and report back, CPD is not just something we enjoy and take notes on and maybe remember to apply in our teaching. Instead, the practical application of what we learn during capacity building to real situations serves to make us better instruction librarians.

Joint training and sharing build a community of practice. Having the experience of learning together and working on projects helped develop team spirit and friendships within libraries and the consortium. Early-career librarians and those who have not yet assumed managerial or supervisory responsibilities rarely have chances to work with and come to know their counterparts at other institutions. Having their libraries encourage training and working across institutions makes for stronger and deeper ties. We learn more and see how different skills and methods can be applied to information literacy in different contexts, making us better librarians and instructors.

Notes

1. Rayjen Munoo, "Trial by Fire, Boot Camps and Brown Bags: How Do We Learn to Teach," *Singapore Journal of Library and Information Management* 47 (2018/19), 126–33.
2. Al Badiri, "Survey of Selected US Academic Library Consortia: A Descriptive Study," *The Electronic Library* 34, no. 1 (2016): 31.
3. Tami Echavarria Robinson, "Professional Development Opportunities Provided by Consortia: What We Can Learn from This Model," in *Revolutionizing the Development of Library and Information Professionals: Planning for the Future*, ed. Hines Samantha Schmehl (Hershey, PA: IGI Global, 2014), 219, https://doi.org/10.4018/978-1-4666-4675-9.ch014.
4. "ACRL Immersed in Hong Kong," *American Libraries, International Supplement* (August 2013), 31.
5. Rebecca K. Miller and Jonathan R. Paulo, "Learning the Language of Information Literacy: Takeaways from ACRL's Immersion Program," *Virginia Libraries* 58 (2): 34, https://doi.org/10.21061/valib.v58i2.1212.
6. Jessica Jerrit and Sue Wozniak, "ACRL Teacher Immersion: Reflections in a Business Library," *Public Services Quarterly* 11, no. 4 (October 2015): 319–23, https://doi.org/10.1080/15228959.2015.1091763.

7. Lisa Nichols, "Pushing Your IL Program Forward: Five Lessons from My Immersion Experience," *Kentucky Libraries* 72 (4): 4–6, https://search-ebscohost-com.lib.ezproxy.hkust.edu.hk/login.aspx?direct=true&db=lih&AN=35285191.
8. Etienne Wenger, *Communities of Practice: Learning, Meaning, and* Identity (Cambridge: Cambridge University Press, 1998), 3–17.
9. Heather Weltin and Nancy Graff Schultz, "Communities of Practice as a Professional Development Tool for Management and Leadership Skills in Libraries," *Library Leadership & Management* 33 (3) (2019): 1–12, https://doi.org/10.5860/llm.v33i3.7347.
10. Alexander J. Caroll and Melissa N. Mallon, "Using Digital Environments to Design Inclusive and Sustainable Communities of Practice in Academic Libraries," *Journal of Academic Librarianship* 47 (5) (2021): 1–10, https://doi.org/10.1016/j.acalib.2021.102380.
11. Elizabeth A. Burns, Jody K. Howard, and Sue C. Kimmel, "Development of Communities of Practice in School Library Education," *Journal of Education for Library and Information Science* 57, no. 2 (2016): 101-111.
12. Saima Qutab, Abid Iqbal, Farasat Shafi Ullah, Nadeem Siddique, and Muhammad Ajmal Khan, "Role of Virtual Communities of Practice (VCoP) in Continuous Professional Development of Librarians: A Case of Yahoo Mailing Group from Pakistan," *Library Management* 43(5) (2022): 317–33, https://doi.org/10.1108/LM-02-2021-0017.
13. Michelle Boule, "(Un)Defining a Camp or Unconference," chap. 2 in *Mob Rule Learning: Camps, Unconferences, and Trashing the Talking Head* (Medford: Information Today, 2011), 17.
14. In the Hong Kong context, "language" mostly refers to English language courses in reading and writing at university level, since seven of the eight universities are English-medium and English is not the native language of the vast majority of the students.
15. Victoria F. Caplan and Lisa Janicke Hinchliffe, "Praxis, Baby, Praxis: Building Capacity in Information Literacy Teaching & Assessment: A Territory-Wide Strategy of the Academic Libraries in Hong Kong" (*International Relations Round Table Poster Session*, ALA Annual Conference and Exhibition, Washington, DC, United States, 23 June 2019), https://hdl.handle.net/1783.1/100672.
16. Ursula K. Le Guin et al., "The Trouble with the Cotton People," in *Always Coming Home* (New York: Bantam Books, 1987), 150–51.
17. Shehzad Ahmad, Sajjad Ahmad, and Ijaz Hussain, "Continuing Professional Development (CPD) of University Librarians: A Case Study," *Pakistan Library & Information Science Journal* 50, no. 1 (2019): 23.
18. Outcomes-based education has been strongly promoted by the UGC and at Hong Kong universities for well over a decade.

Bibliography

American Libraries, International Supplement. "ACRL Immersed in Hong Kong." August 2013, 31.

Ahmad, Shehzad, Sajjad Ahmad, and Ijaz Hussain. "Continuing Professional Development (CPD) of University Librarians: A Case Study." *Pakistan Library & Information Science Journal* 50, no. 1 (2019):15–28.

Al Badiri, Saleh A. "Survey of Selected US Academic Library Consortia: A Descriptive Study." *The Electronic Library* 34, no. 1 (2016): 24–41.

Boule, Michelle. "(Un)Defining a Camp or Unconference," chap. 2 in *Mob Rule Learning: Camps, Unconferences, and Trashing the Talking Head.* Medford: Information Today, 2011.

Burns, Elizabeth A., Jody K. Howard, and Sue C. Kimmel. "*Development of Communities of Practice in School Library Education.*" *Journal of Education for Library and Information Science* 57, no. 2 (2016): 101–11.

Caplan, Victoria F., and Lisa Janicke Hinchliffe. "Praxis, Baby, Praxis: Building Capacity in Information Literacy Teaching & Assessment: A Territory-Wide Strategy of the Academic Libraries in Hong Kong." *International Relations Round Table Poster Session, ALA Annual Conference and Exhibition, Washington, DC, United States, 23 June 2019.* https://hdl.handle.net/1783.1/100672.

Carroll, Alexander J., and Melissa N. Mallon. "Using Digital Environments to Design Inclusive and Sustainable Communities of Practice in Academic Libraries." *Journal of Academic Librarianship* 47 (5) (2021): n.p. https://doi.org/10.1016/j.acalib.2021.102380.

Hong Kong University of Science and Technology, The. "ACRL Information Literacy Immersion Program." Accessed October 12, 2022. https://library.hkust.edu.hk/events/staff-workshops/acrl/.

Jerrit, Jessica, and Sue Wozniak. "ACRL Teacher Immersion: Reflections in a Business Library." *Public Services Quarterly* 11, no. 4 (October 2015): 319–23. https://doi.org/10.1080/15228959.2015.1091763.

Le Guin, Ursula K. "The Trouble with the Cotton People." In *Always Coming Home,* 142–53. New York: Bantam Books, 1987.

Miller, Rebecca K., and Jonathan R. Paulo. "Learning the Language of Information Literacy: Takeaways from ACRL's *Immersion Program.*" *Virginia Libraries* 58 (2) (2012): 33–36. https://doi.org/10.21061/valib.v58i2.1212.

Nichols, Lisa. "Pushing Your IL Program Forward: Five Lessons from My Immersion Experience." *Kentucky Libraries* 72 (4) (2008): 4–7.

Munoo, Rajen. "Trial by Fire, Boot Camps and Brown Bags: *How Do We Learn to Teach.*" *Singapore Journal of Library and Information Management* 47 (2018–19), 126–33.

Qutab, Saima, Abid Iqbal, Farasat Shafi Ullah, Nadeem Siddique, and Muhammad Ajmal Khan. "Role of Virtual Communities of Practice (VCoP) in Continuous Professional Development of *Librarians: A Case of Yahoo Mailing Group from Pakistan.*" *Library Management* 43(5) (2022): 317–33. https://doi.org/10.1108/LM-02-2021-0017.

Robinson, Tami Echavarria. "Professional Development Opportunities Provided by Consortia: *What We Can Learn from This Model.*" In *Revolutionizing the Development of Library and Information Professionals: Planning for the Future,* edited by Hines Samantha Schmehl, 209–29. Hershey, PA: IGI Global, 2014. https://doi.org/10.4018/978-1-4666-4675-9.ch014.

Weltin, Heather, and Nancy Graff Schultz. "*Communities of Practice as a Professional Development Tool for Management and Leadership Skills in Libraries.*" *Library Leadership & Management* 33 (3) (2019): 1–12. https://doi.org/10.5860/llm.v33i3.7347.

Wenger, Etienne. *Communities of Practice: Learning, Meaning, and Identity.* Cambridge: Cambridge University Press, 1998.

CHAPTER 16

Increasing Inclusive Instruction:

Building a Bespoke In-house Teacher Training Programme at the University of Cambridge

Kirstie Preest and Claire Sewell

LEARNING OUTCOMES

Readers will be able to

- recognise the need for librarians undertaking teaching to have a thorough grounding in pedagogical approaches;
- evaluate different online tools for delivering teaching;
- explain the importance of the inclusive classroom in modern teaching; and
- apply the principles of equality, diversity, and inclusivity to their own teaching.

Introduction

Increasing numbers of academic librarians are being asked to take on teaching roles. In 2004, Bell and Shank identified what they referred to as the growing ambiguity of the librarian's professional role in light of new technologies where librarians were perfectly placed to evolve into new roles that combined "the traditional skills set of librarianship …

and the instructional or educational designers ability to apply technology appropriately in the teaching-learning process."[1] In order to do this, however, they recognised "strategies, techniques and skills are needed that will allow all academic librarians … to proactively advance their integration into the teaching and learning process."[2] However, it is fair to say that although some librarians undertake brief teaching skills courses organised by libraries or professional associations, the theory and pedagogy underpinning teaching are not taught in depth at many library schools. This sentiment is highlighted by Gammons et al. within the US context where they state that the core "MLIS curriculum fails to adequately prepare graduates to meet these demands."[3] In the UK, recent changes to the Quality and Standards Conditions will also affect the skills needed by library staff to teach, stating that they need to "have and maintain: an expert knowledge of the subject they design and/or deliver, teaching qualifications or training, and teaching experience, appropriate for the content and level of the relevant higher education course and the required knowledge and skills as to the effective delivery of their higher education course."[4]

As a result of these changes, more and more librarians are undertaking a postgraduate qualification in teaching and learning to learn the skills they need. Many also develop them whilst in employment, but, as Carroll and Klipfel[5] point out, "Without a professional culture that values growth and deliberate practice" in the area of teaching, this can be a difficult process.

Cambridge Context

The Cambridge context is certainly no different, and there is a growing need for staff at a range of levels to develop teaching skills. Whether teaching is a core part of their role, they only teach occasionally, or they are working at a service desk, there are many opportunities for teaching skills to be put into use.

Many institutions are increasingly realising that having pedagogic knowledge is important for their teaching staff and have started to offer in-house courses to address these needs. Most of these programmes are mapped to professional standards frameworks, such as the UK-based AdvanceHE, meaning that users leave with a recognised qualification. The University of Cambridge itself has a Postgraduate Certificate in Teaching and Learning in Higher Education, which is open to all teaching staff, including those from the libraries, and runs a Teaching Associate Programme (TAP). However, these courses are mainly aimed at university teaching staff, lecturers, and supervisors who operate different teaching models from their library colleagues. They do not address scenarios specific to the library, such as one-shot sessions, induction tours, or dealing with questions on the reference desk. The assumption that library staff have the same training needs regarding teaching as academic staff means that these in-house programmes often have limited use to library staff who have difficulty translating the lessons outlined to their own teaching practice.

The in-house Teaching and Learning for Librarians course (waiting to be accredited), developed over the last decade, aims to fill this gap and provides a specific teaching course designed by librarians for librarians. The course aims to give library staff a thorough grounding in pedagogy so that they can build an understanding of their teaching initiatives and make the best of the often-limited time they have with their students.

Given the number of libraries within the Cambridge collegiate university, ensuring that all library staff involved in teaching have access to the teaching skills now required by the Office for Students is no easy task. There are over one hundred libraries including those within the colleges, the facilities and departments, and the University Library itself. The disparate nature and geographical spread of libraries across Cambridge make organising suitable training difficult. Staff have previously reported that working patterns, staffing requirements, and travel time have all impacted their ability to attend suitable training.

Course Development and Content

From its inception, the course has aimed to break these barriers to learning and give library staff the pedagogic/andragogic knowledge required to underpin their teaching practice. The development of the course itself has been an iterative process spanning more than a decade and culminating in the current flexible online offering. Established with the aim of building the confidence and skills of librarians in all aspects of teaching, the course covers the whole process from planning through to evaluation and reflection as well as providing the opportunity to practice active teaching in a supportive peer environment.

The first iteration of the course ran biennially from 2014 to 2018 in order to fit in with the working patterns of all the staff involved with course delivery. Delivered in person, the course ran over three half-days spaced out over a week to allow for maximum attendance. The structure and elements of the course are included in Table 16.1.

For the nano-teach element, participants were encouraged to choose a topic that they felt comfortable teaching for fifteen minutes rather than stipulating a topic in advance. The nano-teach is to assess their teaching style and ability to plan and deliver a session rather than their knowledge on any one topic.

The Cambridge Information Literacy Network (CILN), launched in 2017, involved librarians from across Cambridge working together to create tangible outputs on the theme of teaching and learning. A key outcome of this process was the creation of an information literacy framework designed to cover the core areas taught by library staff at the university. As part of the CILN output to look at staff training, the Teaching and Learning course was further revised to encompass this framework and ensure that participants would leave with not only a solid understanding of pedagogy but also how this related to the local approach to information literacy teaching.

This necessitated an expansion of the course so that all relevant content could be covered. Starting in September 2019, the course was re-launched as a nine-month blended programme delivered in person and via a virtual learning environment. This expansion also presented an opportunity to think about the potential outcomes for learners in the form of a recognised qualification. We mapped the existing content to the Cambridge TAP programme, which already had accreditation from AdvanceHE. This mapping exercise was invaluable for identifying similarities and gaps between the TAP and TLFL courses, including highlighting the in-depth pedagogical elements that were missing from TLFL.

TABLE 16.1

Structure of the three-day Cambridge Teaching and Learning for Librarians course, 2014–2018.

Day one	Learning objective
Are librarians teachers?	Introduces learners to debate over the role of the librarian in teaching and whether they identify as teachers.
Who are our students?	Asks learners to consider who the target audience for their teaching is and how the need of this audience impacts the interventions offered. Introduces learners to information literacy and how it impacts student learning.
Learning styles	Introduces learners to various learning styles and your own learning preferences. Encourages learners to evaluate these concepts and critique their effectiveness.
Lesson planning: SMART objectives, teaching methods, assessment methods, creating resources and sample lesson plans	Introduces learners to the concept of using a template to plan learning objectives and teaching activities to achieve these. Explores the creation of various teaching materials and how learning can be assessed.
Reflective practice	Introduces learners to the concept of reflective practice in teaching.
Day two	
Handouts as teaching resources	Introduces learners to the importance of handouts as teaching resources.
Reflective practice, peer review, and constructive feedback	Recap on reflective practice in teaching. Introduces learners to peer review/observation and how to give and receive constructive feedback.
Teaching demonstration	Example teaching demonstration enables learners to put peer observation and giving constructive feedback into practice.
What to do when it all goes wrong	Acknowledges that not all teaching goes to plan and offers learners strategies to help avoid potential problems.
Nano-teach	Introduces learners to the nano-teach and sets out instructions and expectations for the practical session.
Day three	
Practical nano-teach sessions	Learners deliver a 15-minute teaching session to other members of the cohort on a topic of their choice. Other learners provide constructive feedback which the presenter can reflect on to improve their teaching.

The TLFL course was also mapped to the AdvanceHE requirements themselves, which brought to attention further gaps that needed to be addressed, such as student assessment. Both mapping exercises enabled us to find synergies within library practice that could be included alongside core pedagogy, such as information literacy, user experience, and communities of practice. Other potential elements for inclusion in a librarian-specific course included developing a teaching philosophy, whether librarians are teachers, observing teaching practice and equality, and diversity and inclusivity principles.

In order to determine exactly which elements should be included in the blended learning programme, a card-sorting exercise of the teaching elements from the original course, alongside the missing pedagogy highlighted through both mapping exercises, was used. This helped planners decide which elements were key to the course, where they should be positioned within the course structure, as well as deciding which elements would be taught face to face and which online. With this structure in place, the backward design model by Wiggins and McTighe[6] was used to create the content. This approach advocates that modules are created in reverse, using the intended outcomes of a teaching intervention to design appropriate learning activities and learning objectives. Underpinning this process was the need to encourage participants to engage with the CILN information literacy framework, so this was made a core element of the programme, and participants were asked to use the CILN teaching template to plan their nano-teach session. We were also keen to showcase different teaching styles during the course, so guest speakers were recruited to deliver some of the in-person content. The final structure of the nine-month blended course can be seen in table 16.2.

TABLE 16.2
Structure of the nine-month 2019–20 blended TLFL course with online and face-to-face content.

Month	Delivery	Content
September	Face to face	Introduction, are librarians teachers, introduction to reflective practice, introduction to peer observation, developing teaching philosophies (flipped learning)
October	Online	Netiquette, communities of practice, teaching observations
November	Face to face	Who students are, inclusivity, diversity and disability (flipped learning), student learning patterns, environmental impacts of learning
December	Online	Learning theories, learning preferences, critique of learning preferences
January	Online	Information literacy frameworks, approaches to information literacy
February	Face to face	Backward design: learning outcomes, active learning techniques and learning methods, formal and informal learning
March	Online	Assessments, creating teaching materials, evaluating and assessing student feedback, introduction to the nano-teach
April	Face to face	Peer review and constructive feedback, teaching demo and critique, when it all goes wrong
May	Face to face	Nano-teaches (15 minutes)

November offered a specific module covering the themes of equality, diversity, and inclusivity in teaching practice. In addition, we felt it was important to use the TLFL programme to set a good example in this area and, as a result, these are themes present

throughout each module. Slides, images, and written content all followed inclusive practices, with attention paid to accessibility, the inclusion of alt-text, and how screen readers
would access the material. Online modules could be worked through in the participants'
own time, allowing for flexibility around work and other commitments whilst forums
offered the chance for participants to discuss the material with each other asynchronously.
Any additional readings included in the course were provided as ebooks to help ensure
equality of access. Although the preferred method would have been to include direct
copies of this material within the course, this was not possible as the course was not
formally accredited by the university.

At the end of each month, participants were asked to reflect on their learning on the
particular topic being covered, whether they would incorporate elements of the topic
into their own practice, and why/why not. These reflections formed a key part of the
formal, summative assessment. A portfolio option was chosen as the best way to reflect
the participants' learning journey throughout the course. In addition to their monthly
reflections, they were asked to include their personal teaching philosophy, the completed
CILN template for their nano-teach, any materials from their session, and a final reflection on the course itself. This portfolio was submitted after the nano-teach assessment
had taken place and assessed by the course tutors who checked that participants had met
learning outcomes and provided feedback. This final element—the nano-teach—was of
key importance to the goals of the programme. It allowed participants to trial new techniques and receive constructive feedback on their approach from both course leaders and
their fellow learners before they must replicate the teaching in a real-world environment.

The final component of the course was focused on participant's pastoral care. The
University of Cambridge has a well-established tutor system for its learners, so each participant was assigned a course leader to act as their personal tutor. This tutor was their key
point of contact for any questions or concerns about either the course itself or workload.
Some participants made use of their tutors to check in throughout the programme, particularly when workloads were disrupted due to the COVID-19 pandemic.

The Move Online

In line with other educational offerings around the world, the arrival of the COVID-19
pandemic in March 2020 meant huge changes for both the programme and its audience.
Library staff were suddenly trying to move all services online, including teaching provision, with very little notice. This, in addition to personal concerns at a time of great change,
meant that the TLFL course was no longer a priority for many participants, which led to
a large number failing to complete the course on its initial run. A total of five from the
initial cohort of fourteen completed the course.

The programme itself also undertook a pivot to online-only provision. Although it
was designed as a blended learning experience, the face-to-face content was an important
element of this. The April in-person session was cancelled to allow time for the course
to be redesigned, although an online optional check-in was provided in May. Material
on using the CILN teaching template was also removed to allow participants to focus

on backward design when planning their session so that they were not overwhelmed. In addition to moving the remainder of the modules online, a new section on teaching and learning online was added. These changes were well-received by participants who reported that guidance on best practices in online instruction was welcome, given the new pressures of their roles. The nano-teach sessions were also moved online, which gave participants a chance to practice in a supportive environment.

Moving forward to the first post-pandemic year in 2021, the course saw more changes in both personnel and content. One of the original course leaders stepped back and was replaced by a new staff member. This provided an opportunity to reassess the content of the course without the emergency nature of the early pandemic. We took the opportunity to reflect on the feedback received so far and make improvements. For example, comments from participants suggested that they would welcome more depth on some topics. Rather than add extra compulsory work to an already busy schedule, we decided to add a basic and optional element to the module on learning theories so that those wishing to dive deeper into the material could do so without overwhelming other learners.

We also reflected on our own experiences of the programme to date and concluded that the original plan to offer a nine-month blended course had been overly ambitious. This was due to a number of factors: learners were often struggling with heavy workloads and could not attend live sessions whilst others were suffering the stresses of the global pandemic. We were also aware that due to the changing situation with the pandemic, we needed to provide a greater level of flexibility for learners in future iterations. To reshape the program, we reflected on the desired outcomes for learners. We were reluctant to remove any of the key objectives but instead used the backward design process to ensure that they were still addressed by the updated content. This review resulted in the reprioritization of the content and helped us to decide which elements could be eliminated. We also considered alternative delivery formats to further enhance flexibility.

As a result, we developed a new six-month completely online course with a mixture of synchronous and asynchronous modules for participants from 2021 onward, with each module released at the start of the month. Some content was removed completely whilst other elements were delivered using a new approach. The module on backward design was changed to a flipped learning model where participants could read through material prior to attending a live online session with a guest lecturer to explore the topic in more detail. Greater use was also made of existing content, both to avoid duplicated effort and to showcase different tools and approaches to teaching. For example, rather than designing, staging, and recording an example of "bad" teaching practice, an existing YouTube video was used for participants to critique. We made the most of the online format to continue using different tools to deliver content. This encouraged participants to have experience with a variety of delivery formats and technology that they may not have had a chance to experiment with before. Live online sessions were delivered using a mixture of Teams and Zoom, as each platform enabled the demonstration of different features—for example, breakout rooms which worked better on Zoom. Optional online live discussion sessions were introduced to replace asynchronous forums on certain topics. Not only did this allow participants to speak directly to course leaders but it also gave them the opportunity to interact with each other—something otherwise missing from the blended approach. Digital bulletin boards such as Padlet were used to deliver in-module activities so participants could answer in their own time but still have the answers visible to other learners. One of the biggest challenges with this approach was how to gather peer feedback from the nano-teach sessions. Collating verbal feedback was time-consuming, and waiting for individuals to send their feedback via email was not a viable option. As a solution, we introduced Google Jamboards. This interactive whiteboard not only offered a solution to the issue of anonymous feedback collection but also exposed participants to another digital learning tool. This exposure was a key feature of the revised course, and an extra module on Moving Teaching Online was developed to engage learners in discussions around the best practices involved in transitioning their in-person sessions to a new format. It was important for learners to recognise that whilst digital tools were useful, they should complement learning outcomes rather than change them.

The final structure of the course from 2021 onward can be seen in table 16.3:

TABLE 16.3

The revised, shortened online course introduced in 2021.

Month	Delivery	Content
January	Mixture of live online presentation and asynchronous online module	Live: introduction and developing teaching philosophies (flipped learning) Asynchronous: are librarians teachers, introduction to reflective practice, introduction to peer observation
February	Asynchronous online module	Learning theories and information literacy frameworks Learning preferences and critique of learning preferences (optional)
March	Mixture of live online presentation and asynchronous online module	Live: backward design and CILN teaching template (flipped Learning session) Asynchronous: backward design and CILN teaching template resources and instructions
April	Asynchronous online module	Inclusivity, diversity and disability, creating teaching materials, and moving teaching online
May	Asynchronous online module	Peer review and constructive feedback, creating teaching materials, evaluations and assessing student feedback, when it all goes wrong, introduction to the nano-teach
June	Live online sessions	Nano-teaches (15 minutes)

The 2021 cohort consisted of twenty-two participants of whom fourteen completed. The online nature of the course also allowed for more flexible completion, and some learners chose to move through the content at a slower pace and rejoin a future cohort. A further thirteen learners joined the 2022 cohort (including an external participant) with six of these completing both the nano-teach and portfolio submission.

Feedback and Lessons Learnt

As the programme has had to adapt to changing circumstances, it has been very important to collect feedback from both cohorts to determine which aspects are working and where improvements can be made. A mixture of quantitative and qualitative feedback was collected using a formal end-of-programme survey and a more informal learner reflection. We also undertook our own reflection as course leaders to see how our experiences had been shaped by our learners.

The learner feedback survey was administered to the 2021 and 2022 cohorts. There was limited opportunity to collect formal feedback for the 2020 group due to ongoing issues relating to the pandemic although some informal comments were recorded.

Overall Programme

Learner feedback on the overall programme was very positive, with 85 percent prepared to recommend future participation to a colleague. The survey questions in this area focused on the format and content of the programme as it was especially important to understand how these had been impacted by the move to a fully online course. Most learners were highly supportive of this change and reported that it had helped their participation as they were able to fit the workload more easily around existing commitments. All respondents had engaged with the taught online sessions, either live or by watching the recordings if they couldn't make it on the day. Those who attended live reported that it was good to have a chance to meet others and exchange experiences and even indicated that they would prefer more of this in future runs of the programme.

The majority of learners also strongly agreed that the topics covered were relevant to their current practice, pitched at the right level, and included issues relevant to the way that they actually teach in a library context—for example, how to deliver a one-shot session. This was a particularly welcome response as it was a key motivator for the development of the programme. For many learners, a highlight was a chance to develop a deeper understanding of the pedagogical approaches that underpin the teaching they offer. All those surveyed felt that the programme had helped to increase their knowledge of theory. As one participant wrote, "I'm finding the theory behind the practical teaching interesting and extremely useful as I've not done the conceptual underpinning before." Others reported similar outcomes and said that it would help them in preparations for future teaching sessions.

Influence on Practice

Building on the theoretical knowledge they gained during the programme, many learners had already begun to make changes to their practice or intended to do so. These changes were focused on three key areas: using backward design to inform planning, making use of a teaching template to design sessions, and embedding inclusive practices in their teaching.

Backward design was new to many of those on the programme, but they reported that it was a practical outcome that they would use in their future planning. Many learners mentioned it as a highlight of the programme, with one commenting that it "changed my view of how to do things." Combining this approach with using a template to help plan sessions step by step meant that learners were able to leave the course with a new strategy for designing sessions for maximum impact. During the programme, several learners struggled with how to fit the content for their sessions into the limited time available—a struggle familiar to many teaching librarians. Backward design using either an Excel spreadsheet or a structured template[7] enabled them to make the best use of the time they had, and as one learner commented, "It makes me think in a concrete way and helped limit what I do."

Inclusive practice was a topic often highlighted by learners, and this was reiterated in the feedback, showing the deep impression the topic made. While some of the comments focused on aspects of accessibility and Universal Design, such as ensuring slides were legible and alternative text was provided for images, others took embedding inclusivity further. They detailed plans to include more diverse examples in their resource instruction sessions, such as ensuring they included books or articles authored by women or minority groups. Other examples focused on the importance of setting clear expectations to create an environment where students felt encouraged to have open discussions. As one learner wrote, "I made sure my presentation was as inclusive as possible, fostering a 'safe space' environment for all to share personal histories," which helped to generate an incredibly useful discussion of a sensitive topic.

Impact on Professional Development

Learners also reported an impact on their personal and professional development. At the start of the programme, participants are asked to rate their confidence and experience levels when it comes to teaching. This is done on a scale from 0 to 10 with 0 representing no confidence/experience and 10 representing full confidence/experience. This exercise is repeated at the end of the programme after learners had completed their nano-teach. They were given a chance to reflect on their experiences of the teaching session and then asked how they would rate themselves using the same scale. Participants were deliberately not told at this point what their initial assessment was, although it is possible that they remembered the score they had given. Over the three cohorts, all learners showed an increase in both areas, with an average increase of four points on the confidence scale and three on the experience scale. Whilst these figures are not scientific proof, it was gratifying to see that learners were rating themselves more highly than before the programme, especially around the key aim of developing confidence. Those learners who had rated themselves lower in confidence at the start of the programme showed the largest improvement at the end, but this is perhaps to be expected given their initial confidence. This increase in confidence was echoed in comments made in the formal feedback survey. Learners wrote that the programme had made them "more confident with each session I deliver" and that "increased confidence means I will feel more comfortable putting myself forward for a wider range of sessions with students and visitors."

Participation also helped learner professional development in other ways. The value of reflective practice was emphasised throughout the course, and many embraced this concept as a way to keep learning from their experiences after the programme had finished. One of the most interesting themes to emerge from the feedback was that taking part in a blended learning course gave participants a new perspective on what the experience was like for their own learners. They were able to observe what worked well and what needed adjustment, and several stated that this was one of the most valuable outcomes of the programme for them. As one learner commented, "It increased my confidence exponentially … by showing me how to be a better student and teacher." Not only did this enhance their own professional development, but it also helped them provide more effective blended and online learning opportunities for their own communities.

Nano-teach and Assessment

As the programme is intended to have practical outcomes for learners, we were keen to get feedback on the nano-teach assessment model. Although members of each cohort reported during the course that the prospect of delivering the session caused them some anxiety, this was not reflected in the formal feedback. All learners who responded agreed that the nano-teach helped improve their confidence, and some even called it a highlight of the course. They particularly welcomed the chance to put what they had learnt into practice in front of a supportive audience of their peers, who offered constructive feedback, and many of them used it as an opportunity to test out sessions that they planned to deliver to students. Those presenting nano-teaches also found that they learned from the experiences of others, commenting that being able to view different approaches to delivering content was not only enjoyable but educational. Some learners commented that one way to alleviate anxiety around the nano-teach would be to have an example session to observe so that they felt better prepared, and this is certainly something that we can consider for future cohorts.

Areas for Improvement

There were still some recommended areas of improvement, however, for us to take into consideration as we plan future programmes.

The content and corresponding workload for each monthly module varies depending on the topic being covered. Although the syllabus[8] is designed to spread this load over the entire programme, there are inevitably months that have more content and so require more time. A good example of this is seen in the first two modules. January's module introduces learners to the programme and asks them to consider teaching philosophies, the role of the librarian as teacher, and reflective practice. Although this is a lot of information to cover, each is a short introduction with links to further details that can be explored later. In contrast, the module for February explores essential learning theories and includes an extra optional module that learners can complete. As one of the main goals of the programme is to offer a thorough grounding in pedagogy, this module goes into greater depth than the previous month, although we have tried to keep this manageable. However, some learners reported that they found this overwhelming, would have preferred more detail of the content, and suggested timings to be made available in advance as this would help them to better plan their study time around other commitments. Whilst we take this feedback on board, we are hesitant to include suggested timings for any module in case it creates false expectations in a programme where people are encouraged to learn at their own pace and explore individual areas of interest.

One potential solution is to open the content of modules in advance of their "official" start date. This would let learners better anticipate the workload and adjust their plans accordingly. We could also release the entire programme in January, but we feel that this would not be feasible as each module is designed to build on previous content and it helps to access this in sequence. Many of these issues are a result of the programme being condensed from a nine- to a six-month programme. When planning this change, we gave serious thought to which material would have to be cut and where modules could be combined to make the best use of time, but it may be that after two cohorts we need to revisit these decisions.

Lessons for Course Leaders

In addition to the feedback received from learners, we as course leaders also developed our own knowledge and experience whilst running the programme. Nowhere was this more evident than in our learning around inclusivity. The term synergy is apt here as the sum of the various parts of the programme resulted in something much greater than predicted. Although the programme emphasised the importance of inclusive practices throughout, these were necessarily influenced by our own lived experiences. Whilst we tried to include as much information as we could, there were always going to be gaps in our knowledge. However, the programme brought together staff from a range of levels across the library system, and each one also brought with them their own diverse experiences that we all could learn from. As a result, we developed knowledge of more accessibility needs, community language, and appropriate adjustments than any of us could have alone. We found that learning from each other in this way was a key part of building trust and broadening our own definitions of what it meant to be inclusive.

We were also pleasantly surprised that other developments challenged our assumptions around creating a programme that was available to all. The initial move to a blended format pre-pandemic had been carefully planned to offer learners the best of both in-person and flexible online learning, and we were worried that the switch to online-only would undermine this. In fact, feedback showed that the result was the opposite. The pivot to online proved to be the catalyst for many learners signing up for the programme as the increased flexibility meant that they could now fit it in around other commitments. Several learners commented that they would not have been able to justify even the blended programme, so it was gratifying to see that this unanticipated change had positive consequences.

Another outcome of this change was that we discovered learners developing their own ways to learn. When designing the online programme, we were careful to offer routes for participants to take so they were not overwhelmed. Although some did use these, many more developed their own successful methods, including peer-support and mentoring groups with close colleagues. Learners would meet separately from the programme to discuss the content and how it related to their own experiences. Not only did this help them develop their knowledge, but it also meant that they had someone to help motivate them through the potentially isolating experience of online learning. As course leaders, we have discussed the potential to formalise some of these initiatives for future cohorts but have decided against it as is it better to allow such things to develop organically rather than disrupt something that is working through (well-meaning) interference.

Perhaps the biggest lesson of all for us is that there is always more to learn about teaching—for us as practitioners, programme designers, and inclusive teachers. The whole experience of delivering the programme has enhanced our own knowledge and professional development opportunities and helped us in our own roles outside the course.

Conclusion and Next Steps

In addition to positive outcomes for learners and course leaders, the programme has reflected positively on the wider perception of librarians within the university. As noted earlier, many lecturers and academics undertake their own teaching qualifications as part of their roles. Having library staff take part in their own tailored programme, covering similar topics, results in a common experience between the different types of staff, helps to raise the profile of librarians, and allows their teaching to be taken more seriously by non-library colleagues. The programme has helped to raise the profile of the teaching offered by libraries and demonstrate that it is based on sound pedagogical knowledge and reflection, further helping to enhance the reputation of the library as an educator. The key immediate goal for the programme is to pursue formal accreditation so that learners who complete are recognised in some way. As the course is mapped to the HEA framework, the aim is to seek accreditation from this awarding body so that learners gain the associate level of fellowship.[9]

Those looking to create similar initiatives in their own institutions will hopefully see that there are many benefits to implementation. The Teaching and Learning for Librarians programme has been designed with academic librarians in mind, but there is no reason that it could not be adapted to cover different sectors depending on local needs. What do school librarians need to know about pedagogy? What about those working in law firms or business? How could the programme be built upon to cater to the way they teach? In addition to pursuing formal recognition for the current programme, we are hoping that by making the syllabus and other materials openly available, we will encourage colleagues from different sectors to think about how they can address the pedagogical needs of their own librarians and build on these foundations to create their own communities of teaching librarians.

Notes

1.   Steven J. Bell and John Shank, "The Blended Librarian: A Blueprint for Redefining the Teaching and Learning Role of Academic Librarians," *College & Research Libraries News* 65, no. 2 (July 2004): 373.

2.   Bell and Shank, "The Blended Librarian."
3.   Rachel W. Gammons, Alexander J. Carroll, and Lindsay Ingle Carpenter, "I Never Knew I Could Be a Teacher," *portal: Libraries and the Academy* 18, no. 2 (April 2018): 334, https://muse.jhu.edu/pub/1/article/690733.
4.   "Quality and Standards Conditions," Office for Students, accessed May 5, 2022, https://www.officeforstudents.org.uk/media/084f719f-5344-4717-a71b-a7ea00b9f53f/quality-and-standards-conditions.pdf.
5.   Alexander J. Carroll and Kevin Michael Klipfel, "Talent, Schmalent: An Instructional Design/Action Research Framework for the Professionalization of Teaching in Academic Libraries," *The Journal of Academic Librarianship* 45, no. 2 (March 2019): 113, https://doi.org/10.1016/j.acalib.2019.01.009.
6.   Grant Wiggins and Jay McTighe, *Understanding by Design*, 2nd ed. (Upper Saddle River: Pearson, 2005).
7.   "Designing Teaching: Teaching Template," Tools for Teaching, Cambridge University Libraries, last modified November 24, 2022, https://libguides.cam.ac.uk/toolsforteaching/teachingtemplate.
8.   Kirstie Preest and Claire Sewell, "Teaching and Learning for Librarians: Course Outline," Knowledge Commons, accessed October 14, 2022, https://hcommons.org/deposits/item/hc:47075/.
9.   Advance HE, Associate Fellowship, 2020, https://www.advance-he.ac.uk/fellowship/associate-fellowship.

Bibliography

Advance HE. Associate Fellowship. 2020. https://www.advance-he.ac.uk/fellowship/associate-fellowship.

Bell, Steven J., and John Shank. "The Blended Librarian: A Blueprint for Redefining the Teaching and Learning Role of Academic Librarians." *College & Research Libraries News* 65, no. 7 (2004): 372–75.

Cambridge University Libraries. "Designing Teaching: Teaching Template." Accessed June 8, 2023. https://libguides.cam.ac.uk/toolsforteaching/teachingtemplate.

Carroll, Alexander J., and Kevin Michael Klipfel. "Talent, Schmalent: An Instructional Design/Action Research Framework for the Professionalization of Teaching in Academic Libraries." *The Journal of Academic Librarianship* 45, no. 2 (March 1, 2019): 110–18. https://doi.org/10.1016/j.acalib.2019.01.009.

Gammons, Rachel W., Alexander J. Carroll, and Lindsay Inge Carpenter. "'I Never Knew I Could Be a Teacher': A Student-Centered MLIS Fellowship for Future Teacher-Librarians." *portal: Libraries and the Academy* 18, no. 2 (2018): 331–62. https://muse.jhu.edu/pub/1/article/690733.

Preest, Kirstie, and Claire Sewell. "Teaching and Learning for Librarians: Course Outline." Knowledge Commons. July 2022. https://hcommons.org/deposits/item/hc:47075/.

Wiggins, Grant P., and Jay McTighe. *Understanding by Design*. Expanded 2nd ed. Alexandria, VA: Association for Supervision and Curriculum Development, 2005.

CHAPTER 17

Communities of Support:
Using the Community of Practice Model for Library Instructor Development

Melissa A. Wong and Laura Saunders

LEARNING OUTCOMES

Readers will be able to
- identify ways a community of practice can provide support and professional development for instruction librarians;
- identify potential structures and considerations for designing a community of practice; and
- implement strategies that facilitate knowledge and skill-building related to inclusive and critical pedagogies as part of a community of practice.

Introduction

Instruction has long been a central aspect of academic librarianship, yet many librarians report feeling underprepared for teaching roles, and many may feel isolated in their work.[1] Recent events, including anti-racist protests and a pandemic that forced most library services online, including instruction, have emphasized the need for librarians to have robust instruction skills and highlighted the importance of equity, diversity, and inclusion (EDI) practices, such as inclusive pedagogy, empathetic teaching, and principles of universal design for learning. Even seasoned instructors may feel overwhelmed by the magnitude of issues impacting their practice, and many instruction librarians seek professional development opportunities and support for improving their practice.

Traditional professional development offerings often utilize an expert-led approach in which an invited speaker delivers a planned presentation. While such offerings may include speaker-led activities and opportunities for participants to ask questions, these models replicate a traditional classroom with an expert speaker in a position of authority determining the content to be learned while attendees are cast into the role of learners. Such an approach replicates the power imbalances of the traditional classroom and risks ignoring or minimizing the knowledge and experience that participants bring to the conversation.

Another drawback to expert-led training is that it may not offer support for the affective aspects of teaching.[2] In addition to the emotional labor inherent in teaching in general, instruction librarians must navigate relationships with faculty members who do not always see them as peers, the challenges of a tenure system that was not designed with their work structures in mind, and heavy administrative loads.[3] Instructors from marginalized identities are likely to face additional challenges, including isolation on campus, microaggressions, challenges to their expertise and authority, and other forms of pushback in the classroom.[4]

Communities of practice offer an alternative model for professional development among instruction librarians. In contrast to expert-led trainings and workshops, communities of practice are participant-led and emphasize shared expertise and mutual learning. In a community of practice, everyone is simultaneously both a learner and a valued professional with expertise to share. Collegial by nature, they offer a low-stakes and low-pressure way for librarians to reflect on their classroom experiences, exchange ideas and pedagogical strategies, and continue learning in order to improve their practice. And because they support sustained interaction between participants, communities of practice can be a place for instructors to find (and offer) support and encouragement for the affective aspects of teaching.

In this chapter, the authors explore the benefits and challenges of using communities of practice for professional development of instruction librarians. Drawing on our experience leading the LIS Pedagogy Chat—an online community of practice—we share advice on designing, launching, and sustaining a local community of practice.

LIS Pedagogy Chat

The authors' interest in communities of practice began when we inadvertently started an online community of practice during the COVID-19 pandemic. Prior to the pandemic, both authors were experienced online instructors. When the pandemic pushed institutions to move face-to-face courses into the online environment on short notice, including those that had never been taught online before, we offered an introductory webinar on online teaching for library and information science faculty.[5] We also found ourselves dispensing advice to colleagues and educator friends via email, phone calls, social media, and informal workshops.

The authors discussed ways to offer more support to colleagues, such as a series of ongoing workshops, but quickly realized that we did not have the capacity (or desire) to develop and deliver a formal workshop every few weeks. We also discussed our desire to improve our own practice as online instructors, not just position ourselves as experts teaching others, and with that, our online discussion group LIS Pedagogy Chat was born.[6]

LIS Pedagogy Chat meets online on a monthly or bi-monthly basis. The topics vary, but all are related to teaching within library and information science and have included feminist pedagogy, dismantling deficit thinking, critical youth studies, and designing authentic assessments. Each session features a guest moderator who provides a brief introduction to the day's topic, presents four to five discussion questions, and then leads a collegial discussion for all participants. The discussion may follow the moderator's planned questions, or it may go in a different direction based on participants' needs and interests. To preserve the environment of a supportive, non-judgmental community, we do not record sessions; however, we do maintain an archive of moderators' slides and collaborative notes from the discussion.

In line with the community of practice model, we have found that participants greatly value the discussion aspect of LIS Pedagogy Chat. The discussion format makes this a true community of practice where we draw on experience and expertise of participants, and while attendees appreciate a brief research overview shared by a moderator, people clearly like coming to a discussion rather than another webinar.

Communities of Practice

Etienne Wenger-Trayner and Beverly Wenger-Trayner define a community of practice as "a group of people who engage in a process of collective learning."[7] In their definition, a community of practice has three essential characteristics. First, members must have a shared domain of interest, one in which they have both a commitment and expertise or direct experience to share. Second, the community must be based on relationships between members; members learn through conversation and interaction with one another. Third, beyond sharing an interest in the domain, members must be practitioners who are engaged in an area of activity and seek to improve their practice through knowledge-sharing. Thus, Wenger-Trayner and Wenger-Trayner note, a webpage of resources is not a community of practice, nor is a group of people who work in the same location but do not gather for mutual learning. Building on this idea that a community of practice is more than a loose collective passively sharing resources, Jesús Oliver and Julia Olkin define a community of practice as a "collaborative, informal network that supports professional practitioners in their efforts to develop shared understandings and engage in work-relevant knowledge building."[8]

Communities of practice take many forms, from the highly informal, such as a group of colleagues who gather to "talk shop" at lunch, to formalized learning programs with predetermined goals and a schedule of regular meetings. They can take place within an organization or, particularly in the age of discussion forums and online meeting software, bring together participants from different locations and organizations.

Communities may focus on a broad area of interest, such as instruction, or coalesce around a very specific topic. For example, Christina H. Gola and Lisa Martin describe a community of practice that focuses on emotional intelligence and its application to the academic library workplace, while the Association of College and Research Libraries' Contemplative Pedagogy Interest Group defines itself as a community of practice with a shared interest in applying contemplative pedagogy to library instruction.[9]

Communities of practice will vary in their structure and activities. Many communities center around exchanging ideas and advice, exploring new developments in a field, and sharing resources. Communities of practice can engage in collaborative problem-solving, whether that involves identifying and addressing recurring challenges or tackling large-scale, emergent problems. David Gomillion et al. describe a community of practice within a business school where faculty met to discuss strategies for embedding the program's newly adopted core competencies into their courses.[10] Oliver and Olkin describe a similar effort using a community of practice to support curricular changes in a mathematics department.[11] The LibCares Team at the University of Washington Libraries began as a place to discuss the challenges of public service and handling difficult patron encounters, then evolved to take on a problem-solving role, arranging training sessions for all front-line staff, creating resource cards with recommended phrases for use in challenging situations, and scheduling dialogues with library and campus officials.[12]

Communities of practice can play a vital role in offering support and encouragement to colleagues and, as mentioned earlier, discussion of the affective aspects of teaching is often a central feature of instruction-related communities of practice. This support and encouragement can be particularly valuable during times of crisis and for instructors who feel isolated in their work. Lynn Jettpace et al. describe how their existing community of practice for instructors pivoted to address online course delivery at the start of the pandemic, noting, "We transitioned immediately from a best practice and research collective to a support structure during a crisis."[13] Renee Jones et al. also emphasize the value of communities of practice as a place for mutual support, describing a community of practice for Black faculty that celebrates one another's accomplishments and alleviates the sense of isolation on campus.[14]

Community of Practice Models

For educators, communities of practice most often blend collegial discussion, exploration of relevant research and literature, idea- and resource-sharing, and/or supportive and constructive conversations about pedagogical challenges. Several models exist for facilitating such idea-sharing and discussions, including journal clubs, peer presentations, and discussion groups.

Journal Clubs

In the journal club model, members gather to discuss pre-selected readings, such as journal articles, book chapters, or entire books. Gola and Martin suggest libraries use free online courses as a structure and source of material for a community of practice, particularly when groups are interested in a short-term, focused learning experience.[15]

Using shared readings or other resources as the basis for a community of practice has many advantages, including giving focus to the discussion, bringing research or data into the conversation, and prompting engagement with new ideas and perspectives. However, the success of a journal club hinges on members' knowledge of the reading as a starting point for discussion. Just as in the classroom, groups may struggle if members have not completed the readings prior to the meeting and, given the many demands on instruction librarians' time, organizers should consider whether this model will work for their community.

Peer Presentations

Similar to how journal clubs use a shared reading as a focal point for gatherings, some communities of practice use presentations to share information and spark discussion. In line with the community of practice ethos, these presentations are often informal and given by participants themselves rather than outside experts and are accompanied by opportunities for robust discussion. A good example of a presentation-based community of practice is morbidity and mortality conferences, in which physicians within a hospital meet to review and discuss cases of adverse patient outcomes.

Presentations can tap into participants' expertise and give structure to meetings, making it easier to keep meetings on track and productive. However, this model does require more work for participants and may dissuade some individuals from participating, especially early-career professionals who feel they do not yet have expertise to share. Organizers may need to identify and encourage potential presenters rather than relying on a sufficient number of volunteers to step forward.

Discussion Groups

In the discussion group model, participants identify a topic of interest and share ideas and experiences through casual conversation. Topics may vary from meeting to meeting or groups may take a deep dive, discussing one topic over an extended period of time. Some groups take a problem-based approach, where members bring challenges they face in their work and the group brainstorms solutions.

Discussion-based communities of practice can be very informal. As Wenger-Trayner and Wenger-Trayner note, a group of nurses that gathers at lunch and shares advice for patient care is a community of practice.[16] However, many discussion-based communities of practice do take a formal approach with a regular meeting schedule and a pre-planned agenda of topics for future meetings. Even with this more formalized approach, the discussion-based model tends to be less labor-intensive since participants do not need to prepare in advance. However, in the absence of firm facilitation or a strong shared agreement to stay on topic, discussion groups can quickly get off track with socializing, tangential conversations, or griping, leaving conversations unproductive and members frustrated.

Organizing a Community of Practice

Regardless of the structure, most communities of practice, even casual discussion groups, require some leadership to establish and sustain them. As a starting point, the community likely needs an organizer who plans when and where to meet, reserves a space or sets up an online meeting, and sends meeting reminders to participants. If the group is organized around readings or presentations, the organizer needs to maintain a schedule of planned readings or presenters. Large or very active groups may want to identify co-organizers who can share the workload or establish a mechanism for rotating organizers on a pre-determined basis, such as each semester or annually.

For example, as part of establishing the LIS Pedagogy Chat, the authors put in several hours creating a format, planning a roster of topics, recruiting discussion moderators, and advertising sessions. We also created a slide template for moderators and wrote templates for emails and advertisements. Once the community was established, one partner took on the task of creating and maintaining our website while the other partner handles registrations. In addition, we still recruit moderators and arrange sessions, help with advertising and registration, open and close each session, and keep the website up to date with the schedule and an archive of past sessions. (The appendices provide examples of some of this work.) Now that we are established, this ongoing work amounts to only one to two hours per week; however, there was definitely an investment in time to get the program off the ground.

Once a group is established, the organizer can serve as the discussion moderator; however, it is not uncommon to rotate moderators so that over time every participant takes a turn leading a session. This spreads out the work of preparing for and leading a discussion, fosters the inclusion of diverse perspectives, and provides an opportunity for participants to develop skills in facilitating discussions. Another benefit of rotating moderators is that moderators may use instructional activities or technologies that are new to other participants, thus modeling new pedagogical approaches that participants can take back to their own classrooms.

As noted earlier, organizers may need to identify and encourage discussion moderators. In our experience, it is not uncommon for potential moderators to initially respond to our invitation by protesting that they are not "experts" and therefore not appropriate moderators. We take this opportunity to discuss how the community of practice format flips the traditional approach so that we are all learning together. This approach has allowed many moderators, including both early-career professionals and more senior colleagues, to explore topics of interest or challenges from a learning perspective.

Establishing a template or set of guidelines for meetings can ease the process of preparing to moderate and ensure that meetings continue to remain true to the group's intentions. Once these guidelines are established, organizers can use them to gently remind moderators of the group's format as well as expectations like the inclusion of critical perspectives.

Organizers should also be ready to help facilitate discussions or support moderators as necessary. We have found that we need to be ready to support our guest moderators, helping them facilitate busy discussions or offering up new discussion questions if the conversation starts to lag. Because we use a presentation and discussion model, moderators and participants used to the more traditional, expert-led webinar model are apt to fall into a pattern where participants direct their questions to the moderator and the moderator answers each question from their own knowledge and experience. If this pattern emerges during a session, sometimes the organizer can redirect the talk back toward discussion. For instance, after a moderator answers a question, the organizer might step in and say something like, "That is really interesting! I wonder if anyone in the group has had a different experience or tried something similar?"

At the same time, organizers should strive to balance adherence to the group's format and goals with an openness to the unexpected. In leading LIS Pedagogy Chat, we do try to maintain the focus of the sessions and have realized that, in the spirit of being a community, we sometimes have to cede some control. Sometimes moderators will take the discussion in a different direction than we expected. For instance, one chat ended up focused on participants' personal experiences as learners rather than instructors. While unexpected, it was a rich conversation that clearly resonated with participants, showing that allowing the discussion to develop organically can be beneficial as well.

Critical Pedagogy and Inclusive Teaching

Communities of practice can offer a valuable space for instruction librarians to explore issues of equity and diversity and share pedagogical strategies that create more inclusive classrooms. While these topics may arise organically as part of discussions, particularly if many members are already familiar with and interested in inclusive teaching, communities that value critical pedagogy and inclusive teaching will likely need to be intentional in integrating this content into their discussions. Francesca Marineo, Chelsea Heinbach, and Rosan Mitola argue that this intentionality is important for many reasons. First, it recenters equity and inclusion work from an individual pursuit to a shared responsibility and, in the case of localized communities of practice, an organizational goal.[17] Second, it stresses the importance of instructors from majority groups learning about and engaging in equity work—work that otherwise falls disproportionately on those from marginalized identities.[18]

At a minimum, communities should establish an expectation that all topics will be explored through an EDI lens and codify this expectation in their guidelines. Organizers can follow through with reminders to discussion moderators as they are scheduling and/or confirming meetings. Organizers can also come prepared with their own questions that raise issues of diversity and inclusion relative to the meeting's topic, and if they are helping moderate the discussion, affirm and build on participant contributions that further diversity-related conversations.

Communities should also schedule discussion topics that explicitly center critical and inclusive pedagogy. For example, LIS Pedagogy Chat has hosted sessions on feminist pedagogy, strengths-based approaches, teaching critical cataloging, critiquing course evaluations, and accessibility. This approach may require more effort on the part of organizers. With LIS Pedagogy Chat, we find ourselves combing the literature and professional presentations to identify topics and brainstorming and reaching out to moderators who could lead a conversation on those topics. We have also consciously worked to invite a diverse group of moderators, including junior colleagues who bring new perspectives, to amplify a range of voices and experiences.

Marineo, Heinbach, and Mitola provide additional guidance for organizers committed to discussions of equity and inclusion. They suggest that organizers reflect on their own positionality and the power dynamics that may bring to the community of practice. They also recommend planning for how one will handle challenging moments in the discussion and being mindful that discussions do not place an undue burden on or retraumatize participants from marginalized identities.[19]

Challenges

Communities of practice can pose some challenges, especially to organizers. Particularly in forming a local community of practice, organizers may need to build departmental or institutional support for participation in the community. While communities of practice typically do not take much in terms of financial resources, they do take some effort and care, especially in the beginning. If managers do not see the value in these activities, they might not support their employees taking the time to organize, facilitate, or participate in a community of practice. To generate buy-in from managers, organizers and participants can point to the benefits, from the learning and professional development to the supportive community aspects that can be especially crucial to more novice librarians as well as those from marginalized identities. Gola and Martin recommend finding an organizational champion—a person in a position of formal leadership who convinces others of the value of the community of practice in addressing an organizational challenge.[20]

Another challenge is that communities of practice can be difficult to assess. Communities of practice tend to be informal, and members may not attend every session, particularly in communities that are discussion-focused and where topics vary from meeting to meeting. Even formalized communities may experience fluctuations in membership as individuals become absorbed in other priorities or leave the institution. In addition, communities of practice may focus on affective areas of teaching, like confidence and efficacy, that are more difficult to assess. One might argue that communities of practice are not necessarily meant to be assessed, but it is a point worth considering for librarians working within institutions or settings that require documentation of the impact of professional development offerings.

Lisa Bosman and Philip Voglewede offer some strategies for assessing the impact of communities of practice, including facilitator observations and surveys of participants. In their study of engineering faculty in a community of practice, Bosman and Voglewede were also able to collect reflections and documentation of course changes. However, it should be noted that the communities of practice these researchers facilitated were formalized and included a stipend for faculty participants, which may have allowed them to ask more of participants in documenting their participation.[21]

Starting Your Own Community of Practice

A number of communities of practice exist, so librarians looking for a support system and place to share ideas might find an established community to join. However, some practitioners might prefer to start their own community, perhaps tailored to their interests, geographic location, career paths, or unique circumstances. One of the first steps to launch a new community of practice is to identify the goals of the group, including what you want to learn and whether you want to have a specific focus like pedagogy, management, equity and inclusion, early career development, and so on. Once you have a set of goals in mind, you can select the structure that seems most likely to support those goals while being manageable from a logistical standpoint.

Organizers should also consider who their intended community might be and how members will be invited (and encouraged) to join, with the caveat that the intended membership and the focus and format will probably inform each other. For instance, if you intend to focus on your own organization or local community, you might find face-to-face meetings most effective, while a community focused on trends in higher education could be of interest to all academic librarians and therefore might be best suited to an online forum. The more intentional organizers are about these decisions, the more likely they are to succeed. Bringing people together to chat without a goal or direction could result in a nice social session but might not lead to tangible outcomes. If participants feel that they did not get anything out of a session, they are less likely to return.

As noted earlier, organizing a community of practice does take some work, especially in the beginning. The organizer should carefully consider logistics such as when and where to meet, keeping in mind the intended audience and what will work for the greatest number of people. For instance, LIS Pedagogy Chat always meets at 2:00 p.m. on Fridays. We chose Fridays because they can be a somewhat lighter day for academic librarians, and we chose 2:00 p.m. because it was neither too early for attendees on the West Coast nor too late for those on the East Coast. A regular day and time are easier for attendees to remember and makes scheduling easier overall.

Organizers should also give some attention to creating an environment of trust, openness, and respect. It may be helpful to establish ground rules for participation and even discuss how violations of the community's guidelines will be addressed. Communities of practice that draw their members from within a single institution—especially if members have differing levels of authority or status on campus—may also need to decide how to address power imbalances while still maintaining a climate of openness and vulnerability.[22]

Once these details are decided, the organizer should consider any other structures that might support success, such as a webpage or listserv for communication, guidelines for moderators, and/or a shared drive to organize schedules, notes, and other files. Other considerations are whether sessions will be recorded and, if so, how they will be archived and shared, and whether the sessions will follow a standard format. For instance, LIS Pedagogy Chat always begins with a framing presentation followed by an open discussion while the University of Illinois Library's AI Infodemic used a Padlet to solicit discussion questions from the day's reading.[23] Martha McAlister recommends finding a balance of structure and freedom, arguing, "Too much structure and the group will suffocate. Not enough structure and the group may experience chaos and confusion."[24]

Organizers will also want to consider who will facilitate discussions. In LIS Pedagogy Chat, the person providing the framing presentation also moderates the discussion. However, we have observed that some of our moderators are more experienced than others at handling a fast-paced discussion that is happening on the mic and in the chat simultaneously, and we often step in to assist. Organizers may need to be prepared to assist in the discussion by helping to keep the discussion on track and drawing out the participants. If the sessions are online, it can also be helpful to have a second person monitor the chat, bring questions forward, and/or provide technical support.

Conclusion

Communities of practice offer a participant-led approach to professional development. By emphasizing shared expertise and mutual learning as well as sustained interactions between participants, they can be a supportive space for instruction librarians to build pedagogical knowledge, identify classroom practices that foster inclusive teaching, and find support and encouragement for both innovation and the affective aspects of teaching. Many academic library-oriented communities of practice already exist, so those interested in participating might find an established community that meets their needs. However, some librarians might be inspired to start their own community, tailoring the focus to their own interests and finding like-minded colleagues with whom to share ideas. Launching a new community of practice takes some work and planning, but the reward is worth the effort.

APPENDIX A
Example of an LIS Pedagogy Chat Schedule

The LIS Pedagogy Chat website includes a schedule of upcoming sessions. The information includes the date and time, topic, and the moderator's name and institutional affiliation along with a link to register. Registrations are captured in a simple Google form and a link to the Zoom session is emailed to registrants the morning of the session. This screenshot provides an example from fall 2021. In more recent semesters, we have also included a brief (one- or two-sentence) description of the scheduled topic.

Schedule & Registration

November 19 – Dismantling Deficit Thinking and Shifting to Strengths-Based Approaches

Moderators: Chelsea Heinbach (UNLV), Rosan Mitola (UNLV), and Erin Rinto (U of Cincinnati)
2:00 p.m. Eastern / 1:00 p.m. Central / 12:00 p.m. Mountain / 11:00 a.m. Pacific
Register

December 3 – Professionalism and Professional Skills for LIS Graduates

Moderator: Kawanna Bright, Heidi Julien, Laura Saunders, & Amy VanScoy
2:00 p.m. Eastern / 1:00 p.m. Central / 12:00 p.m. Mountain / 11:00 a.m. Pacific
Register

APPENDIX B
Sample Email to Invite a Moderator

The following is an example of an email we send to colleagues inviting them to lead an LIS Pedagogy Chat session. In some cases, moderators have attended a previous session and expressed interest in a topic; in other cases, we suggest a topic based on something they have recently published or presented. This is our first opportunity to ensure that potential moderators understand our discussion-based format.

Dear [colleague],

Greetings! I hope this email finds you well!

You may have seen on social media that Melissa Wong and I run an online professional development series, LIS Pedagogy Chat (https://www.lispedagogychat.org/). As the name implies, it is a discussion-based series focused on teaching in library and information science.

We were wondering if you would be willing to moderate a discussion in Fall 2023? We hope you would be willing to lead a discussion about [topic].

Our moderators provide a brief presentation (15-20 minutes) that frames the day's topic, and then lead a large group discussion for all participants, community of practice style. We ask moderators to prepare 4-5 questions to jumpstart the discussion, but have found that the discussion may move in other directions based on participants' interests. Since you are an experienced instructor, we are confident you would be a capable discussion facilitator, however we would also be happy to assist with the discussion portion of the session, if you prefer.

Please let us know if you might be interested. We usually schedule one session per month, always on a Friday at 2pm ET, and right now our fall schedule is wide open.

Best,

Laura & Melissa

APPENDIX C
Sample Email to Moderators to Confirm a Session

The following is an example of an email we send to moderators approximately ten days before their scheduled session. In addition to addressing logistics, the email reminds moderators of the discussion-based format of LIS Pedagogy Chat.

Dear [moderator],

We are looking forward to your upcoming LIS Pedagogy Chat session, Friday, [date], at 2 pm ET, on [topic]. Laura will email you a link to the Zoom session a few days in advance. Please plan to meet us about 10 minutes before your session for a mic check.

We will handle the advertising, registration, and Zoom meeting. We advertise on Twitter and a few library listservs. You are welcome to share information about your session with colleagues and on social media as well. People can register to attend on our website at https://www.lispedagogychat.org/.

As a reminder, our format is for moderators to provide a brief presentation that frames your topic (no more than 15–20 minutes) and then lead a large group discussion for all participants, community of practice style. The discussion is a great place for folks to share their own strategies and challenges in teaching the topic and as the moderator, your role is to keep the conversation flowing, but do not need to have all the answers. It is very helpful if you come with 3-4 discussions questions (e.g., How do you…? What challenges have you faced with…?). Please let us know if you would like help moderating! We usually have some folks on the mic and some participating via chat, and if you/we can pull the two streams together, it is a great conversation.

We take a set of collaborative notes during the discussion and make it and any slides you share available in our archive. If you could email us a copy of your slides the day of the session, we would be very appreciative.

Thank you, and please let us know if you have any questions,

Melissa

Notes

1. Charlene Seymour, "Ethnographic Study of Information Literacy Librarians' Work Experience: A Report from Two States," in *Transforming Information Literacy Programs: Intersecting Frontiers of Self, Library Culture, and Campus Community*, eds. Carroll Wilkinson and Courtney Bruch (Chicago: ACRL Publications, 2012), 45–72.
2. Heidi Julien and Shelagh K. Genuis, "Emotional Labour in Librarians' Instructional Work," *Journal of Documentation* 65, no. 6 (December 2009): 926–37, https://doi.org/10.1108/00220410910998924; Lorraine Evans, "Emotional Labor of Instruction Librarians: Causes, Impact and Management," in

The Emotional Self at Work in Higher Education, eds. Ingrid Ruffin and Charissa Powell (Hershey, PA: IGI Global, 2021), 104–19.

3. Veronica Arellano Douglas, "Innovating Against a Brick Wall: Rebuilding the Structures that Shape Our Teaching," *Libraries + Inquiry* (blog), June 12, 2019, https://veronicaarellanodouglas.com/critlib/innovating-against-a-brick-wall-rebuilding-the-structures-that-shape-our-teaching-tilc-2019-keynote/; Veronica Arellano Douglas and Joanna Gadsby, "All Carrots, No Sticks: Relational Practice and Library Instruction Coordination," *In the Library with the Lead Pipe* (July 10, 2019), http://www.inthelibrarywiththeleadpipe.org/2019/all-carrots-no-sticks-relational-practice-and-library-instruction-coordination/.

4. Frank Tuitt et al., "Teaching in the Line of Fire: Faculty of Color in the Academy," *Thought and Action,* Fall 2009, 65–74; S. Renée Jones et al., "Fostering a Sense of Community Among Black Faculty Through a Faculty Learning Community," *Adult Learning* 32, no. 4 (2020): 165–74.

5. Laura Saunders and Melissa A. Wong, "Yes, You Can! Tips for Moving Online at Short Notice," ALISE, March 19, 2020, https://ali.memberclicks.net/alise-webinar-march-2020-moving-online.

6. LIS Pedagogy Chat, https://www.lispedagogychat.org/.

7. Etienne Wenger-Trayner and Beverly Wenger-Trayner, "Introduction to Communities of Practice: A Brief Overview of the Concept and Its Uses," Wegner-Trayner, June 2015, https://wenger-trayner.com/introduction-to-communities-of-practice/.

8. Jesús Oliver and Julia Olkin, "A Community of Practice Model for Infusing Active Learning in the Classroom," *PRIMUS* 31, no. 3-5 (2021): 252–68, https://doi.org/10.1080/10511970.2020.1746452.

9. Christina H. Gola and Lisa Martin, "Creating an Emotional Intelligence Community of Practice: A Case Study for Academic Libraries," *Journal of Library Administration* 60, no. 7 (2020): 752–61; Nancy F. Gibson and Matthew T. Regan, "On the Journey to a Contemplative Library: Reflections from a Professional Community of Practice," *International Information & Library Review*, 53, no. 3 (2021): 264–71.

10. David Gomillion et al., "Learning How to Teach: The Case for Faculty Learning Communities," *Information Systems Education Journal* 18, no. 4 (2020): 74–79.

11. Oliver and Olkin, "A Community of Practice Model."

12. Heather Cyre et al., "LibCares: A Community of Practice and a Community of Caring," *Alki* 37, no. 3 (December 2021): 32–38.

13. Lynn Jettpace et al., "With a Little Help from Our Friends: Teaching Collectives as Lifelines in Troublesome Times," *Journal of Teaching and Learning with Technology* 10 (April 2021): 127–34.

14. S. Renée Jones et al., "Fostering a Sense of Community Among Black Faculty Through a Faculty Learning Community," *Adult Learning* 32, no. 4 (2020): 165–74.

15. Gola and Martin, "Creating an Emotional Intelligence Community of Practice," 759.

16. Wenger-Trayner and Wenger-Trayner, "Introduction to Communities of Practice."

17. Francesca Marineo, Chelsea Heinbach, and Rosan Mitola, "Building a Culture of Collaboration and Shared Responsibility for Educational Equity Work through an Inclusive Teaching Community of Practice," *Collaborative Librarianship* 13, no. 1 (2022): 63, https://digitalcommons.du.edu/collaborativelibrarianship/vol13/iss1/8.

18. Marineo, Heinbach, and Mitola, "Building a Culture of Collaboration," 63.

19. Ibid., 69.

20. Gola and Martin, "Creating an Emotional Intelligence Community of Practice," 755.

21. Lisa Bosman and Philip Voglewede, "How Can a Faculty Community of Practice Change Classroom Practices?," *College Teaching* 67, no. 3 (2019): 177–87, https://doi.org/10.1080/87567555.2019.159414 9.

22. Martha McAlister, "Emerging Communities of Practice," *Collected Essays on Learning and Teaching* 9 (2016): 129, http://files.eric.ed.gov/fulltext/EJ1104499.pdf.

23. AI Infodemic: Interrogating Algorithms of Information Seeking, University of Illinois Urbana-Champaign, https://publish.illinois.edu/infodemic/.

24. McAlister, "Emerging Communities of Practice," 130.

Bibliography

Bosman, Lisa, and Philip Voglewede. "How Can a Faculty Community of Practice Change Classroom Practices?" *College Teaching* 67, no. 3 (2019): 177–87. https://doi.org/10.1080/87567555.2019.1594149.

Douglas, Veronica Arellano. "Innovating Against a Brick Wall: Rebuilding the Structures that Shape Our Teaching." *Libraries + Inquiry* (blog), June 12, 2019. https://veronicaarellanodouglas.com/critlib/innovating-against-a-brick-wall-rebuilding-the-structures-that-shape-our-teaching-tilc-2019-keynote/

Douglas, Veronica Arellano, and Joanna Gadsby. "All Carrots, No Sticks: Relational Practice and Library Instruction Coordination." *In the Library with the Lead Pipe* (July 10, 2019). http://www.inthelibrarywiththeleadpipe.org/2019/all-carrots-no-sticks-relational-practice-and-library-instruction-coordination/.

Cyre, Heather, David K. Frappier, Johanna Jacobsen Kicimen, Ruba Sadi, and Elliott Stevens. "LibCares: A Community of Practice and a Community of Caring." *Alki* 37, no. 3 (December 2021): 32–38.

Evans, Lorraine. "Emotional Labor of Instruction Librarians: Causes, Impact and Management." In *The Emotional Self at Work in Higher Education*, edited by Ingrid Ruffin and Charissa Powell, 104–19. Hershey, PA: IGI Global, 2021.

Gibson, Nancy F., and Matthew T. Regan. "On the Journey to a Contemplative Library: Reflections from a Professional Community of Practice." *International Information & Library Review* 53, no. 3 (2021): 264–71.

Gola, Christina H., and Lisa Martin. "Creating an Emotional Intelligence Community of Practice: A Case Study for Academic Libraries." *Journal of Library Administration* 60, no. 7 (2020): 752–61.

Gomillion, David, Aaron Becker, Jordana George, and Michael Scialdone. "Learning How to Teach: The Case for Faculty Learning Communities." *Information Systems Education Journal* 18, no. 4 (2020): 74–79.

Jettpace, Lynn, Leslie Miller, Mary Ann Frank, Michelle Clemons, and Nancy Goldfarb. "With a Little Help from Our Friends: Teaching Collectives as Lifelines in Troublesome Times." *Journal of Teaching and Learning with Technology* 10 (April 2021): 127–34.

Jones, S. Renée, Christina Cobb, Jeremiah O. Asaka, Chandra R. Story, Michelle C. Stevens, and Michaele F. Chappell. "Fostering a Sense of Community Among Black Faculty Through a Faculty Learning Community." *Adult Learning* 32, no. 4 (2020): 165–74.

Julien, Heidi, and Shelagh K. Genuis. "Emotional Labour in Librarians' Instructional Work." *Journal of Documentation* 65, no. 6 (December 2009): 926–37. https://doi.org/10.1108/00220410910998924.

LIS Pedagogy Chat. https://www.lispedagogychat.org.

Marineo, Francesca, Chelsea Heinbach, and Rosan Mitola. "Building a Culture of Collaboration and Shared Responsibility for Educational Equity Work through an Inclusive Teaching Community of Practice." *Collaborative Librarianship* 13, no. 1 (2022): 62–77. https://digitalcommons.du.edu/collaborativelibrarianship/vol13/iss1/8.

McAlister, Martha. "Emerging Communities of Practice." *Collected Essays on Learning and Teaching* 9 (2016): 125–32. http://files.eric.ed.gov/fulltext/EJ1104499.pdf.

Oliver, Jesús, and Julia Olkin. "A Community of Practice Model for Infusing Active Learning in the Classroom." *PRIMUS* 31, no. 3-5 (2021): 252–68. https://doi.org/10.1080/10511970.2020.1746452.

Saunders, Laura, and Melissa A. Wong. "Yes, You Can! Tips for Moving Online at Short Notice." ALISE. March 19, 2020. https://ali.memberclicks.net/alise-webinar-march-2020-moving-online.

Seymour, Charlene. "Ethnographic Study of Information Literacy Librarians' Work Experience: A Report from Two States." In *Transforming Information Literacy Programs: Intersecting Frontiers of Self, Library Culture, and Campus Community*, edited by Carroll Wilkinson and Courtney Bruch, 45–72. Chicago: ACRL Publications, 2012.

Tuitt, Frank, Michele Hanna, Lisa M. Martinez, Maria del Carmen Salazar, and Rachel Griffin. "Teaching in the Line of Fire: Faculty of Color in the Academy." *Thought and Action*. Fall 2009, 65–74.

University of Illinois Urbana-Champaign. AI Infodemic: Interrogating Algorithms of Information Seeking. https://publish.illinois.edu/infodemic/.

Wenger-Trayner, Etienne, and Beverly Wenger-Trayner. "Introduction to Communities of Practice: A Brief Overview of the Concept and Its Uses." Wegner-Trayner. June 2015. https://wenger-trayner.com/introduction-to-communities-of-practice/.

PART VI

CASE STUDIES:
TRAINING NEW LIBRARIANS

CHAPTER 18

We're All in This Together:

Holistic Approaches to Training New Instruction Librarians

Randi Beem, Marc Bess, Ryan Harris, Abby Moore, Natalie Ornat Bitting, Catherine Tingelstad, and Angel Truesdale

LEARNING OUTCOMES

Readers will be able to

- describe the benefits of developing a holistic training program for new instruction librarians;
- identify specific methods for providing complementary professional development and training opportunities for new instruction librarians, such as peer observation, workshops, mentorship, and instruction unit meetings;
- plan and implement cross-unit collaborations to support the development of new instruction librarians;
- explain the importance of mentoring relationships in an instructional training program; and
- create professional development opportunities for experienced instructional librarians to share their knowledge with new library instructors.

Background

New instruction librarians typically bring a variety of backgrounds, knowledge, and experience to their roles. Whether new librarians have a background in classroom teaching or have never taught an instruction session, thoughtful, interactive, and dynamic training is critical to a new librarian's success in instruction. To this end, the Research and Instructional Services (RIS) unit at J. Murrey Atkins Library at UNC Charlotte approaches training new instruction librarians from a holistic perspective by promoting continuous professional development throughout the librarian's career. The unit utilizes a range of ongoing professional development initiatives to build the skills of instruction librarians, introduce them to new technologies and instructional approaches, and prepare them to further the library's instructional mission in their subject areas. The RIS unit has created a comprehensive training program for new instruction librarians as well as established librarians who are interested in learning about new teaching topics and updating their instruction. This program involves instruction librarians from throughout the library to ensure that all librarians have opportunities to learn from each other's unique experiences and insights. Training components include a mentoring program, monthly instruction meetings, a summer workshop series, and a peer observation program. Each component of the program is planned and implemented by the Instruction and Pedagogy Working Group, a small team of instruction librarians who have a significant amount of experience with teaching. Each part of the overall initiative is designed to complement the others in order to build a robust instructional training experience.

Library instruction at Atkins Library is primarily provided by librarians in the RIS unit. Additionally, specialized instruction that involves special collections and archives and technology resources is led by librarians in Special Collections and Digital Scholarship and Innovation respectively. The Research and Instructional Services unit is made up of two subunits—subject librarians in the Research Services subunit and librarians in the Instruction and Curriculum Engagement subunit. Research Services and Instruction and Curriculum Engagement have different areas of focus regarding library instruction, with Research Services librarians working on subject-specific instruction and the Instruction and Curriculum Engagement team focusing on first-year students and writing courses. Both groups work together to provide an engaged and dynamic program of instructional services to support student success. In a group of sixteen librarians, there is a range of instruction backgrounds and experience. Some librarians in the unit have backgrounds in education, others have learned about instruction on the job, and others are recent graduates from library science programs who have limited experience with teaching. Due to librarians' varied experiences with instruction, the department developed an ongoing training program that fosters and supports all librarians no matter what stage of their careers they are in to enhance and further their instruction skills.

Supporting instruction at all levels is essential to ensure that teaching is effective and makes a positive impact on student success. Scott Walter suggests, "On-the-job training is common among instruction librarians, as it is among members of the classroom faculty. Likewise common among the two professional groups is the preference for attendance at workshops sponsored by professional associations, campus teaching centers, and other organizations, as a means of instructional improvement."[1] New librarians with limited or no instructional coursework and experience often face challenges as they begin working at academic libraries. Library science graduate programs do not always provide their students with a strong foundation in teaching and instructional design. This can lead to a need for supervisors of new librarians to spend time teaching basic library instruction skills.[2] The results of a study by Lund et al. provided encouraging news when it revealed that "library schools better prepare students for instructional roles compared to past decades. Expectations for preparation have also increased."[3] However, there continues to be a strong need for providing instructional training, programming, and mentorship opportunities for librarians in positions requiring library instruction.

Approaches
Mentorship of New Librarians

When new librarians join the Research and Instructional Services team, the head of the unit pairs them with a mentor. These mentors are teaching librarians who have been with the department for at least two years. Mentors are available to help guide new librarians as they begin teaching instruction sessions and to answer any questions they might have about how library instruction is implemented. At their initial meetings, the new librarians and their mentors develop goals for the mentorship. To help facilitate the relationship, a research guide provides new librarians and mentors with helpful resources and guidelines for their collaboration. Mentors will often invite their new colleagues to co-teach or team teach with them in order to gain instructional experience. Additionally, mentors are encouraged to share lesson plans, active learning strategies, and teaching methods that can be used in instruction sessions. The head of Research and Instructional Services, the head of Instruction and Curriculum Engagement, and the new librarians' mentors observe the librarians teaching mock instruction sessions, provide immediate feedback, and ask constructive questions about the librarians' instructional techniques. This allows the new librarians to acclimate themselves to the department's instructional program early during their tenure and better prepares them to provide library instruction to students in their assigned subject areas.

Mentorship within the department can take a variety of forms in addition to the formal relationship established between the official mentors and the new librarians. New librarians are encouraged to observe and meet with other veteran instruction librarians in the department to learn from their experiences and gain ideas to incorporate into their own instruction sessions. They can meet before and after they observe an experienced librarian's instruction session to discuss content and strategies. In some cases, a new librarian will assist veteran librarians during the session by passing out handouts or acting as a student if a demonstration is necessary. This provides exposure to different teaching styles and provides new librarians with a sense of how library instruction is implemented in classes across a variety of subject areas.

Instruction and Pedagogy Working Group

In early 2018, the library's head of Research and Instructional Services charged a small team of instruction librarians with developing training and educational opportunities for librarians who teach information literacy and research skills. This meant including not only those librarians in the Research & Instructional Services unit but also teaching librarians in Special Collections & University Archives, Digital Scholarship, and Area 49 (the library's technology spaces). This team of librarians serves as the Instruction and Pedagogy Working Group, which meets monthly to set the direction for educational initiatives for the library's instruction team.

Recognizing that the library's instruction team benefits from ongoing educational experiences, the head of Research and Instructional Services tasked the group with developing an ongoing program of instruction meetings, peer observation, and summer workshops. The need for training opportunities for instruction librarians aligns with the findings of a recent study by Lund et al., which identified that instruction librarians need opportunities to gain teaching experiences beyond those provided in library school.[4] These initiatives allow teaching librarians to learn about educational theory and pedagogy, teaching practices such as scaffolding and active learning, student engagement strategies, and approaches to assessment, among other topics.

While several members of the instruction team at Atkins Library have an educational background (undergraduate degrees and K-12 teaching experience), the majority of the group learned about teaching and student learning by observing other teachers, attending workshops and conferences, and gaining experience on the job. Brecher and Klipfel state, "To succeed as an instruction librarian, or as any librarian with an instructional aspect to his or her position in the 21st-century library, an understanding of how students learn is critical."[5] This knowledge about student learning, whether self-taught or gained through traditional education, is essential for librarians who are teaching students research skills, critical thinking strategies, and information literacy concepts.

At Atkins Library, the instructional philosophy of Research and Instructional Services includes the tenet that when one librarian gains experience and expertise, the whole team becomes stronger. To that end, the department focuses on exploring instructional topics, theories, and strategies that might be new to some members of the team while others may be more familiar with the concepts and content. This approach provides the group with the chance for more experienced instructors to share their knowledge by leading sessions, contributing to discussions, and providing examples from their backgrounds. This model of collaboration and partnership helps avoid a siloed environment in which those with less teaching experience and education are reluctant to ask for input, express concerns, and seek advice from peers.

The Instruction and Pedagogy Working Group develops a year-long slate of meetings and workshops keeping the demands of the academic instructional calendar in mind. The team schedules sessions on more scholarly, reading-intensive topics for months with less instruction while creating opportunities for instruction librarians to interact and share experiences during the months with a heavier instruction load. These more interactive sharing sessions allow for collaboration and growth. Martinez and Forrey suggest that sharing stories and learning about the experiences of others can reinforce the idea that trying something new can be good even if it doesn't work.[6] The library's workshop series is scheduled for the summer when instruction librarians have time to take a deeper dive into topics and to learn and explore during two- to three-hour sessions. Planning these educational opportunities while considering the requirements of the academic calendar provides opportunities for personal and professional growth without placing unrealistic demands on teaching librarians.

Instruction Meetings

Instruction meetings at Atkins Library are held once a month and take the place of a regularly scheduled Research and Instructional Services unit meeting. While not mandatory, all instruction librarians are encouraged to attend. The Instruction and Pedagogy Working Group sets the agenda for these meetings. At the beginning of each fall and spring semester, the group collects topics and ideas for meetings from library instructors to address the needs and interests of teaching librarians. Many academic librarians who find themselves in instruction positions may feel unprepared to teach. In fact, "many of these librarians lack the education necessary to excel in these positions."[7] Therefore, regular instruction meetings are designed to help instruction librarians as they develop effective instructional practices and prepare them to deliver high-quality library instruction to students.

Topics for meetings focus on practical methods for improving library instruction and analysis of teaching and learning theory to advance the development of teaching librarians. Instruction meetings may address big-picture topics, such as critical librarianship and anti-racist pedagogy, or teaching and assessment tools that librarians can seamlessly incorporate into their instruction sessions. The meetings are positive and engaging and serve as a safe space not only to learn but also to share ideas and frustrations and to consider teaching as part of the librarians' professional identity.

The structure of instruction meetings looks different from meeting to meeting. Often, the goal is to model a teaching technique while the group is engaging with the topic of the month. For example, the group utilizes think-pair-shares, jigsaws, brainstorming, and debate-like activities. Recently, the meeting incorporated a matching activity based on the article, "The Many Faces of Instruction: An Exploration of Academic Librarians' Teaching Personas" by Elena Azadbakht.[8] In small groups, the librarians matched personality traits to teacher archetypes. No matter what topic is discussed, open dialogue is encouraged and anecdotal evidence from teaching experiences is shared in hopes of improving librarians' instructional skills. Topics of note from instruction meetings include challenges from recent instruction sessions, ideas about how to better teach online, and incorporating assessments.

Instruction meeting time is also used to highlight exemplary work and acknowledge expertise. Presentations about formative assessments, instructional infographics, and presentation slide design have been conducted by librarians within and outside the RIS unit during our instruction meetings. Recently, lightning talks were presented by four librarians on different aspects of their instruction practices. Occasionally, presenters from outside the department are invited to meetings to share their expertise and offer suggestions. For example, the assessment librarian presents an overview of the instructional statistics that each librarian submits throughout the semester. This allows the group opportunities to discuss insights and trends derived from the statistics to plan for upcoming semesters.

Instruction meetings can take on a variety of forms: formal or informal, highly organized or unstructured, mandatory or non-mandatory. The overall goal of instruction meetings is to provide the time and space to discuss ways to improve and enhance library instruction. These meetings serve as a place for librarians to feel comfortable discussing not only their fears and concerns about teaching but also to share instructional successes. The meetings operate on the idea that professional growth takes place in spaces where librarians can speak freely about their experiences without judgment. Humble brags and venting sessions are not uncommon during instruction meetings. Someone observing these meetings might note that the format, content, and tone are different each month; however, the main goal of providing a space conducive to professional development is almost always achieved.

Workshop Series

Every summer, the Instruction and Pedagogy Working Group organizes a series of three to five workshops that focus on specialized topics related to instruction. While the department's monthly instruction meetings are geared toward librarians who have instructional responsibilities as part of their regular job duties, the summer workshop series is open to anyone in the library regardless of whether they regularly engage in library instruction. The goal of the summer workshop series is to connect library faculty and staff with a variety of new pedagogical approaches, technologies, and teaching strategies. This allows all library faculty and staff to think about how they can apply these ideas to their work.

The Instruction and Pedagogy Working Group begins the process of planning and scheduling the workshop series during the spring semester. The planning process is initiated by a general discussion about which instruction-related topics might be interesting not only to instruction librarians but also to other library faculty and staff. After an initial discussion about workshop topics, the group narrows down the list of ideas to between three to five possible session topics and asks a member of the group or another instruction librarian to plan and facilitate each workshop. Often, multiple librarians will work together to plan and lead a workshop. The planning process presents opportunities for collaborations with library faculty and staff from departments other than Research and Instructional Services. For example, RIS librarians partner with faculty and staff from Special Collections and Digital Scholarship and Innovation to plan and conduct workshops that incorporate their unique expertise in archives and emerging technologies. Each summer, the Instruction and Pedagogy Working Group invites a librarian from another educational institution to speak about a topic such as critical pedagogy or backward design at one of the workshops. This practice of featuring an outside speaker allows Atkins librarians to explore a new and often unfamiliar pedagogical concept.

The Instruction and Pedagogy Working Group does not typically assign a common theme for workshops in the series. This gives the group the latitude to address topics that are of the most interest to library faculty and staff at that point in time rather than being constrained by a common theme. The group also considers suggestions for workshop topics from faculty and staff throughout the library; this ensures that the workshops have genuine interest from faculty and staff and are responsive to their needs.

Workshops within the series have addressed a wide variety of topics, including lesson planning, learning principles, critical pedagogies, and visual design concepts. No matter what the subject of a session may be, workshop organizers are encouraged to provide attendees with practical applications of the content. Organizers are also strongly encouraged to incorporate active learning into their workshops to provide attendees with an opportunity to practice what they are learning and think about how they could apply these concepts to their professional practice. This ensures that the sessions will present learners with a highly engaging experience that will result in long-term knowledge retention.

This approach is exemplified in one of the most well-attended summer workshops: a session devoted to design principles for librarians. The session was developed due to an expressed interest by library faculty and staff who do not typically engage with design principles but were interested in how they could utilize these concepts in their work. In this session, the library's First Year and Online Learning librarian teamed with the Technology and Multimedia Production coordinator to plan and facilitate a session focused on basic principles of visual design and multimedia learning and how those principles can be applied to common projects in library work. The facilitators explained how principles such as segmenting content and visual hierarchy make it easier to communicate through instructional media such as infographics and video tutorials. This focus on the basic need to communicate to library users, no matter what one's role in the library may be or which method of communication is being utilized, made it more applicable to a wide range of library faculty and staff. The session began with a brief tutorial on the concept of visual design and multimedia design principles. The workshop facilitators described basic visual design principles such as contrast and repetition alongside selected concepts from Mayer's Principles of Multimedia Learning, such as segmentation, coherence, and signaling. The facilitators also provided examples of how these principles could be applied in scenarios that were relevant to library work. The attendees were then organized into groups and participated in an activity that required them to identify applications of the principles in infographics that focused on communicating information about using the library. Feedback from workshop participants was positive, particularly regarding the interactive nature of the session and the focus on infographics in the active learning activity.

The intent of these workshops is to introduce new concepts and provide librarians with the opportunity to apply them to their work. Feedback from workshop participants is critical to understanding how learners perceive the overall value of the sessions and is useful in helping inform the design and focus of future workshops. For example, positive feedback from the session that centered around design principles helped shape the development of a workshop focused on designing infographics while also incorporating elements from design thinking. The infographics/design thinking session also provided librarians in Research and Instructional Services with another opportunity to collaborate with colleagues from Digital Scholarship and Innovation.

Workshops that involve collaboration with faculty from Special Collections are also an indispensable part of the workshop series. While Special Collections is a separate unit from the Research and Instructional Services unit, the instruction archivist is considered an integral part of the instruction team. Much of the instruction archivist's work focuses on providing library instruction that incorporates the rare and unique materials that are part of the library's Special Collections. Library instruction that involves Special Collections materials commonly takes place in the Special Collections reading room, and instruction workshops focusing on Special Collections are also typically held in this space to allow attendees the opportunity to see how instruction takes place in context. These workshops showcase a variety of different active learning activities that are utilized during library instruction sessions involving Special Collections materials. Activities include examining archival materials and finding commonalities among the artifacts. The materials used include manuscript collections that focus on Charlotte, NC-based activists, urban renewal, and regional maps. Special Collections instruction workshops encourage participants to collaborate with faculty across the university as well as the Research and Instructional Services team and the instruction archivist. The Special Collections workshops are always well-attended and illustrate how primary source literacy can be incorporated into library instruction.

The ultimate value of the summer workshop series lies in its ability to provide library faculty and staff opportunities to think about skills and concepts they may not encounter regularly in their day-to-day duties and to forge connections among colleagues throughout the library. The Instruction and Pedagogy Working Group has created a workshop series that engages library employees with new ideas and approaches to teaching, informing, and helping users.

Peer Observation Program

Peer observation is a common professional development technique in the field of teaching and broadly involves one colleague attending another colleague's class, observing their teaching practice and resulting student behavior, and providing constructive feedback and ideas after the session. While there is a wide range of practices and models for peer observation, the ultimate goal is to assess and improve teaching performance and, as a result, increase student success. Several studies point to the positive impact peer observation may have on both the teacher being observed and departmental culture. These programs can increase individual teacher confidence in the classroom and may play a role in developing a strong instructional climate.[9]

Peer observation programs also serve as a reminder that no classroom is an island and that both observer and observed can mutually benefit from the assessment process. While it may appear so at first glance, peer observation is not one-sided. While the observed librarian may receive constructive feedback to improve their performance, the observer can benefit from the exposure to different teaching techniques and styles. As Hendry, Bell, and Thomson explore in their study on peer observation at a large research-intensive institution, not only does the observer potentially gain new teaching ideas, but they can see their current work affirmed when the observed successfully implements a shared teaching practice.[10] As most teaching librarians do not have a formal background in education and learning, these experiences of seeing the effectiveness of their adopted techniques and practices can be powerful moments in building confidence and identities as educators.

David Gosling identifies three models for peer observation in a report frequently cited in the literature on peer observation in higher education settings.[11] The evaluation model has a figure of authority serving as the observer in order to appraise the performance of the instructor. The development model sees a highly experienced teacher or instructional leader observe to assess teaching competencies and then share their expertise in relation to measured deficiencies. The peer review model makes more authentic use of the term "peer" by having instructors observe each other to engage in productive discussion and professional reflection. An extension of Gosling's peer review model may be seen in the "critical friends" approach of peer observation taken by instruction librarians at the University of Washington-Bothell and Cascadia College Campus Library, where the elements of self-reflection and peer trust are viewed as essential to an effective program.[12] The purpose of the Atkins Library peer observation program is to encourage both the individual professional growth of our instruction librarians and to strengthen the overall effectiveness of the instruction team. Our program is most closely aligned with Gosling's peer review model, where members of the Research and Instructional Services unit are observed by their peers in a non-judgmental, constructive fashion. Following the ethos of Gosling's third model, observations are conducted in a formative rather than summative manner and are meant to foster professional growth. Our program is, notably, not part of our annual review, reappointment, or promotion process.

At the start of each fall semester, the head of the department places instruction librarians in pairs. These pairs alternate as both observer and librarian being observed, allowing each librarian the opportunity to give and receive feedback on their teaching. Pairs are guided to hold a pre-instruction meeting that takes place a few days before a scheduled observation to identify session goals. Pre-observation questions are provided to guide the conversation and identify areas on which the observed may want targeted feedback. These questions include "What are the plans or learning activities that you will use in order to achieve these goals?" and "What would you like me to focus on during this instruction session?" The pre-observation questions generally remain the same from year to year, but the group is open to making revisions based on feedback from participants. The librarian being observed is encouraged to share their lesson plan and other instructional materials with their observer beforehand.

During the observation session, the observer utilizes a rubric to provide specific, constructive feedback to the librarian being observed. This rubric is available as a worksheet that the observer can reference during the instruction session. The worksheet lists several areas related to key elements of a library instruction session, such as content organization and instructor delivery. As the librarian teaches the session, the observer uses the rubric to note that these elements were observed during the instruction. The worksheet also includes space for the observer to make notes about parts of the session that were done well and aspects that the librarian could improve in future sessions.

After the observation occurs, the pair is encouraged to meet soon after and talk about the session. The observer may review portions of the worksheet with their colleague, sharing their thoughts on the overall effectiveness of the session, offering suggestions for improvement where needed, and brainstorming ideas for other activities, assessment techniques, or approaches that could be taken by the instructor in the future. As highlighted by Dimmit, Maxwell, and Nesvig, trust and self-reflection are critical components at this stage in the observation process.[13] Conversations should be honest and constructive, grounded in the principles of mutual respect and collegiality, and most importantly, confidential. For effective peer observation programs, trust between observer and librarian being observed is key to maintaining a supportive and positive observational environment.

Our program reflects many of the benefits and challenges seen by other peer observation programs. Similar to the case of a peer observation program detailed by Bell and Cooper, our program allows for the furthering of a supportive learning environment, where teaching librarians can turn to each other as colleagues for support or draw on each other as a group of educators with their own unique set of strengths and skills in the classroom.[14] In enhancing a spirit of community and open discussion around teaching strategies and techniques, individuals can feel less isolated, an impact found by Hendry, Bell, and Thomason's survey on academics' experience of observation.[15] As the group learns from one another and adopts each other's effective practices and techniques, they can become a more cohesive, consistent, and ultimately effective instructional program.

Peer observation programs can raise anxiety on both the part of the observer and observed. As noted in the detailing of a peer review teaching program for pre-tenure librarians, the observer may find it difficult to offer feedback that is more critical in nature while the observed may find receiving either praise or constructive criticism to be difficult.[16] In our case, this peer observation program is just one component of a larger program of instructional professional development. The stress and anxiety that may come from the observation experience can be mitigated when observations are done within a holistic program that frames the individual practice of library instruction within a growth mindset and provides colleagues with structured and supportive opportunities to disclose and discuss their challenges in the classroom.

Conclusion and Future Directions

The Instruction and Pedagogy Working Group views each of its approaches to training instruction librarians as essential in helping librarians build their instructional skills. The mentorship program and peer observation sessions provide specialized support and feedback to librarians both at the beginning of their time at Atkins Library and throughout their careers. Initiatives such as the workshop series and instruction meetings provide forums for librarians to share ideas and learn from each other in supportive settings. Taken together, all these approaches provide librarians with opportunities to learn and improve at every stage of their careers.

As the group moves forward with building the library's program of instructional training and development, it is exploring ways to engage with academic institutions in the region to foster connections between Atkins librarians and other instructional librarians. Due to the success of the summer workshop series, the group is planning to invite librarians from other institutions in the region to future sessions. These workshops could be beneficial to librarians from a variety of institutions. This would provide all participants with the opportunity to learn from others' professional experiences and to collaborate with peers from other libraries.

The group is also planning to establish a separate monthly meeting for teaching librarians that focuses on complex questions that arise from reference interactions. In addition to teaching library sessions, instructional librarians at Atkins Library assist library users with research and reference questions in a variety of ways, including at the information and research desk, through the library's chat service, and through in-person and virtual consultations. In the proposed meeting, librarians with specialized experience and expertise in areas such as primary source research, data services, and assisting with systematic reviews will demonstrate how to respond to requests for help on these topics. While some librarians encounter such questions more than others due to their assigned subject areas, all librarians benefit from gaining some knowledge about these types of specialized questions.

Every year, the Instruction and Pedagogy Working Group assesses its membership to ensure that the range of programmatic and pedagogical experience among the teaching librarians is adequately represented in the group. New members are regularly added to ensure that the group continues to cultivate innovative ideas and engages new librarians in the work of providing robust professional development opportunities.

Instruction at Atkins Library is constantly evolving as teaching librarians build new collaborations with faculty, become embedded in both online and in-person courses, and incorporate new concepts into their teaching. The instruction program will respond to these changes by continuing to create meaningful opportunities for internal development and training to ensure that all teaching librarians, particularly those who are new to the profession, have the support that they need to succeed in their professional roles.

Notes

1. Scott Walter, "Instructional Improvement: Building Capacity for the Professional Development of Librarians as Teachers," *Reference and User Services Quarterly* 45, no. 3 (2006): 213–18.
2. Kimberly Davies-Hoffman, Barbara Alvarez, Michelle Costello, and Debby Emerson, "Keeping Pace with Information Literacy Instruction for the Real World," *Communications in Information Literacy* 7, no. 1 (2013): 9–23.
3. Brady D. Lund, Michael Widdersheim, Brendan Fay, and Ting Wang, "Training and Practice of Instructional Librarians: Cross-Population and Longitudinal Perspectives," *The Reference Librarian* 62, no. 2 (2021): 126–43.
4. Lund et al., "Training and Practice," 126–43.
5. Dani Brecher and Kevin Michael Klipfel, "Education Training for Instruction Librarians: A Shared Perspective," *Communications in Information Literacy* 8, no. 1 (2014): 43–49.
6. Jessica Martinez and Meredith Forrey, "Overcoming Imposter Syndrome: The Adventures of Two New Instruction Librarians," *Reference Services Review* 47, no. 3 (2019): 331–42.
7. Brecher and Klipfel, "Education Training," 43–49.
8. Elena Azadbakht, "The Many Faces of Instruction: An Exploration of Academic Librarians' Teaching Personas," *Communications in Information Literacy* 15, no. 1 (2021): 57–74.

9. Alan Barnard, Waveney Croft, Rosemary Irons, Natalie Cuffe, Wasana Bandara, and Pamela Rowntree, "Peer Partnership to Enhance Scholarship of Teaching: A Case Study," *Higher Education Research and Development* 30, no. 4 (2011): 435–48.

10. Graham D. Hendry, Amani Bell, and Kate Thomson, "Learning by Observing a Peer's Teaching Situation," *The International Journal for Academic Development* 19, no. 4 (2014): 318–29.

11. David Gosling, "Models of Peer Observation of Teaching," Learning and Teaching Support Network: Generic Centre (2002).

12. Laura Dimmit, Caitlan Maxwell, and Chelsea Nesvig, "Librarians as Critical Friends: Developing a Sustainable Peer Observation Process," *College & Research Libraries News* 80, no. 4 (2019): 216.

13. Dimmit et al., "Librarians as Critical Friends," 216.

14. Maureen Bell and Paul Cooper, "Peer Observation of Teaching in University Departments: A Framework for Implementation," *The International Journal for Academic Development* 18, no. 1 (2013): 60–73.

15. Hendry, Bell, and Thomson, "Learning by Observing a Peer's Teaching Situation," 318–29.

16. Jaena Alabi, Rhonda Huisman, Meagan Lacy, Willie Miller, Eric Snajdr, Jessica Trinoskey, and William H. Weare, "By and for Us: The Development of a Program for Peer Review of Teaching by and for Pre-Tenure Librarians," *Collaborative Librarianship* 4, no. 4 (2012): 165–74.

Bibliography

Alabi, Jaena, Rhonda Huisman, Meagan Lacy, Willie Miller, Eric Snajdr, Jessica Trinoskey, and William H. Weare. "By and for Us: The Development of a Program for Peer Review of Teaching by and for Pre-Tenure Librarians." *Collaborative Librarianship* 4, no. 4 (2012): 165–74.

Azadbakht, Elena. "The Many Faces of Instruction: An Exploration of Academic Librarians' Teaching Personas." *Communications in Information Literacy* 15, no. 1 (2021): 57–74.

Barnard, Alan, Waveney Croft, Rosemary Irons, Natalie Cuffe, Wasana Bandara, and Pamela Rowntree. "Peer Partnership to Enhance Scholarship of Teaching: A Case Study." *Higher Education Research and Development* 30, no. 4 (2011): 435–48.

Bell, Maureen, and Paul Cooper. "Peer Observation of Teaching in University Departments: A Framework for Implementation." *The International Journal for Academic Development* 18, no. 1 (2013): 60–73.

Brecher, Dani, and Kevin Michael Klipfel. "Education Training for Instruction Librarians: A Shared Perspective." *Communications in Information Literacy* 8, no. 1 (2014): 43–49.

Davies-Hoffman, Kimberly, Barbara Alvarez, Michelle Costello, and Debby Emerson. "Keeping Pace with Information Literacy Instruction for the Real World." *Communications in Information Literacy* 7, no. 1 (2013): 9–23.

Dimmit, Laura, Caitlan Maxwell, and Chelsea Nesvig. "Librarians as Critical Friends: Developing a Sustainable Peer Observation Process." *College & Research Libraries News* 80, no. 4 (2019): 216.

Gosling, David. "Models of Peer Observation of Teaching." Learning and Teaching Support Network: Generic Centre (2002).

Hendry, Graham D., Amani Bell, and Kate Thomson. "Learning by Observing a Peer's Teaching Situation." *The International Journal for Academic Development* 19, no. 4 (2014): 318–29.

Lund, Brady D., Michael Widdersheim, Brendan Fay, and Ting Wang. "Training and Practice of Instructional Librarians: Cross-Population and Longitudinal Perspectives." *The Reference Librarian* 62, no. 2 (2021): 126–43.

Martinez, Jessica, and Meredith Forrey. "Overcoming Imposter Syndrome: The Adventures of Two New Instruction Librarians." *Reference Services Review* 47, no. 3 (2019): 331–42.

Walter, Scott. "Instructional Improvement: Building Capacity for the Professional Development of Librarians as Teachers." *Reference and User Services Quarterly* 45, no. 3 (2006): 213–18.

CHAPTER 19

Learning What Works:
The Impact of Change on Training New Library Instructors

Josette M. Kubicki, Tonya D. Dority, Thomas C. Weeks, and Emma Kate Morgan

LEARNING OUTCOMES

Readers will be able to
- gain two approaches to training library instructors;
- identify external and internal influences that can impact training;
- comprehend how other institutions have successfully trained library instructors; and
- take away a proposed model for training library instructors.

Introduction

Hiring new librarians can be an exciting time of change as they bring new ideas in and adjust to the culture of their new library. However, training these new librarians can also present challenges when they must teach but have little experience in instruction and may not have had curricula in their library graduate programs. This can be especially true when the new librarians' primary role is not instruction and their training occurs during times of change. Times of change can be unexpected and chaotic, such as the COVID-19 pandemic. Other times of change are planned, like a change in management and organizational restructuring. Whether planned or unplanned, change often reveals strains in our educational systems. This is true of how we onboard new instruction librarians as well. Change forces us to rethink existing paradigms and rethink what we value. In this chapter, we describe how library instruction and how librarians prepare for this role have evolved in our academic library from one approach into another due to the influences of a world crisis, changes in management, new institutional requirements, and reorganization, and how this evolution can improve future processes. Upon reflecting on our own experiences, we agree that our master of library and information science (MLIS) (or equivalent) programs left us feeling ill-prepared for library instruction, especially in changing environments. Through the literature review and sharing of our personal experiences, we describe how MLIS programs' coverage of teaching and instruction is generally misaligned with today's academic library environment and how internal training programs have answered this need. To address this, we discuss how some libraries have implemented effective training programs for their teaching librarians and how we have learned from these to craft our version(s).

Looking closer at various models of instruction can help provide context for challenges to instruction training. Instruction programs have become entrenched in the culture of the academic library and have shifted toward the trend of teaching units that focus solely on instruction. ACRL's *Characteristics of Programs of Information Literacy that Illustrate Best Practices: A Guideline* states that library administration should "[assign] information literacy leadership and responsibilities to appropriate librarians, faculty, and staff.[1] "But who are the "appropriate librarians" to teach information literacy? Where does this leave those still performing traditional librarian functions, such as collection development, cataloging, and circulation, who must also teach? Reese Library is one of two libraries that serves a mid-sized university. During the timeframe of this project, Reese Library had seven librarians working out of eight faculty librarian positions: the director of Reese Library, the director of Library Technology and Systems, two reference and instruction librarians, an access services librarian, an e-resources librarian, and a cataloging and metadata librarian. The special collections librarian position was vacant at the time.[2] Four of these librarians shared instruction, and three were new and required training—the e-resources, access services, and cataloging librarians. These librarians have limited teaching duties, but because of Reese Library's shared instruction model, they are also expected to teach. They contribute to the library instruction for gen-ed courses and teach library instruction for their liaison areas.

On-the-Job Instruction Training

There are many ways libraries and librarians have attempted to remedy the lack of preparedness on the part of library and information science (LIS) graduate programs. In 2010, Click and Walker found that 24 percent of librarians reported receiving "very little" instruction training in the workplace upon hire.[3] This indicates that although many libraries have provided instruction training for new hires, in order to make up gaps in LIS education, almost a quarter of librarians still feel that their on-the-job training inadequately prepared them for conducting instruction. Goodsett and Koizura found many new librarians have had to supplement their graduate degrees and on-the-job training with some form of self-education.[4] Conferences, webinars, and ACRL programs, such as the Immersion program, offer new career librarians options for self-education. Still, institutions are best positioned to mold future instruction librarians for their needs, seeing as so few have consistent experiences in their MLIS education. In their study, Martinez and Forrey found that while most new career librarians they surveyed felt unprepared to teach, the respondents felt supported by their institutions, including co-teaching opportunities, formal and informal mentorship, robust onboarding procedures, and communities of practice.[5] Many organizations have sought to increase preparation for instruction librarians by creating instruction training programs within the new hire onboarding process. However, inconsistencies in how libraries provide this training leave many new instruction librarians feeling ill-prepared as they begin teaching, even if they went through training programs.[6]

Some standardized training programs can be found in the literature, but the models vary. This indicates that not all libraries approach training in the same manner and choose models that best fit their needs. The Libraries at McGill University partnered with the university's Teaching and Learning Services department to create an intensive course on library instruction, Designing and Delivering Effective Information Skills Sessions.[7] Before the development of this course, their liaison librarians attended a generic instruction workshop that covered learner-centered course design. However, after receiving feedback, they found that the course had been useful, but did not address their specific needs. The libraries' response to this was to reach out to Teaching and Learning Services to create a course specifically geared toward preparing librarians to teach information literacy. This course is a 1.5-day workshop that is now required for all new librarians. The course starts with surveys to gather background information on teaching and other educational or reference experience. Throughout the course, the attendees are required to rework a selected course. Using a mix of background probes and active learning, it was determined that participants finished the workshop feeling empowered, and overall, they recommend collaborations such as theirs with Teaching and Learning Services to create a program that is replicable, malleable, and enduring.

Another popular choice for training is the peer-coaching model. At the University of Colorado at Boulder, librarians had experienced teaching librarians working with new librarians to co-teach and serving as mentors as they develop their teaching skills.[8] As they discuss, "Peer coaching has proven to enliven teaching librarians individually and to nurture a community of teachers at UCB."[9] Brady also used a peer-coaching model for instruction.[10] Instead of librarians training each other, they had librarians train graduate assistants in psychology to teach *their* peers information literacy. This allows for true peer-to-peer teaching networks at the graduate level. Similarly, Sobel describes training LIS graduate students to teach through graduate assistantships within the library.[11] They used mentorship by an experienced teacher, observation, and co-teaching to train the graduate assistants. Peer-coaching models are closest to what Reese Library currently does but only with other librarians, not graduate students. However, as shown in the literature, the success of this approach is variable based on the institutional needs, resources, and processes. Another emerging approach for training is not a standalone program but one that is a combination of any of the above methods. We implemented such an approach, described later in this chapter. Communities of practice can offer open dialogue among peer support networks and can lead to rich discussions about instructional practice.[12]

Original Approach: Training New Library Instructors Coordinated by the Chair of Reference and Education Services

Until recently, Reese Library's organizational structure included a chair of reference and education services who reported to the associate director of Reese Library. This chair was responsible for coordinating the reference, instruction, and government documents services for Reese Library. As mentioned, all Reese librarians participate in the shared library instruction program for general education (gen-ed) courses, including first-year and second-year English composition, communications, and first-year experience courses. The number of courses taught varies—over the last few years, we taught an average of thirty-seven of these general education courses each academic year. Each Reese librarian also has at least one subject liaison area. Teaching faculty would contact the chair of reference and education services,[13] either by filling out an online library instruction request form or emailing her directly. Gen-ed library instruction requests were fielded to all librarians to see who could teach which class. Requests for library instruction for upper-division and graduate courses were forwarded directly to the appropriate liaison librarian. The two reference and instruction librarians take on more library instruction sessions than the others because teaching makes up most of their job descriptions. However, all Reese librarians are expected to teach some library instruction sessions throughout the year and document it in their faculty self-evaluation during the yearly evaluation period.

With many librarians of different backgrounds and varying levels of expertise involved in the shared instruction program, the chair saw the need for some standardization in library instruction so that all librarians have a common baseline for teaching students. Liaising with the chair, the reference and instruction librarians developed a basic lesson plan format for all librarians. This lesson plan format outlines how to structure a typical one-shot library instruction session and the basic knowledge and skills we want students to develop for the various classes a librarian may be asked to teach. The lesson plans were designed so that plenty of room is left for flexibility for the librarian to make the lesson their own.

For further standardization, the reference and instruction librarians developed informal summative assessment activity pro formas using Google Forms (now we use LibWizard) for students to undertake during the library instruction session. They saved these in a Google Drive account they established for all librarians to access. The activities have tasks reflecting specific frames of the ACRL *Framework for Information Literacy for Higher Education*, particularly Authority as Constructed and Contextual, Searching as Strategic Exploration, and Information Has Value. Again, there is room for flexibility. Each of the librarians would duplicate the informal assessment before their class, and they could either leave it as is or modify it to suit the librarians' or class's needs. But the chair expected that common content would be assessed. For example, could students undertake a search on our discovery search, find two articles, generate a citation, and evaluate them for credibility and relevance? Could students do the same when searching two relevant databases in their subject area? With the informal assessment not being a requirement, completion rates vary. If the librarian has the time to implement it in the library session, they typically see a near 100 percent completion rate. If they shared the link to it toward the end of the session and encouraged students to complete it in their own time, the completion rate is generally low. The assessment is used only to inform one's practice. It is expected that each librarian would log in to view and reflect on what the students recorded. Supervisors do not log in to view these results.

After finalizing the new lesson plan format and informal assessment forms, the chair arranged a training session for one of the reference and instruction librarians to train all the librarians in the backward design of lesson planning, followed by an induction/refresher on an overview of the libraries' PROT (peer review of teaching). This training was not mandatory to participate in, but it was strongly encouraged. The reference and instruction librarian would explain using the summative assessment activities and lesson plan format to implement backward design. This training was successful because the librarians started sharing lesson plans to see what we were teaching and how. PROT, the libraries' "peer review of teaching," is where a librarian formally evaluates another librarian on their instruction according to a rubric and documents this evaluation and any final comments on a PROT form. Librarians evaluate each other on content knowledge, teaching methods, interaction, presentation, and assessment (see appendix A). Librarians are expected to submit two PROT forms for their performance evaluation. This training on backward design in lesson planning and the PROT process formed some of the instruction training for new librarians.

If only one new librarian were starting, the chair would organize a reference and instruction librarian to train them one-on-one, following the peer coaching model. However, if more than one librarian were beginning around the same time, the chair would organize for one of the reference and instruction librarians to run a more formalized training session. All other librarians and library staff would also be invited to the training session so they could undertake a refresher.

The reference and instruction librarian first covered the overview of the lesson plan format Reese Library uses for designing lessons. The lesson plan format (see appendix B) includes sections for learning outcomes, supplemental materials, introduction, lesson body, and assessment. He then instructed on each of these sections. For the learning outcomes, he taught how to create learning outcomes that map to at least a couple of the ACRL frames. For example, the outcome of "Students will use research tools and indicators of authority to determine the credibility of sources" is mapped to the ACRL frame of Authority is Constructed and Contextual. For supplemental materials, he shared examples of teaching aids that could be useful for the lesson, like whiteboard markers, a research guide (LibGuide) suited for that class, and useful links for background research, like procon.org, and to have these ready before the class begins so that one is not wasting time looking for these materials during the class. For the introduction, he explained creating student buy-in over typically three steps: (1) introduce oneself in a friendly manner, (2) engage the class in a brief discussion about why they are there, and (3) inform them what we want them to learn. The longest part of the training session was spent on the lesson body. The reference and instruction librarian instructed that librarians have the autonomy to design the lesson as they wish but to ensure that they cover certain concepts so that students have a baseline of knowledge on Reese Library's services and where and how to locate and evaluate sources. Specifically, these concepts include the following:

- Finding background information on a topic—e.g., by undertaking a web search
- Refining a topic so it is "searchable"
- Main features of the Reese Library website:
  o ways to get help—e.g., chat with a librarian, research consultations
  o discovery search box
  o pertinent links underneath, like databases, library catalog, and research guides
- Developing a basic search strategy:
  o identifying key terms in their topic
  o brainstorming synonyms and related terms
- Implementing the search strategy in discovery search:
  o "exact phrase search" technique
  o using Boolean operators to include synonyms and exclude unwanted terms
  o limiters—useful ones and the ones to apply caution with
- Brief examination of results page and a record:
  o structure of the record
  o subject headings—what they are, how they are useful
  o saving, emailing, generating citations of results (warning on accuracy)
  o selecting the link to activate the link resolver to see if we have full-text access, interlibrary loan, and document delivery option
- Searching the same topic in two separate databases:
  o finding recommended databases in the research guide
  o similarities and differences with discovery search
  o implement same search strategy – compare results to discovery search
- Evaluating sources:
  o the importance of evaluating sources, even if found on library platforms
  o brief overview of one source evaluation rubric—e.g., CRAAP test
  o finding more information on source evaluation in Research Guide
- Citing sources:
  o the importance of citing sources—acknowledgment, prevent plagiarism
  o finding guidelines for main citation manuals in the research guide

Lastly, for the assessment section, the reference and instruction librarian explained that the class should be given an activity to work on. This activity assessed students' ability to find two sources for their assignment, one using the discovery search tool and one using an individual database, and then evaluate these sources according to an evaluation rubric. Following the tasks was a brief survey of the instruction session. The reference and instruction librarian instructed librarians how to find the pro formas of activities in Reese Library's Google Drive account and how to duplicate an assessment form and customize it to the class they are teaching. For example, they could shorten the assessment if it is a fifty-minute session instead of a seventy-five-minute one. He then showed how to create a custom shortened URL of the assessment using Bitly.

Following this training session, the chair assigned new librarians to observe library instruction sessions taught by other experienced librarians. This was not a formal observation experience with no guidelines formalized to support the observation process. It was an unwritten expectation that the observer would take notes. Observers were encouraged to ask questions. The chair would arrange for them to watch different librarians' teaching sessions because although everyone is expected to follow the basic lesson plan and cover the concepts outlined earlier, each librarian has a unique teaching style. For example, a librarian may use analogies to break down certain concepts; another may integrate humor. As noted earlier, there is a formal observation process—the PROT—but this was not used to train the librarians at this time. Later, PROT was introduced in training.

New Approach: How Instruction Training Evolved Due to Change

In this section, we discuss how instruction training has evolved into a second approach due to the following influences, some of which overlap: an international crisis, a change in management, new institutional requirements, and reorganization. We informally surveyed two of the co-authors of this chapter, Morgan and Dority, on their library instruction training experiences impacted by two of these changes: a change in management and the COVID-19 crisis. We surveyed them on how many sessions they observed and any other experiences that were part of their instruction training. Their reflections are interspersed in the discussion.

Changes in Management Alongside the Crisis

In 2019, the chair of reference and education services was promoted to associate director and another librarian outside of reference and education services became the chair. No new librarians had started between the management change and COVID-19; therefore, no training was conducted. Later, two new librarians joined Reese Library right before the pandemic: Morgan and another librarian. A hiring freeze was set in place. Meanwhile, the associate director retired during the hiring freeze and the chair of reference and education services became interim associate director. When the hiring freeze was lifted, a third librarian, Dority, was hired as the cataloging and metadata librarian. However, the vacant chair of reference and education services position remained frozen because more change was on the horizon—the university was recruiting an inaugural dean of libraries, and they wanted to allow the new dean to rethink the position.

These changes, against the backdrop of the crisis, impacted instructional training. Due to shifting priorities—the interim associate director straddling both roles, scrambling to focus on the crisis and how to adapt library services—the formal training sessions the previous chair of reference and education services had organized had fallen by the wayside. It could also be because the interim associate director was unaware of this training experience that the previous chair had arranged.

Crisis

The two new librarians who joined immediately before the pandemic did not undertake any instructional training in the spring and summer of 2020. Augusta University partially reopened in the fall of 2020. While some departments continued to work remotely, the university libraries were considered essential and reopened. Many classes were still online, but some transitioned face-to-face with masking and social distancing protocols. Because of the considerably fewer instruction requests (we offered virtual instruction, but many did not utilize this) and social distancing requirements not allowing guests, it was far more difficult for the new Reese librarians to acquire observation and teaching experiences. Morgan and the other new librarian undertook training during "peak pandemic" in the fall of 2020. Dority undertook training while we transitioned to a "new normal" in the fall of 2021. The interim associate director allocated the new librarians to observe a library instruction session whenever possible. Before each observation, the librarians received the course assignment and the teaching librarian's lesson plan so they could follow along.

Because there were few opportunities to observe and not many lower-division classes to teach, the interim associate director organized a mock library instruction session for a hypothetical first-year English class, conducted in person. She arranged this for Morgan and the other new librarian after they had the opportunity to observe at least a few sessions. She invited other library faculty and staff to be the "class" and undertake a mock "peer review of teaching" for feedback. Morgan reached out to a colleague for lesson plans to help her plan her session. This mock peer review followed the same template the PROT librarians use for each other at least twice a year for performance evaluations. The PROT evaluation was repurposed as a training document so trainee librarians could learn what is considered sound instruction practice. This repurposed training document also gave the training librarians a heads-up on what their peers would formally evaluate them on. The interim associate director compiled the feedback, reviewed it with each librarian, and decided whether they felt ready to teach independently. Morgan received the green light, but there were still not enough library instruction requests to take on. The other librarian did not receive the green light and was asked to undertake more observations and conduct another mock training session later. When Morgan eventually started teaching in the summer of 2021, she had a more experienced Reese librarian present in the room for the first two sessions she taught to provide support if needed during the session and feedback at the end. However, she continued to observe library instruction between sessions that she taught because there were comparatively few instruction requests. She remembered observing around nine or ten sessions. Meanwhile, the other librarian left our institution before having the opportunity to conduct another mock training session.

With vaccine availability, more and more classes transitioned to face-to-face in 2021, and social distancing requirements began to ease. Dority, who started in September 2021, had the opportunity to observe more classes, and observation became the focus of her training. She learned from observing nine library instruction sessions and talking to the librarians who conducted the sessions from September through February. Because there was much more opportunity for observation, the interim associate director did not arrange a mock instruction session. Instead, she asked Dority if she felt ready to begin instructing on her own, with the offer of co-teaching. Dority said she felt ready and would try independently. She started teaching in March 2022. She did not have a more experienced librarian present. The formal training session had not been re-instituted. This left the new librarians to learn about the informal summative assessment tools on their own, from observation and talking to the librarians who already conducted the sessions.

External Institutional Enforcement

When the libraries had adapted to operating with the crisis, the interim associate director later organized additional training for all librarians. This was due to another change—the university's division of institutional effectiveness started requiring the libraries, besides other units, to report on the achievement of undergraduate student learning outcomes. The libraries' administration designed standardized assessment tools, one for Reese Library and a different one for our library on the health sciences campus, to implement toward the end of each undergraduate library instruction session. The interim associate director conducted a training session for all librarians on what this tool assessed and how to access and implement it. This assessment, called "The Reese Instruction Survey," assesses students in three ways to evaluate the quality of a source, followed by optional questions on three things they learned. If time remained in the session, the librarians could then implement the existing informal summative assessment. The training session then covered spending greater time on source evaluation in the instruction sessions and reducing the time spent on other concepts, for example, only demonstrating how to search within one database instead of two. This session was followed by another training session on backward design, which she arranged for one of the reference and instruction librarians to conduct. However, this session occurred after Morgan had already started teaching.

Libraries' Reorganization

The final change that has impacted the training of library instructors at Reese Library is the reorganization of the university libraries' structure. In the fall of 2022, the dean of libraries implemented a new organizational structure for the university libraries, entailing new positions and the elimination of others. This included eliminating the reference and education services positions that were now vacant in both libraries. The reference and education services teams continue to report directly to the associate directors, and the associate directors continue to oversee the training of library instructors. With the Reese associate director juggling many responsibilities, a formal training program has never been reinstituted; however, she reinstated the mock instruction session. Training library instructors remains much the same as it was for Morgan during the COVID-19 crisis era:

1. The librarian-in-training observes as many classes as possible over the course of one semester.
2. After observing several classes, they co-teach with other librarians. Before the class, the librarian shares their lesson plan with the librarian-in-training who selects which parts they are willing to co-teach. After the class, the librarian gives them informal feedback.
3. Toward the end of the semester, the associate director arranges for the librarian-in-training to undertake a mock library instruction session and invites all Reese Library faculty and staff to attend. Faculty undertake a PROT.
4. The associate director collates feedback from the PROTs and shares it with the librarian-in-training. She informs the librarian whether they can begin conducting library instruction independently or if they need to observe more classes.
5. The librarian-in-training starts to conduct library instruction independently while continuing to co-teach in other classes. After a few times of teaching independently, they stop co-teaching.

The training session on backward design was never reinstituted.

Evaluation of the Library Training Experiences

We also surveyed the librarians on their comfort level before and after, how many sessions they observed, any other experiences that were part of their instruction training, and any suggestions for improvement. Both librarians, Morgan and Dority, reported having low confidence in providing instruction before commencing instruction training at our library; however, only Morgan reported a significant increase in confidence at the end. Dority had rated the same level of confidence. Morgan noted she found the mock training session to be very helpful to practice library instruction in a safe space and to gain feedback on what went well and how she could improve. She also found that "observing was really helpful, especially when I was provided with the professor's assignment and the instructor's lesson plan ahead of time."

Dority, who rated no improvement in confidence, had only undertaken observation and did not have a more experienced librarian present to provide support for the first couple of sessions she taught, although she was offered to have a co-teacher. She lamented, "I could have taken up her offer, but I felt bad because I had already observed many instruction sessions and thought I better just jump in there and start teaching." Dority recognized that observation is but one element of instruction training. Waiving the offer to co-teach, she feels, impacted her growth as an instructor. Co-teaching could have improved her confidence and effectiveness. Both librarians recommend having a formal training program to introduce new librarians to library instruction would be helpful, with Dority expressing, "I would recommend a formal training program where new instructors have access to the same experiences, resources, and supports."

What Worked Well, Lessons Learned, and Moving Forward

The mock library instruction session and plenty of observational experiences with the lesson plan and course assignment provided ahead of time were beneficial. However, there were disparities in the breadth and depth of training experience between the two librarians we interviewed due to the timing of when they began. These disparities were unintentional—the mock instruction session was instituted to replace a void, and with that void filled, we had gone back to "what we used to do" without the training session that was in place pre-crisis. It wasn't until another new librarian was hired that the mock instruction session was reinstituted. When both librarians heard we used to have a formal training session, they expressed they wished they had that. Below is an analysis of the components of what we found worked well between the previous and the current approaches at Reese Library:

Previous approach	Current approach	Both approaches
Formal training session covering developing outcomes, lesson plan format, components, and summative assessment	Co-teaching opportunities	Observation over one semester or until librarian feels comfortable
Formal training session on backward design	Mock instruction session	
	Collating and sharing feedback from PROTs	

Given our collective experiences, we recommend instituting a formal training program similar to the one that the Libraries at McGill University ran; however, an online module for the first part was composed of the following components:

- Online modules on library instruction, expanding on the original formal training session, including topics such as:
  - backward design
  - creating student learning outcomes and examples of them
  - the typical lesson structure and content
  - the mandated and optional summative assessments; how and when to access and implement them
- A minimum number of observational experiences of different librarians' instruction sessions
- A mock library instruction session in a safe space in which PROTs are undertaken whereby constructive feedback is noted. The associate director reviews the compiled feedback with the librarian.
- Having a more experienced librarian present to provide support and feedback in the first two sessions the new librarian teaches.
- Informal one-on-one peer coaching with new librarian(s) after they have taught a few sessions independently.

We intend to recommend this formal training program to the libraries' administration, and we hope that they will take it on board for future hires. Going through the pandemic forced us to think of new strategies to train librarians, which were found to be quite helpful. What made it helpful was the collegiality involved when the training librarians would observe the experienced librarians teach and due to the largely informal nature of these observations. It would be worth our while to incorporate what we did into a formal training program, as suggested above, and gather research on its effectiveness in training new librarians over time.

Conclusion

We hope that our description of how Reese Library's training program has evolved due to internal and external changes provides ideas to other academic libraries in developing or building on their library instruction training program. We learned that the training strategies we used at the peak of the crisis are helpful for librarians new to instruction to build their skills and confidence levels regardless of whether a crisis is happening or not. We also hope that the lessons we have learned will prevent others from making the same mistakes, particularly assuming that the librarians-in-training will suffice to undertake observation alone. In our experiences, along with the experiences of other academic libraries documented in the literature, a varied instruction training program of teaching theory and giving opportunities for practice is most effective.

APPENDIX A
PROT Form

Peer Review of Teaching Observation Form

Instructor	Observer	Date			
Course	**Audience** o Undergraduate o Graduate/Professional o Faculty/Staff o Other _____				
CRITERIA	DESCRIPTION	RATING (Circle a number)			
Content Knowledge	• Selected class content worth knowing and appropriate to the course • Included material appropriate to student knowledge and background • Minimized use of jargon, explained terms and concepts • Made distinction between fact and opinion • Presented divergent viewpoints when appropriate • Incorporated examples relevant to students to clarify class content • Matched stated objectives of the class to the class content	**1** Needs Improvement	**2**	**3** Meets Expectations	**4**	**5** Exceeds Expectations
Comments					
Teaching Methods	• Showed enthusiasm for topic • Made effective use of visual aids, handouts, slides, guides, etc. • Used appropriate styles(s)—problem-solving, problem-based learning, information transfer (lecture), discussion	**1** Needs Improvement	**2**	**3** Meets Expectations	**4**	**5** Exceeds Expectations
Comments					

CRITERIA	DESCRIPTION	RATING (Circle a number)				
Interaction	• Actively engaged students with the project at hand • Provided students with opportunity to ask questions • Paced lesson for note-taking • Addressed non-verbal communication such as confusion, boredom, or curiosity • Had professor clarify any confusion about research assignment • Used helpful examples for students to follow	**1** Needs Improvement	**2**	**3** Meets Expectations	**4**	**5** Exceeds Expectations
Comments						
Presentation	• General demeanor appropriate (voice, diction, and articulation were clear; body language and eye contact good; limited use of repetitive phrases; showed enthusiasm for subject) • Well-paced environment (started and stopped on time; solicited questions and waited a sufficient amount of time for students to respond; listened to student questions/comments and provided feedback; demonstrated efficient use of class time) • Presented material in a knowledgeable, clear, and organized fashion • Teaching strategy appropriate to topic and effectively used (lecture, demonstration, student participation, exercises (independent/group), question and answer, and other activities)	**1** Needs Improvement	**2**	**3** Meets Expectations	**4**	**5** Exceeds Expectations
Comments						

CRITERIA	DESCRIPTION	RATING (Circle a number)				
Assessment	• Assessed the existing information needs of students at the beginning of the class • Asked questions to monitor student progress • Employed active learning strategies as appropriate • Designed appropriate assessments into the instruction in order to demonstrate accomplishment of learning outcomes for the class	**1** Needs Improvement	**2**	**3** Meets Expectations	**4**	**5** Exceeds Expectations
Comments						
Overall Assessment		**1** Needs Improvement	**2**	**3** Meets Expectations	**4**	**5** Exceeds Expectations
Additional Comments						

APPENDIX B
Reese Library Lesson Plan Format

COURSE CODE: Professor's last name

Learning outcomes

- Students will…
- Students will…
- Students will…
- Students will…

Supplemental materials

Introduction

Lesson

Assessment

Notes

1. Information Literacy Best Practices Committee, *Characteristics of Programs of Information Literacy That Illustrate Best Practices: A Guideline* (Instruction Section of the Association of College and Research Libraries, January 2019), https://www.ala.org/acrl/standards/characteristics.
2. Since then, a few positions have since changed. The e-resources librarian has been replaced with a student success librarian; the cataloging and bibliographic management librarian is now known as librarian for acquisitions and metadata, and the access services librarian now oversees access services at both libraries.
3. Amanda Click and Claire Walker, "Life After Library School: On-the-Job Training for New Instruction Librarians," *Endnotes* 1, no. 1 (May 2010): 3.
4. Mandi Goodsett and Amanda Koziura, "Are Library Science Programs Preparing New Librarians? Creating a Sustainable and Vibrant Librarian Community," *Journal of Library Administration* 56, no. 6 (2016): 707–08.
5. Jessica Martinez and Meredith Forrey, "Overcoming Imposter Syndrome: The Adventures of Two New Instruction Librarians," *Reference Services Review* 47, no. 3 (2019): 331–42, https://doi.org/10.1108/RSR-03-2019-0021.
6. Martinez and Forrey, "Overcoming Imposter Syndrome."
7. April L. Colosimo, Sara Holder, and Amber Lannon, "Walking the Walk, Talking the Talk: A Learning-Centered Approach to the Design of a Workshop on Teaching for McGill Librarians," *Practical Academic Librarianship* 2, no. 2 (2012): 18–35.
8. Caroline Sinkinson and Stephanie Alexander, "Providing the 'Right' Instructional Development Opportunities," *LOEX Quarterly* 34, no. 4 (2008): article 3; Caroline Sinkinson, "An Assessment of Peer Coaching to Drive Professional Development and Reflective Teaching," *Communication in Information Literacy* 5, no. 1 (2011): 9–20, https://doi.org/10.15760/comminfolit.2011.5.1.99.
9. Sinkinson, "An Assessment of Peer Coaching," 18
10. Frances Brady, "Training Peer Teachers to Teach First Year Graduate Level Information Literacy Sessions," *Journal of Academic Librarianship* 47, no. 2 (2021): 1–12, https://doi.org/10.1016/j.acalib.2020.102308.
11. Karen Sobel, "Teaching Them to Teach: Programmatic Evaluation of Graduate Assistants' Teaching Performance," *Public Services Quarterly* 12, no. 3 (2016): 189–213, https://doi.org/10.1080/15228959.2016.1168724.
12. Martinez and Forrey, "Overcoming Imposter Syndrome"; Jessica Louque, "Exploring the Value of Communities of Practice in Academic Libraries," *Codex* 6, no. 1, (2021): 54–76.

Bibliography

Association of College and Research Libraries. Information Literacy Best Practices Committee. *Characteristics of Programs of Information Literacy That Illustrate Best Practices: A Guideline.* Instruction Section. January 2019. https://www.ala.org/acrl/standards/characteristics.

Brady, Frances. "Training Peer Teachers to Teach First Year Graduate Level Information Literacy Sessions." *Journal of Academic Librarianship* 47, no. 2 (2021): 1–12. https://doi.org/10.1016/j.acalib.2020.102308.

Click, Amanda, and Claire Walker. "Life After Library School: On-the-Job Training for New Instruction Librarians." *Endnotes* 1, no. 1 (May 2010): 1–14.

Colosimo, April L., Sara Holder, and Amber Lannon. "Walking the Walk, Talking the Talk: A Learning-Centered Approach to the Design of a Workshop on Teaching for McGill Librarians." *Practical Academic Librarianship* 2, no. 2 (2012): 18–35.

Goodsett, Mandi, and Amanda Koziura. "Are Library Science Programs Preparing New Librarians? Creating a Sustainable and Vibrant Librarian Community." *Journal of Library Administration* 56, no. 6 (2016): 697–721. https://doi.org/10.1080/01930826.2015.1134246.

Jaguszewski, Janice M., and Karen Williams. *New Roles for New Times: Transforming Roles in Research Libraries.* Washington, DC: Association of Research Libraries, August 2013. https://www.arl.org/wp-content/uploads/2015/12/nrnt-liaison-roles-revised.pdf.

Louque, Jessica. "Exploring the Value of Communities of Practice in Academic Libraries." *Codex* 6, no. 1 (2021): 54–76.

Martinez, Jessica, and Meredith Forrey. "Overcoming Imposter Syndrome: The Adventures of Two New Instruction Librarians." *Reference Services Review* 47, no. 3 (2019): 331–42. https://doi.org/10.1108/RSR-03-2019-0021.

Sinkinson, Caroline. "An Assessment of Peer Coaching to Drive Professional Development and Reflective Teaching." *Communication in Information Literacy* 5, no. 1 (2011): 9–20. https://doi.org/10.15760/comminfolit.2011.5.1.99.

Sinkinson, Caroline, and Stephanie Alexander. "Providing the 'Right' Instructional Development Opportunities." *LOEX Quarterly* 34, no. 4 (2008): article 3.

Sobel, Karen, Susan Avery, and Ignacio J. Ferrer-Vinent. "Teaching Them to Teach: Programmatic Evaluation of Graduate Assistants' Teaching Performance." *Public Services Quarterly* 12, no. 3 (2016): 189–213. https://doi.org/10.1080/15228959.2016.1168724.

PART VII

CASE STUDIES:
TRAINING NEW AND EXPERIENCED LIBRARIANS

CHAPTER 20

Planning for Instruction Training:

Implementing an On-the-Job Training for Library Instructors

Livia Piotto

LEARNING OUTCOMES

Readers will be able to

- design a training plan to support on-the-job training for new instruction librarians;

- adapt library instruction theoretical frameworks into practical approaches to design an on-the-job training that can be easily adjusted to different individuals;

- identify institute-specific practices that have an impact on library instruction to recognize instructional needs and opportunities; and

- assess basic instructional design principles and frameworks to develop their own instruction toolkit for improving their teaching skills.

Introduction

The need for instruction training for librarians is not new because, as Oakleaf et al. noted, "Librarians teach. It might not be what we planned to do when we entered the profession, or it may have been our secret hope all along. Either way, we teach."[1] However, it is also evident that there is no one-size-fits-all approach when it comes to instruction training.[2]

The majority of newly hired instruction librarians receive their training on the job, and this type of training remains the "primary means of learning" in academic libraries.[3]

This chapter describes the implementation of an instruction training plan developed to assist early-career librarians and librarians with no previous instruction experience with developing the basic skills for teaching information literacy in an academic environment. The existing literature on this topic is already plentiful. There are general and comprehensive guides, explorations of the topic with a practical approach, and the many publications that provide sample lesson plans for the library instructor to use as guides and inspiration.[4] Building from the existing literature, this case study offers a real-life example of how an instruction training program meant to support an on-the-job approach to training new instruction librarians can be implemented.

Institutional Context

John Cabot University (JCU) is an American liberal arts university based in Rome, Italy, and through the years it has grown into a university that attracts an international body of students, of which most are Italians and Americans. In time, the Frohring Library at JCU has become a vital ally for ensuring that students grow to become savvy researchers and critical learners.[5] Instrumental to this end was the development of an instruction program that was started in 2006 when I was hired as reference and instruction librarian. Once I started the job at JCU, I realized quickly that this was more than a standard reference job. When I learned that I would be responsible for providing instruction in the form of library orientations and information literacy instruction, I did what anyone would have done: I started reading and learning about information literacy instruction. Unfortunately, I was alone in this endeavor without someone to mentor or teach me how to teach. This meant I had to learn by trial and error. There was a lot of error. I ultimately discovered that this on-the-job training was very common, and I could not have learned what I did in a classroom during my formal preparation for librarianship. It is frequent for instruction librarian training to occur primarily in the workplace, and few librarians learn to teach after receiving formal training, as noted by Kilcullen in 1998: "Librarians are self-taught and teach other librarians to teach. Instruction librarians learn how to teach library instructional sessions by trial and error, by reading the literature, by communicating with colleagues, and by attending conferences and workshops on teaching…. They are constantly teaching and learning how to teach."[6]

In time, the needs of the instruction program grew so much that the library needed to hire new instruction librarians. Initially, the training of the new librarians was simply an informal passing of the knowledge acquired in the field, then I realized that this knowledge could have been the basis of a more structured instruction training for future colleagues. The instruction training plan that was then developed aimed to teach librarians with no previous instruction experience the basics of what it means to be a library instructor. The training plan builds its strengths on a mix of theoretical learning, observation activities, and practical applications. The recent need to hire, and therefore train, new instruction librarians has provided an opportunity to update and formalize the training plan. JCU did not invent anything special, we just adapted the answer to a common need in our context.

The instruction training plan is based on the ACRL documents and guidelines related to instructional practices, including the ACRL *Framework for Information Literacy for Higher Education*[7] and the *Roles and Strengths of Teaching Librarians*.[8] These documents, which may not necessarily be known by librarians with a non-American library science background, informed the best practices of the instruction program at JCU.

Development of On-the-Job Training for Library Instructors

JCU library is relatively small, and the entire staff participates in shifts at the central circulation desk, the only staffed workstation during evenings and weekends. This makes the onboarding experience for new employees very comprehensive and time-consuming. Training cannot just focus on instruction. Moreover, the instruction training cannot happen overnight, and past experience suggests that the new instruction librarian should spend at least one semester familiarizing with how the university works and with how the organizational structure might have an impact on the teaching job.

Ideally, the instruction training should not take place when the term is in full swing, as there is not much time left for regular training sessions when the rest of the staff are already busy with their duties. There is always the risk that the new instruction librarian will be left to figure things out on their own. Training instruction librarians requires a lot of time and energy and, above all, constant dedication. Therefore, the onboarding procedure can be scaffolded in such a way as to cover the initial broad responsibilities expected of all staff members, especially if training is to take place after the semester has already begun. More in-depth training for reference work can be provided later, while the newly hired librarian can begin to use the knowledge gained by becoming familiar with the institution and interacting with students and faculty. Finally, the new instruction librarian can start their formal teaching training. Because the line between reference and instruction work is often blurred anyway, we can easily use reference work as one-on-one instruction practice that can help the new instruction librarian overcome "stage fright" by familiarizing with resources and assignment requirements.[9] This scaffolded training plan is also intended to allow for a more gradual teaching experience.

Keeping in mind that a one-size-fits-all approach is not ideal for training library instructors, the plan developed at JCU presents a focus on analyzing the Frohring Library and the university environment as factors influencing how teaching is understood in our specific context. Backward design is the primary strategy implemented to help newly hired instructional librarians develop measurable learning outcomes, create instructional activities that foster authentic learning, and apply appropriate assessment techniques. The training plan itself follows a backward design approach. After setting the learning outcomes, we worked backward to develop the assessments and the activities that would enable the new instruction librarian to get started with the new job.

JCU Training Plan Learning Outcomes

- Analyze the organizational and instructional environment to identify instructional needs and opportunities and to define audiences.
- Recognize the various roles instruction librarians play in various contexts.
- Familiarize with basic instructional design principles (e.g., backward design, big ideas, outcomes, learning assessment, and activity sequencing).
- Apply backward design to a variety of library instruction services, both within and beyond classroom instruction (e.g., one-shot sessions, course co-design, learning objects).
- Develop an understanding of assessment techniques to evaluate instructional opportunities.

The training plan is also designed to accommodate a variety of teaching techniques and learning styles by including: an extensive list of reading recommendations (to help those who favor a verbal learning style or simply to read more about the topic);[10] experiential learning opportunities to accommodate those who prefer learning by doing; and opportunities for observing other colleagues teaching in a real-life setting (to favor those that need to see how things happen not just in an abstract sense).

Where We Teach: The Environmental Scan

Given that we firmly believe that "instruction is an institute-specific scenario,"[11] it is fundamental for a new instruction librarian to become familiar with the organizational culture and therefore with its teaching culture. In our training plan, the newly hired librarian needs to spend a significant amount of time getting to know the characteristics that define the institution, starting from the university and library missions. Instead, librarians who move from different positions to become instruction librarians should already be familiar with the institutional context, so less time should be spent on this initial step of the training. In either case, however, it is worth starting the training with an environmental scan to better understand both the library environment, its instruction practices, and the broader organizational environment.

Although time-consuming, an environmental scan is a good way to learn about the organizational context in which new instruction librarians will be expected to teach. In the case of frequent turnover of instruction librarians, this exercise can also be of great benefit for the library as an organization, as it offers the possibility to monitor how the institutional environment changes and to react to these changes. If the library does not have a programmatic document for environmental scanning, a good tool is "Analyzing Your Instructional Environment: A Workbook."[12] While this was developed before the implementation of the ACRL Framework and it still refers to the *Information Literacy Competency Standards for Higher Education*, the workbook provides a structure for drawing a comprehensive picture of the "unique situation" that defines the instruction program.

After gaining an insight into the macro-environment in which the instruction program is placed, the new instruction librarian needs to better understand how the library teaching efforts should relate to the broader academic curriculum. To this end, our training plan includes engaging in a curriculum mapping activity. Ideally, using this activity as an iterative assessment of the sequencing of library instruction practices should become part of the regular library operations. Curriculum mapping allows the library to examine the academic curriculum offered by the university, align the information literacy teaching with what is actually taught in the classroom, and identify information literacy instruction gaps and opportunities. This is time-consuming and difficult to carry out on a regular basis, but it is helpful when things change drastically—for example when the general curriculum is revised, new majors are implemented, or when new library staff is hired. Curriculum mapping provides the means to understand the institutional context from a strictly teaching perspective: what is taught? What are the general education prerequisites? What types of assignments are the students required to work on? In short, curriculum mapping can support library instruction at the point of need, and it provides a blueprint to create a programmatic engagement within the academic curriculum. Moreover, as Jacobson and Gibson noted, "information literacy librarians will need to conduct systematic curriculum analyses and design curriculum maps to identify those courses and programs that are the most natural "fit" or homes for the six frames"[13] in order to better incorporate the Framework discourse into a broader conversation that would go beyond the walls of the library and would then foster collaboration with the faculty.

Knowing the curriculum alone is not enough, it is also essential to get to know the people with whom the instruction librarian will then have to collaborate, who they are, their faces, what they do and teach in class, what they ask the students to do, and what their research interests are. A new instruction librarian first needs to get a sense of the place where they landed and who could become a potential teaching partner and collaborator. This is even more important in a small institution like JCU, where everybody knows each other and their roles. Getting to know the people is vital to create lasting relationships and build trust.

This phase of the training plan can take anywhere from one week to a few months. There is no way that an instruction librarian can teach confidently without knowing the surrounding environment and the contextual practices linked to the curriculum. Becoming familiar with the broad context in which the teaching takes place and getting to know the people who shape that environment is just as important as learning how to teach.

One Librarian, Different Roles

Inevitably, as the new instruction librarian learns about the environment, the organizational culture, and the academic curriculum, they begin to develop an understanding of the different roles they must play in their day-to-day job. As many have noted in recent years,[14] the profession and practice of an instruction librarian typically involve a range of different roles and responsibilities, which are, of course, institution-specific.

Knowing which roles an instruction librarian is expected to play is an essential part of the training of new instructors at JCU, where, for example, the instruction librarians, in addition to their in-classroom teaching responsibilities, provide reference services to the community (both walk-in and scheduled consultations),[15] act as a liaison for two to four academic departments, support the collection development within the disciplines in which they specialize, and provide support as instructional technologists for the LMS platform. All of these roles require specific training, which in some cases overlaps from role to role (i.e., reference is a kind of instruction, curriculum knowledge for reference and instruction is essential for collection development as well, and being an instructional technologist requires providing some kind of instruction to the faculty). In any case, the specific organizational culture of JCU has a major impact not only on the content and modalities of library instruction but also on the extensive training that we need to put in place to coach newly hired instruction librarians.

There is No Training without Theory First

However, when creating our plan for instruction training, we decided to prioritize only the roles of instructional designer and teacher, leaving the training for the other roles to be completed separately. For new instruction librarians, especially those who did not have the opportunity to receive any formal training about theoretical and practical aspects of teaching in library school, these two roles—despite having been the subject of extensive study over the past few years—remain the main roadblocks.[16] The training plan that we developed at JCU includes a brief overview of the major learning theories that are typically used in information literacy instruction: behaviorism, which focuses on observable behaviors and how these can be influenced by external motivations; cognitivism, which emphasizes what happens in the brain during learning; and constructivism, which emphasizes the role of the learner in the learning process. We then move on to the fundamental concepts of instructional design, including the basic models used in instructional design, such as the ADDIE framework (analysis, design, development, implement, evaluate), and other models that were inspired by it (USER,[17] the Teaching Tripod Approach,[18] Understanding by Design[19]).

This part of the training, because it is largely based on theoretical concepts, is mostly carried out with a series of reading assignments recommended to the newly hired instruction librarian. While the training provides a preliminary summary of learning theories and instructional design frameworks, the new instruction librarian has the opportunity to delve into concepts that may have already been covered in library school. For those librarians who are completely new to the idea of also becoming teachers and instructional designers as part of their job, this phase of the training is a good opportunity to explore the basis of these two roles. Reading about the theories is then completed by reflection and discussion with the trainer, who provides further guidance integrated with their personal experience.

During an on-the-job training program like the one JCU uses, learning theories and instructional design models are easily overlooked. The reason can be traced to the fact that instructional design frameworks and theories are usually applied to semester-long teaching contexts, while library instruction does not necessarily follow the same modalities.[20] To accommodate the specific needs of the library teaching context, instructional design models must be scaled down. We believe it is essential to incorporate these theories in the training program because instructional design models give librarians the framework they need to create engaging lessons. However, learning about instructional design frameworks is rarely fully applicable to the constrained time provided by on-the-job training such as the one developed at JCU. Therefore, the time devoted to this theoretical part of the training may vary significantly depending on many factors, including the new instruction librarian's prior knowledge of the topic. Moreover, if the training is set to start before the beginning of the term, theories and frameworks can be examined more thoroughly, whereas, once the semester has already begun and the training needs to start, priorities need to shift, and the theoretical background is likely to be left aside.

Lesson Plans: Where Theory and Practice Meet

In addition to focusing on what it means for an instruction librarian to become a teacher and an instructional designer and to learn the theories behind these two roles, the core of the training plan developed at JCU aims to establish a connection between these theories and their practical application in the classroom. Our training plan, therefore, places a lot of emphasis on designing the teaching (and, hopefully, learning) experience and how to create a lesson plan, which is the bridge between the design theories applied by the librarians in their role as instructional designer and what actually happens in the classroom during the teaching practice. As librarians learn to apply instructional design theory in the classroom, the roles of instructional designer and teacher become intertwined.

At JCU, we have chosen to use a backward design approach to design our instruction training plan because this is also the structured approach that we recommend for outlining teaching and learning experiences. Within this approach, evidence of learning is identified through assessment and then a plan is developed that allows the instructor to appropriately sequence the content to be delivered and the activities that will be employed to enforce student learning and understanding.[21]

It is true that developing a lesson plan is time-consuming, but what we try to emphasize during the training is that spending more time at the beginning engaging in thorough lesson plan development means that the instruction librarian will end up spending less time in the long term. Once developed, lesson plans can be reused for sessions that are repeated over time, for sessions that are similar in content and structure, and they can be tailored to suit different needs in different contexts. At JCU, we have outlined a lesson plan template that all librarians are encouraged to use, so we don't have to create something new whenever we are asked to prepare a session.[22] We have developed the content for our template based on what Benjes-Small and Miller have identified as the essential components of an effective lesson plan.[23] Moreover, lesson plans can easily be reused and shared among librarians and, ideally, with faculty as well. We have created a shared repository of all lesson plans created by the instruction librarians, and we reuse and adapt these documents based on the specific needs.

As part of their training, the new instruction librarian is encouraged to access and review the shared lesson plans to become familiar with the structure of the template that we use and to better understand the components of a well-developed lesson plan. Reviewing and revising lesson plans created by others is an introductory activity in preparation for creating lesson plans from scratch. After the new instruction librarian has become familiar with the organization and design of a lesson plan, the training starts focusing on its three main components: the learning outcomes, the assessment, and the instructional strategies and learning activities they will employ in the classroom.

Developing Learning Outcomes

Learning outcomes that outline what the librarian envisions the students will be able to know and do after the instruction session are the most important part of the lesson plan. The training plan implemented at JCU places an emphasis on learning outcomes, as learning outcomes are likely to be the foundation upon which lessons are structured. Extensive literature already discusses how learning outcomes should be developed, and we follow the models that are already commonly used in library instruction.[24]

Our training for instruction librarians not only focuses on developing specific learning outcomes. At JCU, we emphasize that "big ideas," which Wiggins and McTighe identify as the concepts that give "meaning and connection to discrete facts and skills,"[25] are central for helping students transfer their learning from one context to the other. Using the backward design process, the instruction librarian can develop learning outcomes starting from these big ideas. Once the abstract big idea has been identified, the instruction librarian can connect it to the specific skills and understanding that the students should gain after the instruction, and therefore they can define the learning outcomes.

The specific model that we have chosen to follow for writing learning outcomes is based on the formula developed by Gilchrist and Zald, which combines verbs from Bloom's Taxonomy with an action phrase demonstrating learning at some level of mastery.[26] This formula is especially helpful for beginners because it breaks down the learning outcomes into discrete parts and it provides a frame that prevents instruction librarians from trying to cover more content than can be realistically included in the allotted instruction time. Having to think about what we want students to learn activates a reflective process that prevents developing more learning outcomes than are needed.

To provide further guidelines to develop meaningful learning outcomes, we have also adapted the SMART method that George T. Doran developed for goals and objectives.[27] Library instruction learning outcomes should be

- student-centered: the focus is on the student learning experience;
- measurable: the librarian should be able to measure or judge the outcomes;
- appropriate: the learning outcome is suitable for the discipline and for the level of understanding of the students;
- realistic: the learning outcome represents what students can realistically accomplish given the time allotted and the assignment the professor has developed; and
- transferable: students should see that they are learning something that will last and that can be transferred to other contexts.[28]

Since practicing the construction of learning outcomes based on the "students will be able to + action verb + in order to" formula might become quite an abstract exercise when taken out of context, we encourage new instruction librarians to rely on course syllabi, conversations with the faculty, and departmental or programmatic learning goals to get a sense on how to develop meaningful outcomes for specific contexts. Additionally, new instruction librarians can practice applying the formula and using the SMART method by revising learning outcomes developed by colleagues for past instruction sessions available in the shared lesson plan repository. Capitalizing on what others have done has proved to be a good way to help librarians understand how learning outcomes work in a given context and how they relate to the actual instructional activities.

In an effort to provide further tools that could guide new instruction librarians in better understanding the learning outcome development process, we have noticed that, compared to the past when instruction librarians could use the practical language of the ACRL Standards to draft learning outcomes, now it is more challenging to combine the abstract language of the ACRL Framework with the one that would be more appropriate for learning outcomes. Some useful tools we have successfully identified that can support librarians in adapting the abstract concepts included in the Framework into skills-based outcomes are the following:

1. The ACRL Framework for Information Literacy Sandbox (https://sandbox.acrl. org/)
2. ACRL Framework for Information Literacy Toolkit (https://acrl.libguides. com/c.php?g=651675&p=4571135)
3. Project Cora (https://www.projectcora.org/)
4. PALNI LibGuide on the Framework for Information Literacy for Higher Education (https://libguides.palni.edu/ilframework)

These tools are all extremely useful to guide librarians in adjusting the language of the "big ideas" of the Framework to the measurable skills of the learning outcomes. The companion documents to the Framework for Information Literacy for Higher Education, which have been made available so far, have also been helpful in practicing with learning outcomes writing. These documents reformulate the abstract concepts that define the Framework into a more concrete form that is easily adaptable as learning outcomes by adapting the frames and, in particular, the knowledge practices and dispositions to a variety of disciplines.[29]

Getting Started with Assessment

Because of their measurable nature, learning outcomes should ideally be developed with an eye toward identifying valid evidence of learning through assessment. Additionally, gathering evidence cannot be separated from the activities that the instruction librarian will then develop. This is the reason why the training plan that we have implemented considers the definition of what the instructor wants to assess and the instructional activities that will be assessed (steps 2 and 3 in the backward design process) as a single conceptual unit of training.

Teaching assessment to new instruction librarians can be challenging because librarians tend to be relegated to teach one-shot sessions, and it can be hard to assess whether any learning has happened in similar situations. This is typically what happens at JCU, where instruction librarians are invited to teach one class session, two if they are lucky. In such contexts, it can be difficult to find the time to assess what the students learn in a meaningful way. This is the reason why learning outcomes become essential in guiding the instruction librarians to create a learning experience that could provide some evidence of learning. When we focus on achieving the intended learning outcomes, assessment becomes less overwhelming. Moreover, assessment can also be used by teachers as a way to improve teaching skills because "when educators assess learning repeatedly and make instructional changes over time, their pedagogical skills increase."[30]

In our prior experience, we have found that the Kirkpatrick model is a good tool for describing what instruction librarians should aim for when it comes to assessment, even for one-shot sessions.[31] The author first heard of this model while she was enrolled in an online continuing education course,[32] and she felt that it would be beneficial to include the model in the training because "it helps clarify what can be evaluated and assessed given the time and resources at your disposal."[33] The four levels outlined in the model can easily be incorporated into library instruction to assess various facets of the teaching and learning process regardless of the duration of the instruction (one or multiple sessions within the same course). During the training at JCU, we encourage new instruction librarians to pay attention to what each level in the Kirkpatrick model measures and on which aspect of the instruction the instruction librarian should focus:

- Level 1: Reaction—measure of the level of satisfaction of the students
  - o Did everything go well during the instruction session? Is there anything that can be improved?
- Level 2: Learning—formative assessment of the evidence of learning
  - o Have the students met the learning outcomes developed for the instruction session?
- Level 3: Behavior—summative assessment to verify whether a change in behavior happened after the instruction.
  - o To what extent have the students changed their research habits after the instruction session? Are they capable of transferring the knowledge acquired to different contexts?
- Level 4: Results—measure of the "return on investment."
  - o This final level goes well beyond the class borders and corresponds more to the strategic goal of having an academic education: becoming a life-long critical thinker.[34]

We typically focus on the first two levels of the Kirkpatrick model, especially in the one-shot library instruction sessions we provide at JCU, and we try to teach new instruction librarians to turn any assignment or classroom activity in which students do or produce something into an opportunity for assessment. We model our assessment on classroom assessment techniques (CATs), as activities that can be scaffolded throughout the library instruction session, and that help students become more effective, self-assessing, and self-directed learners. CATs provide a way to assess the students' reaction to the instruction, giving the librarian the opportunity to hone their teaching skills.

The training on CATs is mostly based on the foundational text by Angelo and Cross[35] and its subsequent application to the world of libraries by Bowles-Terry and Kvenild.[36] At JCU, we encourage new instruction librarians to familiarize with both texts to gain a general understanding of classroom assessment techniques in general and to get a sense of which CATs can be meaningfully adapted and incorporated in a library instruction setting. To start experimenting with and learning how to apply different CATs, one exercise that can be effective is to work with the shared lesson plans and identify teaching moments that might require alternative CATs. However, learning which classroom assessment techniques are effective in which context depends once again on individual practice, trying and applying specific techniques, maybe failing in using them in the wrong context, reflecting on errors, and transforming these techniques into new activities that might be more fitting for a specific instructional context. For this reason, our training plan also encourages new instruction librarians to observe an experienced colleague during their instruction session. Observing how others integrate CATs into their instructional plan to engage with students and assess specific aspects of their learning experience is a great way to familiarize themselves with the concept of assessment.

Sharing, Observing, Teaching, Reflecting

As we have mentioned several times, working with more experienced colleagues and observing what others have already done are major components of the training plan developed at JCU. Using and revising shared teaching materials is an exercise that helps new instruction librarians practice skills learned during the training, but it also provides the opportunity to receive constructive feedback from a double perspective. For example, the new librarian can receive feedback on their progress in creating clear, specific, and measurable learning outcomes, while the rest of the team can gain a fresh perspective that they could use to revise the learning outcomes in line with recent changes in the instructional context.

Moreover, in the first couple of months, the new instruction librarian is not only encouraged to learn about instructional design theories and practical ways to develop lesson plans in their entirety, but they are also encouraged to observe as many information literacy sessions as possible in a variety of disciplines and settings (one-shot sessions, workshops, embedded sessions). Observations can be very helpful for librarians new to the profession in overcoming any initial anxiety they may have about being in front of an audience. At the same time, shadowing experienced instruction librarians can help the new librarian understand what happens in the classroom. Observing and taking notes about how colleagues incorporate active learning techniques, assess student understanding, and integrate CATs to engage students and then debriefing after an instruction session allow the new instruction librarian to seek clarifications on specific events that happen in the classroom. Observations help put theory into practice and give a sense of common and shared practices within the library instruction program. This practice also allows the new instruction librarian to see different teaching styles in action, different ways of delivering content, and, potentially, different communication styles, while becoming familiar with the basics of instructional design.

After learning the theory and observing others putting it into practice comes the moment in which the new instruction librarian has to start experiencing what it means to be in the classroom. All the theoretical training sessions are accompanied by activities that are meant to replicate—and potentially prepare for—real-life classroom situations (rewriting learning outcomes for observed instruction sessions, ideating or adapting assessment activities, and creating a full lesson plan in collaboration with other colleagues), but eventually the librarian has to start teaching in the classroom. And, of course, after observing more experienced colleagues, the following step is to ask to reciprocate and to have the new instruction librarian observed as they start teaching solo. Receiving feedback allows them to adjust their pace, timing, the organization of the content, and the clarity of the exposition. Observing and being observed in the classroom encourage discussions and stimulate constructive feedback and suggestions for improvement.[37]

With its focus on participatory learning and observations, the training plan that we use at JCU encourages the use of reflection as a tool for reviewing what goes well and what goes wrong during the teaching time, to learn from mistakes, adjust imperfections, and constantly improve. Reflection cannot be forced; it is a personal activity that can, however, become a transformative experience since it induces learning by simply thinking about one's own experiences and actions and by reflecting on observation feedback. Each part of the training can stimulate reflection both as an individual practice and as a team activity. All training exercises can become opportunities to discuss the rationale for specific instructional choices, from the chosen learning outcomes to the classroom assessment techniques implemented. Reflection is one of the most powerful professional development tools available to instruction librarians. As Reale noted, by being reflective, instruction librarians become aware of their strengths and weaknesses, they are not afraid of engaging with their emotions in a classroom setting, they are aware of their purpose in the classroom, they recognize when they are wrong by admitting their mistakes and trying to correct them, and they strive for learning from those mistakes.[38]

Conclusion

Although an instruction librarian's first few months on the job are very important, training does not stop there because it is impossible to cover everything that has been said and written about teaching techniques and practices in the library world in just a few training sessions. The on-the-job training is a necessary component of the job in and of itself. It continues as circumstances change and as teaching practices evolve in response to what happens in the classroom and outside of the classroom in the broader institutional environment. The teaching itself is part of the learning, and "the more that librarians teach, the more they may realize how much there is to learn about teaching. The learning becomes an ongoing process."[39]

At JCU, we strive to provide the tools necessary for ongoing training, and one way to do this is by promoting active participation in the teaching activities as an integral component of the training itself. On-the-job training allows instruction librarians to immediately apply their knowledge in a practical sense. This type of training allows the new instruction librarian to engage in teamwork from the very beginning, and it provides the new librarian with the opportunity to become the fresh eye that can help revise old practices. Moreover, since library instruction can happen in a variety of contexts, and it can be approached in multiple ways, from reference services to the development of instructional materials (research guides and online tutorials), from co-design collaboration for creating assignments, learning outcomes, or entire courses to credit-bearing information literacy courses, the on-the-job training promotes adaptability as instruction librarians have to face a variety of teaching situations and challenges as needs evolve.

However, one of the downsides of an on-the-job training plan such as the one we advocate for at JCU is that it does not allow for formal planning or a formalized structure. This type of training can surely follow certain guidelines, but it mostly depends on multiple factors, including the new librarian's prior knowledge regarding library instruction and the timing of when the training happens. This is the reason why, despite all the efforts to create a training plan that could be reused every time one needs to train a new instruction librarian, "a training plan is something that should be unique to each individual you hire" because each new individual would necessarily have a different background and experience.[40] We also need to take into consideration that on-the-job training can be very time-consuming, especially if the hire happens mid-semester when there is not enough time for a general onboarding and finding dedicated time for training activities is not so easy. Nevertheless, on-the-job training is what most instruction librarians get, and we need to try and create the most meaningful opportunity for providing guidance in a job that constantly changes.

APPENDIX A

Instruction Plan

Title or topic of the lesson plan.

Optional: class for which the lesson plan has been initially developed.

- It is important to know in which broader context the library instruction session is going to fit in because that context has an impact on what and how the librarian will teach.

Frames Addressed

List 1 or 2 that are the primary focus of the session.

- It is important, although not essential nor required, to put the session within the Framework context and try to identify the "big ideas" that underlie the teaching plan.
- The "big ideas" represent the response to those bottlenecks where students get stuck in their learning. The bottlenecks are the core concepts for a discipline, and they provide an opportunity for the instruction librarians to link information literacy concepts to specific disciplines, thus creating collaboration opportunities to work with faculty that have both content expertise of their discipline and knowledge of how and where students get typically stuck.

Learning Outcomes

Include 2 or 3 learning outcomes.

- Learning outcomes are usually tied to the frames addressed, and they are also linked to the assessment that will be chosen for the instruction session. They define what students will know and what they will be able to do.

Estimated Total Time Required

Indicate the total time requested by the professor.

- Knowing the real time allotted for the library instruction session is vital. The professor requesting the session might expect the librarian to free up some time at the end to allow the professor to collect papers or talk about future assignments and homework. A good strategy is to plan for less time than the full class period but be ready to add more content or more backup activities in case there is some extra time left.

Outline and Activities

Use the table to create an outline for the instruction session. Include the step-by-step of what you do in the lesson (lecture time, activities, group discussion) and the estimated time for each part. The content of the lesson plan can be as detailed as a real script, or it could only be a bullet point list of concepts and tools that you would like to include in the session.

You can include here the modality to deliver the content (lecture, point-and-click demonstration, Socratic conversation, etc.).

Besides the content to be shared, the lesson plan should also include:

- Activities for learners to engage with ideas
  - o Learning activities are essential because they promote active learning, they create a more engaging experience for the students, they can be used as assessment, and they allow the instruction librarian to move "From sage on the stage to guide on the side."
- Anticipated length of time for content-sharing and learning activities
  - o Each part of the lesson plan (both content and activities) should be timed to provide a temporal framework that can help structure the lesson plan and make good use of the time allotted. As previously mentioned, planning for less time but preparing backup activities in the case of running too fast is always a good strategy.

Plan	Time in minutes
Introduction	
Wrap-up and conclusion	

Assessment Method

What strategies or assignments will you use to assess student learning? How will you know that they have made progress toward your learning outcomes?

- This should include classroom assessment techniques during this lesson. You may also have other assessments that are longer term, which are integrated into the course you work with.
- The assessment method used really depends on many factors, including the learning outcomes developed for the session, the learning activities that you want to incorporate, and the actual time that can be dedicated to the assessment itself.

Tools, Materials, and Resources

- Including what is going to be needed during the session (e.g., technology, materials for group activities, handouts) helps you remember that logistics also have a crucial role in instruction delivery.

Notes

1. Megan Oakleaf et al., "Notes from the Field: 10 Short Lessons on One-Shot Instruction," *Communications in Information Literacy* 6, no. 1 (2012): 6.
2. Candice M. Benjes-Small and Rebecca K. Miller, *The New Instruction Librarian: A Workbook for Trainers and Learners* (Chicago: ALA Editions, 2017).
3. Sheril J. Hook et al., "In-House Training for Instruction Librarians," *Research Strategies* 19, no. 2 (2003): 100, https://doi.org/10.1016/j.resstr.2003.12.001.
4. See for example: Candice M. Benjes-Small and Rebecca K. Miller, *The New Instruction Librarian: A Workbook for Trainers and Learners* (Chicago: ALA Editions, 2017); Patricia Bravender, Hazel McClure, and Gayle Schaub, *Teaching Information Literacy Threshold Concepts: Lesson Plans for Librarians* (Chicago: Association of College and Research Libraries Library Association, 2015); Christopher N. Cox and Elizabeth Blakesley, *Information Literacy Instruction Handbook* (Chicago: Association of College and Research Libraries, 2008); Samantha Godbey, Susan Beth Wainscott, and Xan Goodman, *Disciplinary Applications of Information Literacy Threshold Concepts* (Chicago: Association of College and Research Libraries, 2017).
5. For a more comprehensive description of JCU's institutional context and the difficulties of being an American institution in a non-American context, see Livia Piotto, "Researching Rome: The Librarian as Research Mediator," in *Library Partnerships in International Liberal Arts Education: Building Relationships Across Cultural and Institutional Lines*, ed. Jeff H. Gima and Kara J. Malenfant (Chicago: Association of College & Research Libraries, 2020), 9–20; Tara Keenan, Manlio Perugini, and Seth N. Jaffe, "Changing a Teaching Culture in an International University Context: Introducing English and Research Competencies for the Price of a Cup of Coffee," in *Library Partnerships in International Liberal Arts Education: Building Relationships Across Cultural and Institutional Lines*, ed. Jeff Hiroshi Gima and Kara Malenfant (Chicago: Association for College and Research Libraries, 2020), 53–62.
6. Maureen Kilcullen, "Teaching librarians to Teach: Recommendations on What We Need to Know," *Reference Services Review* 26, no. 2 (1998): 11, https://doi.org/10.1108/00907329810307623.
7. *Framework for Information Literacy for Higher Education*, Association of College & Research Libraries, American Library Association, February 9, 2015, https://www.ala.org/acrl/standards/ilframework.
8. *Roles and Strengths of Teaching Librarians*, Association of College & Research Libraries, American Library Association, May 15, 2017, https://www.ala.org/acrl/standards/teachinglibrarians.
9. Melissa N. Mallon, *Partners in Teaching and Learning: Coordinating a Successful Academic Library Instruction Program* (Lanham, MD: Rowman & Littlefield, 2020).

10. The full list of readings can vary depending on availability of resources.

11. Caitlin A. Bagley, *Fundamentals for the Instruction Coordinator*, ALA Fundamentals Series (Chicago: ALA Neal-Schuman, 2022), 33.

12. "Analyzing Your Instructional Environment: A Workbook," *ACRL's Instruction Section* (blog), December 2010, https://acrl.ala.org/IS/instruction-tools-resources-2/higher-education-environment/analyzing-your-instructional-environmen/.

13. Trudi Jacobson and Craig Gibson, "First Thoughts on Implementing the Framework for Information Literacy," *Communications in Information Literacy* 9, no. 2 (2015): 104, https://doi.org/10.15760/comminfolit.2015.9.2.187.

14. *Roles and Strengths of Teaching Librarians*, Association of College & Research Libraries; Benjes-Small and Miller, *The New Instruction Librarian*; Jessica Cole, "Instructional Roles for Librarians," in *Curriculum-Based Library Instruction: From Cultivating Faculty Relationships to Assessment*, ed. Amy Blevins and Megan Inman (Lanham, MD: Rowman & Littlefield, 2014); Janice M. Jaguszewski and Karen Williams, "New Roles for New Times: Transforming Liaison Roles in Research Libraries" (Association of Research Libraries, 2013), https://www.arl.org/resources/new-roles-for-new-times-transforming-liaison-roles-in-research-libraries/.

15. The training for the reference work is done separately for those newly hired librarians who are new to this work. Although this training also benefits from a knowledge of the institution and the academic curriculum, it mostly focuses on the reference interview process and an analysis of the complexity of the librarian/patron interaction following the standard behavioral guidelines developed by RUSA.

16. Dani Brecher and Kevin Michael Klipfel, "Education Training for Instruction Librarians: A Shared Perspective," *Communications in Information Literacy* 8, no. 1 (2014), https://doi.org/10.15760/comminfolit.2014.8.1.164; Eveline Houtman, "'Trying to Figure It Out': Academic Librarians Talk about Learning to Teach," *Library and Information Research* 34, no. 107 (October 9, 2010): 18–40, https://doi.org/10.29173/lirg246; Eveline Houtman, "Asking 'Good Questions' about How Academic Librarians Learn to Teach," in *The Grounded Instruction Librarian: Participating in the Scholarship of Teaching and Learning*, ed. Melissa Mallon et al. (Chicago: Association of College & Research Libraries, 2019), 17–30; Sandra J. Valenti and Brady D. Lund, "Preparing the Instructional Librarian: Representation of ACRL Roles and Strengths in MLS Course Descriptions," *College & Research Libraries* 82, no. 4 (2021): 530–47, https://doi.org/10.5860/crl.82.4.530.

17. Char Booth, *Reflective Teaching, Effective Learning: Instructional Literacy for Library Educators* (Chicago: American Library Association, 2011).

18. Joan R. Kaplowitz, *Designing Information Literacy Instruction: The Teaching Tripod Approach* (Lanham: Rowman & Littlefield Publishers, 2017).

19. Grant Wiggins and Jay McTighe, *Understanding by Design*, 2nd edition (Alexandria, VA: ASCD, 2005).

20. At JCU, most of the library instruction sessions are one-shot sessions. Often, multiple sessions are delivered within the same course, but there is minimal programmatic organization, and faculty tend to request sessions when they think these sessions best fit in their courses.

21. Wiggins and McTighe, *Understanding by Design*.

22. See Appendix A.

23. Benjes-Small and Miller, *The New Instruction Librarian*.

24. Debra Gilchrist and Anna Zald, "Instruction & Program Design through Assessment," in *Information Literacy Instruction Handbook*, ed. Christopher N. Cox and Elizabeth Blakesley (Chicago: Association of College and Research Libraries, 2008), 164–92, https://digitalscholarship.unlv.edu/cgi/viewcontent.cgi?referer=&httpsredir=1&article=1145&context=lib_articles.

25. Wiggins and McTighe, *Understanding by Design*, 5.

26. Debra Gilchrist, "Writing Student Learning Outcomes," https://www.youtube.com/watch?v=1Z7E9vHuyX4; Gilchrist and Zald, "Instruction & Program Design through Assessment."

27. George T. Doran, "There's a S.M.A.R.T. Way to Write Management's Goals and Objectives," *Management Review* 70, no. 11 (1981): 35.

28. Piotto and Spasov, "Co-Designing Information Literacy Experiences." Another checklist, adapted from Gilchrist, says that outcomes should be: measurable or "judgeable," clear to students, faculty, and librarians, integrated within the session, within the course, within the program, developmental and sequenced, transferable, related to institutional definitions and documents (including the

Framework), matched to the level (course, 50-minute session, program, etc.), balanced (using a variety of levels in the Bloom Taxonomy), representative of what the students will do. Gilchrist, "Writing Student Learning Outcomes."

29. "Politics, Policy, and International Relations: Companion Document to the ACRL Framework for Information Literacy for Higher Education," Association of College & Research Libraries, 2021, https://www.ala.org/acrl/aboutacrl/directoryofleadership/sections/ppirs/acr-ppirsec; "Research Competencies in Writing and Literature: Companion Document to the ACRL Framework for Information Literacy for Higher Education," Association of College & Research Libraries, 2021, https://www.ala.org/acrl/standards/researchcompetenciesles; "Social Work: Companion Document to the ACRL Framework for Information Literacy for Higher Education," Association of College & Research Libraries, 2021, https://acrl.libguides.com/ld.php?content_id=62704385; "Women's and Gender Studies: Companion Document to the ACRL Framework for Information Literacy for Higher Education," Association of College & Research Libraries, 2021, https://www.ala.org/acrl/standards/wgs_framework; "Journalism: Companion Document to the ACRL Framework for Information Literacy for Higher Education," Association of College & Research Libraries, 2022, https://www.ala.org/sites/default/files/acrl/content/standards/Framework_Companion_Journalism.pdf; "Science, Technology, Engineering, and Mathematics: Companion Document to the ACRL Framework for Information Literacy for Higher Education," Association of College & Research Libraries, 2022, https://www.ala.org/acrl/sites/ala.org.acrl/files/content/standards/Framework_Companion_STEM.pdf; "Sociology: Companion Document to the ACRL Framework for Information Literacy for Higher Education," Association of College & Research Libraries, 2022, https://www.ala.org/sites/default/files/acrl/content/standards/framework_companion_sociology.pdf; "The Framework for Visual Literacy in Higher Education: Companion Document to the ACRL Framework for Information Literacy for Higher Education," Association of College & Research Libraries, 2022, https://www.ala.org/sites/default/files/acrl/content/standards/Framework_Companion_Visual_Literacy.pdf.

30. Megan Oakleaf, "The Information Literacy Instruction Assessment Cycle: A Guide for Increasing Student Learning and Improving Librarian Instructional Skills," *Journal of Documentation* 65, no. 4 (2009): 541, https://doi.org/10.1108/00220410910970249.

31. Kirkpatrick Partners, "The Kirkpatrick Model," 2022, https://www.kirkpatrickpartners.com/the-kirkpatrick-model/.

32. Eric Ackermann and Candice Benjes-Small, "Crash Course in Assessing Library Instruction," Library Juice Academy, 2017.

33. Dominique Turnbow and Annie Zeidman-Karpinski, "Don't Use a Hammer When You Need a Screwdriver: How to Use the Right Tools to Create Assessment That Matters," *Communications in Information Literacy* 10, no. 2 (2016): 145.

34. Candice Benjes-Small, "A Primer for New Teachers," *The Future Academic Librarian's Toolkit*, January 1, 2019, https://scholarworks.wm.edu/librariesbookchapters/1.

35. Thomas A. Angelo and K. Patricia Cross, *Classroom Assessment Techniques: A Handbook for College Teachers*, 2nd ed, The Jossey-Bass Higher and Adult Education Series (San Francisco: Jossey-Bass Publishers, 1993).

36. Melissa Bowles-Terry and Cassandra Kvenild, *Classroom Assessment Techniques for Librarians* (Chicago: Association of College and Research Libraries, a division of the American Library Association, 2015).

37. Katelyn R. Tucker, "Teaching Me to Teach: A New Librarian's Experience with a Structured Training Program for Information Literacy Instruction," *Virginia Libraries* 59, no. 1 (2013).

38. Michelle Reale, *Becoming a Reflective Librarian and Teacher: Strategies for Mindful Academic Practice* (Chicago: ALA Editions, 2017), 42–43.

39. Houtman, "Asking 'Good Questions," 23.

40. Benjes-Small and Miller, *The New Instruction Librarian*.

Bibliography

Ackermann, Eric, and Candice Benjes-Small. "Crash Course in Assessing Library Instruction." Library Juice Academy. 2017.

Angelo, Thomas A., and K. Patricia Cross. *Classroom Assessment Techniques: A Handbook for College Teachers*. 2nd ed. The Jossey-Bass Higher and Adult Education Series. San Francisco: Jossey-Bass Publishers, 1993. http://catdir.loc.gov/catdir/toc/onix07/92033901.html.

Association of College & Research Libraries. "Analyzing Your Instructional Environment: A Workbook." *ACRL's Instruction Section* (blog), December 2010. https://acrl.ala.org/IS/instruction-tools-resources-2/higher-education-environment/analyzing-your-instructional-environmen/.

———. *Framework for Information Literacy for Higher Education*. American Library Association. February 9, 2015. https://www.ala.org/acrl/standards/ilframework.

———. "Journalism: Companion Document to the ACRL Framework for Information Literacy for Higher Education." 2022. https://www.ala.org/sites/default/files/acrl/content/standards/Framework_Companion_Journalism.pdf.

———. "Politics, Policy, and International Relations: Companion Document to the ACRL Framework for Information Literacy for Higher Education." 2021. https://www.ala.org/acrl/aboutacrl/directoryofleadership/sections/ppirs/acr-ppirsec.

———. "Research Competencies in Writing and Literature: Companion Document to the ACRL Framework for Information Literacy for Higher Education." 2021. https://www.ala.org/acrl/standards/researchcompetenciesles.

———. *Roles and Strengths of Teaching Librarians*. American Library Association. May 15, 2017. https://www.ala.org/acrl/standards/teachinglibrarians.

———. "Science, Technology, Engineering, and Mathematics: Companion Document to the ACRL Framework for Information Literacy for Higher Education." 2022. https://www.ala.org/acrl/sites/ala.org.acrl/files/content/standards/Framework_Companion_STEM.pdf.

———. "Social Work: Companion Document to the ACRL Framework for Information Literacy for Higher Education." 2021. https://acrl.libguides.com/ld.php?content_id=62704385.

———. "Sociology: Companion Document to the ACRL Framework for Information Literacy for Higher Education." 2022. https://www.ala.org/sites/default/files/acrl/content/standards/framework_companion_sociology.pdf.

———. "The Framework for Visual Literacy in Higher Education: Companion Document to the ACRL Framework for Information Literacy for Higher Education." 2022. https://www.ala.org/sites/default/files/acrl/content/standards/Framework_Companion_Visual_Literacy.pdf.

———. "Women's and Gender Studies: Companion Document to the ACRL Framework for Information Literacy for Higher Education." 2021. https://www.ala.org/acrl/standards/wgs_framework.

Bagley, Caitlin A. *Fundamentals for the Instruction Coordinator*. ALA Fundamentals Series. Chicago: ALA Neal-Schuman, 2022.

Benjes-Small, Candice. "A Primer for New Teachers." *The Future Academic Librarian's Toolkit*. January 1, 2019. https://scholarworks.wm.edu/librariesbookchapters/1.

Benjes-Small, Candice M., and Rebecca K. Miller. *The New Instruction Librarian: A Workbook for Trainers and Learners*. Chicago: ALA Editions, 2017.

Booth, Char. *Reflective Teaching, Effective Learning: Instructional Literacy for Library Educators*. Chicago: American Library Association, 2011. http://site.ebrary.com/id/10469288.

Bowles-Terry, Melissa, and Cassandra Kvenild. *Classroom Assessment Techniques for Librarians*. Chicago: Association of College and Research Libraries, a division of the American Library Association, 2015.

Bravender, Patricia, Hazel McClure, and Gayle Schaub. *Teaching Information Literacy Threshold Concepts: Lesson Plans for Librarians*. Chicago: Association of College and Research Libraries Library Association, 2015.

Brecher, Dani, and Kevin Michael Klipfel. "Education Training for Instruction Librarians: A Shared Perspective." *Communications in Information Literacy* 8, no. 1 (2014). https://doi.org/10.15760/comminfolit.2014.8.1.164.

Cole, Jessica. "Instructional Roles for Librarians." In *Curriculum-Based Library Instruction: From Cultivating Faculty Relationships to Assessment*, edited by Amy Blevins and Megan Inman. Lanham: Rowman & Littlefield, 2014.

Cox, Christopher N., and Elizabeth Blakesley. *Information Literacy Instruction Handbook*. Chicago: Association of College and Research Libraries, 2008.

Doran, George T. "There's a S.M.A.R.T. Way to Write Management's Goals and Objectives." *Management Review* 70, no. 11 (1981): 35–36.

Gilchrist, Debra. "Writing Student Learning Outcomes." December 10, 2015. https://www.youtube.com/watch?v=1Z7E9vHuyX4.

Gilchrist, Debra, and Anna Zald. "Instruction & Program Design through Assessment." In *Information Literacy Instruction Handbook*, edited by Christopher N. Cox and Elizabeth Blakesley, 164–92. Chicago: Association of College and Research Libraries, 2008. https://digitalscholarship.unlv.edu/cgi/viewcontent.cgi?referer=&httpsredir=1&article=1145&context=lib_articles.

Godbey, Samantha, Susan Beth Wainscott, and Xan Goodman. *Disciplinary Applications of Information Literacy Threshold Concepts*. Chicago: Association of College and Research Libraries, 2017.

Hook, Sheril J., Marianne Stowell Bracke, Louise Greenfield, and Victoria A Mills. "In-House Training for Instruction Librarians." *Research Strategies* 19, no. 2 (2003): 99–127. https://doi.org/10.1016/j.resstr.2003.12.001.

Houtman, Eveline. "Asking 'Good Questions' about How Academic Librarians Learn to Teach." In *The Grounded Instruction Librarian: Participating in the Scholarship of Teaching and Learning*, edited by Melissa Mallon, Lauren Hays, Cara Bradley, Rhonda Huisman, and Jackie Belanger, 17–30. Chicago: Association of College & Research Libraries, 2019.

———. "'Trying to Figure It Out': Academic Librarians Talk about Learning to Teach." *Library and Information Research* 34, no. 107 (October 9, 2010): 18–40. https://doi.org/10.29173/lirj246.

Jacobson, Trudi, and Craig Gibson. "First Thoughts on Implementing the Framework for Information Literacy." *Communications in Information Literacy* 9, no. 2 (2015): 102–10. https://doi.org/10.15760/comminfolit.2015.9.2.187.

Jaguszewski, Janice M., and Karen Williams. "New Roles for New Times: Transforming Liaison Roles in Research Libraries." Association of Research Libraries. 2013. https://www.arl.org/resources/new-roles-for-new-times-transforming-liaison-roles-in-research-libraries/.

Kaplowitz, Joan R. *Designing Information Literacy Instruction: The Teaching Tripod Approach*. Lanham: Rowman & Littlefield Publishers, 2017.

Keenan, Tara, Manlio Perugini, and Seth N. Jaffe. "Changing a Teaching Culture in an International University Context: Introducing English and Research Competencies for the Price of a Cup of Coffee." In *Library Partnerships in International Liberal Arts Education: Building Relationships Across Cultural and Institutional Lines*, edited by Jeff Hiroshi Gima and Kara Malenfant, 53–62. Chicago: Association for College and Research Libraries, 2020.

Kilcullen, Maureen. "Teaching Librarians to Teach: Recommendations on What We Need to Know." *Reference Services Review* 26, no. 2 (1998): 7–18. https://doi.org/10.1108/00907329810307623.

King, Alison. "From Sage on the Stage to Guide on the Side." *College Teaching* 41, no. 1 (1993): 30–35. https://doi.org/10.1080/87567555.1993.9926781.

Kirkpatrick Partners. "The Kirkpatrick Model." 2022. https://www.kirkpatrickpartners.com/the-kirkpatrick-model/.

Mallon, Melissa N. *Partners in Teaching and Learning: Coordinating a Successful Academic Library Instruction Program*. Lanham: Rowman & Littlefield, 2020.

Oakleaf, Megan. "The Information Literacy Instruction Assessment Cycle: A Guide for Increasing Student Learning and Improving Librarian Instructional Skills." *Journal of Documentation* 65, no. 4 (2009): 539–60. https://doi.org/10.1108/00220410910970249.

Oakleaf, Megan, Steven Hoover, Beth Woodard, Jennifer Corbin, Randy Hensley, Diana Wakimoto, Christopher Hollister, Debra Gilchrist, Michelle Millet, and Patricia Iannuzzi. "Notes From the Field: 10 Short Lessons on One-Shot Instruction." *Communications in Information Literacy* 6, no. 1 (2012): 5–23.

Piotto, Livia. "Researching Rome: The Librarian as Research Mediator." In *Library Partnerships in International Liberal Arts Education: Building Relationships Across Cultural and Institutional Lines*, edited by Jeff H. Gima and Kara J. Malenfant, 9–20. Chicago: Association of College & Research Libraries, 2020.

Piotto, Livia, and Krasimir Spasov. "Co-Designing Information Literacy Experiences." Presented at the AMICAL 2017, American College of Thessaloniki, May 18, 2017. https://www.amicalnet.org/sessions/co-designing-information-literacy-experiences.

Reale, Michelle. *Becoming a Reflective Librarian and Teacher: Strategies for Mindful Academic Practice*. Chicago: ALA Editions, 2017.

Tucker, Katelyn R. "Teaching Me to Teach: A New Librarian's Experience with a Structured Training Program for Information Literacy Instruction." *Virginia Libraries* 59, no. 1 (2013).

Turnbow, Dominique, and Annie Zeidman-Karpinski. "Don't Use a Hammer When You Need a Screwdriver: How to Use the Right Tools to Create Assessment That Matters." *Communications in Information Literacy* 10, no. 2 (2016).

Valenti, Sandra J., and Brady D. Lund. "Preparing the Instructional Librarian: Representation of ACRL Roles and Strengths in MLS Course Descriptions." *College & Research Libraries* 82, no. 4 (2021): 530–47. https://doi.org/10.5860/crl.82.4.530.

Wiggins, Grant, and Jay McTighe. *Understanding by Design*. 2nd edition. Alexandria, VA: ASCD, 2005.

CHAPTER 21

Supporting Librarian Teachers:

The Learning-Centered Librarian Instruction Program at the University of Victoria

Karen Munro, Cynthia Korpan, Matt Huculak, and Michael Lines

LEARNING OUTCOMES

Readers will be able to

- recognize the value of partnerships between academic libraries and learning and teaching units (on campus) to enhance librarians' pedagogical skills;
- discover a process and curriculum for developing pedagogical programs for librarians (based on the work of learning and teaching units);
- analyze how the challenges inherent in librarian instruction impact pedagogical program design (in and outside the library); and
- realize the value of program evaluation.

Introduction

This chapter documents a collaboration at the University of Victoria (UVic) between the UVic Libraries and the Learning and Teaching Support and Innovation team (LTSI), a unit tasked with providing professional development and teaching enhancement opportunities to instructors. The goal of our collaboration was to create a pedagogical professional development program specifically designed for librarians.

The University of Victoria, located in Victoria British Columbia, is a Canadian public research university serving approximately 22,000 students in undergraduate and graduate programs. UVic Libraries employs around thirty-five librarians, about fifteen of whom have responsibility for instruction. There is no dedicated position responsible for overseeing all instruction at UVic Libraries—instead, instruction is designed and delivered in a relatively decentralized model, with leadership provided through both the library's unit and committee structures. The Libraries and LTSI have a strong and collaborative relationship with a history of cross-appointments, and many of LTSI's staff are officed in the Libraries, where they provide direct academic and writing support for students in Libraries' spaces.

The decision to collaborate on a pedagogical program specifically for librarians made sense for two reasons. First, LTSI offers pedagogical training programs designed to support the semester-long, graded instruction model that most faculty use, rather than the one-shot and ungraded instruction model that librarians mainly use. Librarians felt they faced distinct teaching challenges due to their modes of instruction and needed a separate pedagogical training program developed specifically for one-shot instruction.

Second, given that most librarians lack formal pedagogical training, Libraries administration wanted to encourage librarians to take a more evidence-based and learning-centered approach to their instruction. For the purposes of this project, "evidence-based" was defined as approaches that have been proven effective and are supported by consensus in education research. "Learning-centered" was defined as instruction offering active learning opportunities as well as design that included clear learning outcomes and relevant assessment. LTSI colleagues were well-situated to guide librarians in both of these respects.

The Libraries and LTSI appointed a team from their ranks to develop the "Learning-Centered Library Instruction Program" (LLIP), a multi-session program designed to support librarians in understanding and using evidence-based, learning-centered pedagogical approaches. The LLIP is based on a longstanding LTSI program called the Faculty Institute of Teaching (FIT). FIT is a multi-session program accredited through the Society for Teaching and Learning in Higher Education and is designed to increase instructors' pedagogical competence and confidence over a full calendar year. LLIP was designed to borrow many of FIT's concepts and strategies but pared down to be a smaller time commitment and more relevant to librarians' specific teaching circumstances.

In this chapter, we discuss the context and specifics of our collaboration, including our goals and the elements of the instruction program we created together. We'll also cover the opportunities and challenges we encountered. We summarize librarians' responses to the LLIP program and recommend areas for further study, such as the outcomes and impact of programs like ours, the effectiveness of shared pedagogy programs on improving librarian teaching and student learning, and the nuances of librarians receiving pedagogical support from non-librarian colleagues.

Literature Review

There is considerable evidence to indicate that many academic librarians don't receive training in evidence-based pedagogical concepts and techniques during their MLIS degree; they instead rely on the training and experiences they receive later in their careers. As early as 1982, Barbara Smith surveyed 145 academic librarians with teaching responsibilities about their pedagogical training and found that although they "acquired education and training appropriate to their assignments… the education and training were not gained as part of their professional degree programs."[1]

In 1993, Shonrock and Mulder surveyed 400 randomly selected members of the Association of College and Research Libraries' (ACRL) Bibliographic Instruction Section (BIS) about how they received training in a range of instructional proficiencies. They found that librarians overwhelmingly felt that they gained their instructional skills through work experience or via self-teaching rather than through their MLIS degree.[2]

After ACRL revised its proficiencies for instruction librarians in 2007, Westbrock and Fabian followed up Shonrock and Mulder's 1993 survey with a new survey of 400 randomly selected members of the ACRL's Bibliographic Instruction Section. Their survey found that librarians still felt they learned most of their instructional skills on the job or via self-teaching; librarians didn't report learning any of their needed instructional skills through their MLIS degree.[3]

In 2021, Lund et al. also followed up on Shonrock and Mulder's original 1993 survey, this time by surveying thirty-seven library administrators, LIS school educators, and instruction librarians in the US and Canada about the ways in which librarians acquired their instructional skills. They found that while instructional training in MLIS degrees has improved since 1993, the demand for instruction in academic libraries has also increased during this time, and there remains a need for greater emphasis on instructional training in the degree.[4]

These studies and a variety of others (Sproles et al.,[5] Bewick and Corrall,[6] Julien and Genuis,[7] Wheeler and McKinney,[8] Vassilakaki and Moniarou-Papaconstantinou,[9] Gammons, Carroll, and Carpenter,[10] Ducas, Michaud-Oystryk, and Speare[11]) show a clear and longstanding gap in librarians' pedagogical training during their professional degree. There is therefore a strong rationale for libraries to provide evidence-based, consistent, and coordinated pedagogical support for librarians who teach.

One way to provide this support is through partnering with campus teaching and learning centers. However, while academic libraries are frequent collaborators with teaching and learning centers—as well as other campus units—many of these collaborations focus on co-developing cross-campus programs or on co-delivering services to faculty and students rather than improving librarians' pedagogical skills. As Walter, Arp, and Woodward write, "Many teaching centers recognize that librarians have something to offer *to* campuswide instructional improvement programs, but fewer appear to recognize how much librarians might benefit *from* participation.[12]

The literature does contain some evidence of academic librarians effectively drawing on the pedagogical expertise of their campus teaching and learning centers. In 2001 Jacobson surveyed 110 instruction and public service librarians at ARL libraries in the US and Canada, asking them about current and future collaborations with teaching centers on their campus.[13] Among the collaborations cited in the responses were partnerships initiated by library and university administrators as well as partnerships initiated by librarians and teaching center staff. Librarian-led partnerships made up the largest proportion and included activities such as attending workshops, seeking pedagogical advice, and reading and borrowing center materials. Mazure et al. surveyed library instructors who participated in the University of Michigan Instructor College, a pedagogical institute offered by the campus teaching and learning unit. Their survey participants reported themselves as "more enthusiastic and refreshed about instruction"[14] and felt the program "helped them… develop confidence as instructors"[15] and gain "foundational knowledge, such as theory, methods, and styles from the perspective of both traditional teaching and library instruction."[16]

More formal, programmatic examples of pedagogical partnership also show value. At the University of Notre Dame, the coordinator of Instructional Services wrote that "it seemed natural and logical to develop a relationship with the teaching center to educate librarians on the most effective ways of teaching."[17] At the University of Toronto, librarians participated in a student success program co-launched by the Centre for Teaching Support & Innovation and the Libraries in 2010.[18] The goal of the program was "to increase capacity for integrative learning and academic excellence within classrooms"[19] through a focus on librarians' development as teachers and deepening relationships between librarians and teaching center staff. The program's participants found that "through formal partnerships such as this, ongoing pedagogical development for librarians can be better supported."[20]

At the University of Colorado, Hoseth describes the participation of librarians in a Master Teacher Initiative offered by the campus teaching center.[21] Librarians who participated received weekly teaching tips by email and joined six lunchtime workshops on topics of particular interest to librarian teachers, such as teaching different generations of students and addressing plagiarism. The positive outcomes of this program included "provid[ing] an environment where concerns and questions about teaching are openly discussed and shared" and "a renewed emphasis on teaching and tangible support for the instruction that librarians provide."[22]

There is a well-documented need for post-MLIS pedagogical training for academic librarians who teach, and the literature shows that teaching and learning centers are valuable partners in meeting this need. The development of library-focused pedagogical training programs with campus teaching and learning center colleagues has been shown to be one effective strategy for improving librarians' pedagogical skills.

Background

UVic Libraries' classroom instruction currently includes a range of activities, including:

- Course-integrated instruction in the disciplines (e.g., "one-shot" instruction), provided mainly by subject liaisons (122 sessions from September 1, 2021, to April 30, 2022)
- Course-integrated instruction in support of the Academic Writing Requirement (AWR), the university's cross-curriculum writing requirement, provided entirely by subject liaisons (51 sessions from September 1, 2021, to April 30, 2022)
- Course-integrated instruction using primary and archival materials, provided mainly by Special Collections and Archives librarians and archivists in collaboration with other librarians (66 sessions from September 1, 2021, to April 30, 2022)
- Workshops in digital and technological skills, provided mainly by non-subject librarians and some non-librarians (392 sessions from September 1, 2021, to April 30, 2022)
- Workshops in general research and citation skills, provided mainly by subject liaisons (71 sessions from September 1, 2021, to April 30, 2022).

These instruction activities are managed, coordinated, and supported through a variety of administrative and supervisory channels. In the absence of a head of instruction with sole administrative oversight, instruction is largely situated in three units: Engagement and Learning, the Digital Scholarship Commons, and Special Collections and Archives. As of 2021, the Libraries has also introduced ongoing working groups into its organizational structure. These groups are composed of librarians and staff from across the Libraries, who work together in broad arenas such as collections and instruction. One of these working groups, the Digital Information Fluency Working Group, provided another structure for instruction planning and support across the Libraries during this period.

As a result of this decentralized structure, UVic Libraries has no explicitly stated common goals, guidelines, or standards for librarians' and archivists' instruction. Little to no formal, coordinated assessment of librarians' and archivists' teaching skills, preparation, or effectiveness has been done. Past instruction assessment has mainly consisted of individuals' efforts to gather student and instructor feedback on individual classes, together with quantitative assessment of the numbers of the overall classes and students taught. Only quantitative assessment was done in a coordinated way, meaning that while we have access to some longitudinal data about our instruction outputs (e.g., number of classes and students taught), we have little to no coordinated data about our instructional outcomes (e.g., impact on student learning, student experience in the classroom, etc.).

Despite the gaps in our instructional data, UVic Libraries' administrative team recognizes that there is an established body of knowledge about how to teach and that our colleagues at LTSI are professional experts in training teachers. To encourage evidence-based instruction practices, the administration has previously supported individual librarians to participate in LTSI's Instructional Skills Workshop (ISW), a multi-day pedagogical skills workshop designed for faculty.

However, this approach was individual rather than programmatic and coordinated, meaning it wasn't required or recognized for all librarians in a consistent way. It also wasn't designed specifically for librarians' instructional context. Unlike academic faculty, librarians typically teach students in ungraded single sessions rather than graded semester-long courses. Librarians also teach skills such as research and citation methods, which students may not see as central to their academic success. For these and other reasons, the Instructional Skills Workshop wasn't an ideal fit or a programmatic solution for improving librarians' pedagogical skills.

Development of the Learning-Centered Library Instruction Program

The catalyst to re-examine librarians' pedagogical training in a more coordinated way came in 2020–21 through another Libraries partnership. UVic's Academic and Technical Writing Program (ATWP) develops and delivers most courses meeting the university's writing requirement. For many years, librarians have provided library instruction for up to 2,000 ATWP students annually enrolled in these courses. In 2020–21, ATWP underwent a reorganization and curriculum refresh. The program's administrators wanted to standardize the library instruction their students received, including common learning outcomes, shared instruction materials, and a consistent, evidence-based approach to classroom teaching. Redesigning our ATWP instruction was an opportunity to support all library instructors in developing a more coordinated, consistent, evidence-based approach to teaching.

In 2020, seven librarians volunteered to participate in an LTSI-facilitated Teaching Square program, observing each other in the classroom and providing appreciative feedback to highlight their existing strengths and skills. In this model, observers learn from observing peers teach and decide what skills they can adapt or adopt from their peers to strengthen their own teaching. This was a first step to encourage librarians to reflect on their teaching effectiveness.

Due to this initial success, the Libraries moved forward on developing an instructional program for librarians. Our overarching goal for this project was to partner with LTSI to develop a multi-session, evidence-based pedagogical institute customized for teaching in the library context—and thereby to support and improve library instructors' teaching skills.

In early 2021, the director of Student Academic Success in the Libraries and the director of Teaching Excellence in LTSI co-developed program-level intended learning outcomes (ILOs) for a library instruction program. It was important for the program to have clear ILOs since one goal of the program was to impress upon librarians the importance of writing ILOs for their instruction. Based on the needs assessment, the initial program-level intended learning outcomes were that participants would

- *Deeply appreciate the strengths you have as an instructor*
- *Explicitly confirm what you value in teaching and learning (what excites you about teaching)*
- *Broadly imagine how to increase the value of your instruction*
- *Effectively develop a plan to enhance your instruction*

- *Competently practice your enhanced instruction*
- *Consistently seek feedback from colleagues and participants*
- *Continuously engage in an ongoing community of practice about enhancing library instruction.*

An initial session, titled Situating Library Instruction, was delivered on Zoom over three hours to approximately thirty librarians. With input from all participants, the ILOs were rewritten as follows:

By the end of the LLIP series, you will:

- *Deeply appreciate the strengths you have as an instructor*
- *Explicitly confirm what you value in teaching and learning (what excites you about teaching)*
- *Broadly imagine how to increase the value of your instruction*
- *Effectively develop a plan to enhance your instruction*

Through active discussion and small group activities, librarians identified their instructional strengths and interests and began to co-create a vision for increasing the effectiveness of their individual teaching. The following graphic was co-created in the Zoom session to help build librarians' sense of ownership in their pedagogical professional development and to capture and document what was discussed for later use.

Librarians articulated their strengths in continual learning, collaborating, and approaching challenges—all helpful points of reflection as they embarked on the development of their skills. They also identified areas for growth in active learning, assessment, student-centered practices, and newer modes of instruction such as flipped, gamified, and technology-enabled instruction.

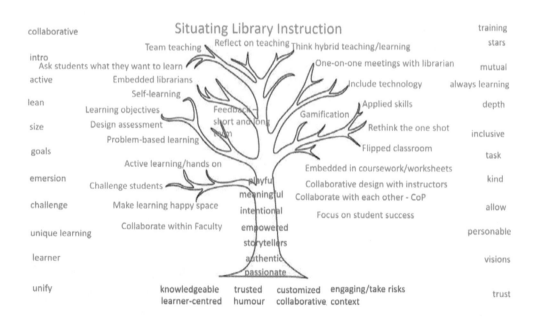

Figure 21.1

Pedagogical strengths and areas of development for UVic librarians.

This activity helped lay the foundation for a more structured program of pedagogical skill-building by engaging librarians first in appreciative reflection and allowing them to contribute ideas for how to build on their teaching strengths. The graphic was useful for reference in later sessions as it reminded librarians of their shared leadership in the program and clearly showed how they had assessed their own strengths and areas for growth.

With this strong foundation in place, a larger group was developed in late fall 2021 to begin planning the LLIP. This group included the director of Teaching Excellence from LTSI and the following positions from the library: the director of Student Academic Success; the head of Advanced Research Services; and a subject liaison librarian for Humanities and Social Sciences. The head of Student Academic Success would later join the group.

Starting with broad librarian input from the initial activities, the LLIP group began to plan the LLIP curriculum. As part of this planning, the group decided to refine the LLIP ILOs. Co-creating the original ILOs was a good way to invite librarians into the conversation in a non-threatening and welcoming way. However, the LLIP group realized that the LLIP curriculum would need more concrete ILOs related to pedagogical skill development in order to be truly meaningful. The group decided to use the co-created ILOs as a basis for revised ILOs for the whole LLIP program as well as for each session within it. The goal was to create ILOs that would reflect the appreciative and supportive spirit of the original co-created ILOs while providing a more specific structure for the course curriculum.

The revised ILOs for the whole LLIP program were as follows:

By the end of the program, you will:

- *Critically examine your underlying assumptions, goals, and pedagogical approaches to teaching and student learning*
- *Thoroughly investigate the principles of a learning-centered approach to teaching*
- *Carefully consider the context of your instruction in relation to student learning*
- *Actively apply backward design and constructive alignment to the development of your intended learning outcomes, assessment, and instructional strategies for your instruction*
- *Appropriately employ educational technology to support intended learning outcomes and student learning*
- *Carefully select teaching strategies that create an inclusive classroom*
- *Deeply reflect on the importance of including a diversity of perspectives in your course*
- *Capably develop a repertoire of learning-centered instructional resources and strategies as evident in a microteaching session.*

The revised ILOs were shared with librarians together with an explanation of the rationale for the revisions and appreciation for the work of all participants to co-create the foundational ILOs that underpin these. The next phase of the LLIP consisted of four sessions that took place between February and June 2022. These sessions composed the bulk of the LLIP experience and required planning a thoughtful curriculum that aligned with librarians' specific teaching modes and self-perceived areas for pedagogical growth as well as the revised ILOs. Each session focused on a different aspect of pedagogical skill development, following a condensed version of the FIT curriculum. The sessions are described below.

Librarians responsible for teaching ATWP courses were strongly encouraged to participate in the LLIP in recognition of the key role they play in introducing large numbers of undergraduate students to the Libraries and to key concepts and skills related to research. Other librarians and staff who teach were also encouraged to attend the sessions. No component of the LLIP was mandatory for any participants, and there was no concrete incentive or recognition for those who chose to participate—apart from the benefit of improved pedagogical skills. All librarians and staff who teach were invited to participate, regardless of how many sessions they were able to attend. Sessions were held primarily in person. Some elements of the in-person sessions (such as content-focused lectures and discussions) were recorded and uploaded to an LLIP site created on the campus LMS, Brightspace.

Thirteen librarians registered at the start of the program, although the actual number of participants for each session varied according to their availability. The Brightspace site hosted all instructional materials for participants to refer to at their leisure, allowed communication among participants, and provided a discussion forum to encourage learning conversations.

Participants were asked to engage in a pre-assessment of the LLIP, which asked them to "describe your observations, hopes, or fears for the LLIP, based on its intended learning outcomes." This garnered thoughtful and reflective responses, indicating the need for and value of the program. Participants were interested in understanding whether and what students learned in their sessions as well as how they could teach more effectively over asynchronous modes, such as video, and how they could apply teaching concepts they were learning about in the pre-reading.

We also asked participants to fill out a survey about their pedagogical background and training to get a sense of the skills and knowledge they were bringing into the program. Most participants who completed the survey had previous teaching experience (defined broadly as teaching a term course or library instruction). One question asked what participants wanted to get out of attending, with several librarians responding that they were looking for strategies to adapt activities to one-shot teaching to strengthen student engagement.

Session 1: Learning-Centered Instruction Design

The ILOs for this session were shared as follows:

By the end of the session, participants will be able to:
- *Fully recognize the difference between teacher-centered/content-oriented teaching and learning-centered/student-oriented teaching*
- *Thoroughly examine the components of a learning-centered approach to designing instruction*
- *Succinctly summarize how constructive alignment and backward design support student learning*
- *Explicitly explain the importance of the learning environment and its impacts on student learning.*

The LTSI director of Teaching Excellence introduced key concepts of learning-centered instruction, including Paolo Freire's critique of the "banking concept of education" and "the pedagogy of the oppressed." Participants were asked to reflect on their experiences as passive learners compared to their experiences with more active and student-centered pedagogical approaches. They then discussed in both small groups and plenary session how they might revisit their approach to teaching in order to create more opportunities for active learning.

The session also introduced participants to the concepts of backward design,[23] constructive alignment,[24] and Universal Design for Learning.[25] In this first session, figure 1 was revisited to remind participants about the work they had done the previous year and to help situate everyone to the curriculum going forward.

Session 2: Designing a Lesson and Intended Learning Outcomes

The ILOs for the session were shared as follows:

By the end of the session, participants will be able to:

- *Correctly identify all three defining components of an intended learning outcome (learning activity, conditions, criteria) when presented with a complete statement of an intended learning outcome*
- *Accurately identify missing component(s) when presented with an incomplete statement of an intended learning outcome*
- *Accurately describe Bloom's taxonomy, Biggs SOLO, and other taxonomies in terms of verbs related to scaffolding and supporting students' learning.*

We asked participants to identify a lesson plan they would develop throughout the LLIP program. Following the backward design approach, our second session focused on developing ILOs for these lesson plans. In this session, participants were guided through the process of developing clear, measurable ILOs with all the necessary components. These components are:

- the learning activity (through what actions learning will be demonstrated, such as writing or speaking);
- the conditions (the context in which learning will be demonstrated, such as within a certain timeline); and
- the criteria (the quantitative or qualitative aspects of how learning will be demonstrated, such as how quickly or how deeply learning will be shown).

In other words, librarians were asked to create ILOs that clearly expressed what students would be able to accomplish, under what conditions, and how well. Librarians practiced color-coding the components of sample ILOs, discussed what they had learned, and then tried writing complete ILOs for their own lessons.

Focusing on lesson design and effective ILOs helped reinforce the learning-centered approach that we introduced in the first session and gave librarians concrete tools to take this approach in their teaching. After the session, librarians were invited to email their draft ILOs to LTSI staff for individual feedback.

Session 3: Aligning Assessment

The ILOs for this session were shared as follows:

By the end of the session, participants will be able to:

- *Clearly explain the value of practice and feedback for student learning*
- *Competently develop classroom assessment techniques (CATs) that align with your learning outcome*
- *Broadly recognize the benefits of an active learning approach (as opposed to passive) to teaching and instruction.*

The head of Student Academic Success led this session by teaching a sample ten-minute lesson that the participants then critiqued. The lesson attempted to model all the concepts covered to that point, including learner-centered design, well-crafted ILOs, and active learning techniques. Participants offered constructive criticism about the assignment's design and delivery, which helped to prepare the group for the final session and which would offer everyone the opportunity to teach and receive critique.

LTSI's director of Teaching Excellence then led participants through a discussion of common Classroom Assessment Techniques (CATs).[26] These included techniques such as one-minute papers, pro and con grids, concept maps, and direct paraphrasing. Participants were then provided with some sample library-focused ILOs and asked to work in groups to come up with CATs that could effectively assess each ILO.

One sample library-focused ILO was, "By the end of today's class, you'll correctly demonstrate how to limit your library catalogue search to peer-reviewed articles within the last 10 years." Participants reviewed lists of potential CATs and suggested several that could work for this ILO, including "asking students to identify the muddiest point," "ask students to model or do the task," "quiz students," and "ask students to write down a real-world application for this knowledge or skill."

This session helped to fulfill the work that participants had done previously to design clear and effective ILOs. Participants could practice connecting assessment, backward design, and ILOs to design their instruction from end to beginning, focusing it on demonstrable student learning.

Session 4: Putting It All into Practice

The fourth and final session asked participants to teach a ten-minute "micro" class from the lesson plan they had been working on so that a small group of their peers could see all elements of lesson design (ILOs, assessment, and instructional activities) in action.

All participants were coached on how to provide respectful and relevant feedback, and moderators from LTSI joined the sessions to help manage them productively. Once the practice teaching session was complete, the moderators guided the participants in providing feedback to the participant. During this process, participants gained valuable feedback from their peers about what worked well and ideas for how the lesson could be enhanced.

Opportunities and Challenges

In our decentralized library instruction environment, the LLIP offers an opportunity to develop a coordinated and evidence-based approach to library instruction. It could become a first step toward an instruction program that is more focused on active learning and that uses consistent ILOs aligned with campus curriculum and campus-level learning outcomes. The LLIP could align librarians through a common set of best practices for teaching—practices that are inclusive and would therefore benefit equity-deserving students and advance the Libraries' equity goals.

In more near-term and concrete opportunities, the Libraries could adapt the LLIP to better align how librarians currently teach in common campus programs such as ATWP. This is an opportunity we are currently pursuing by encouraging librarians who teach ATWP 135 to participate in future iterations of the LLIP.

Among our challenges are the constraints on our capacity. The Libraries is navigating a recent structural reorganization that has redistributed capacity to various needed areas, and only recently have we rebuilt our teaching and learning staffing to full levels. We expect to have greater ability to pursue the opportunities outlined above in the coming years.

Another challenge is the polarity between librarian autonomy and the need for a programmatic approach to instruction. Particularly in the arena of instruction, some librarians feel strongly about receiving advice, encouragement, or critique of their skills or expertise, particularly from non-librarian colleagues. This meant that the LLIP had to be sensitively co-developed with librarians themselves to reduce potential sources of friction and ensure the greatest possible uptake. At times, this meant that we had to reconsider our approach, such as when we revised the program ILOs. It was sometimes challenging to balance administration's desire to foster evidence-based instruction practices with the need to involve librarians in the planning process for maximum uptake.

Finally, the LLIP's impact was inherently limited by its design. Because the LLIP was an opt-in program without penalties or incentives beyond learning, it only benefited librarians who chose to participate. Teaching is an activity that relies strongly on intrinsic values and buy-in. Ironically, the individuals with the strongest pre-existing focus on student learning may be the ones most inclined to participate in a program like the LLIP, while those who are less inclined to reflect or improve may be less inclined to participate. In this way, librarians' pedagogical improvements from participating in LLIP may be uneven and may most benefit those whose teaching skills are already strongest. We currently lack an assessment framework to determine whether this is the case.

Future Research

There are several areas in which further study would extend our understanding of this type of project. A study of the effects of this training on librarians' pedagogical practice would be revealing although potentially challenging to carry out if librarians are concerned about being evaluated as teachers. Such a study would need to clearly and carefully identify its goals as well as the evidence-based metrics it uses to identify successful pedagogical practices.

Other potential areas for further study include the effectiveness of libraries sharing pedagogy programs with campus partners such as LTSI, the benefits or drawbacks of designing pedagogy programs for librarians' specific teaching modes, and the facets of librarian response to receiving pedagogical support from non-librarian colleagues. Greater knowledge about each of these areas would help to construct more effective partnerships between libraries and teaching centers and would support greater development of librarians' pedagogical skills.

Finally, given the increased focus on instruction in libraries evidenced through ACRL guidelines, it would be fruitful to study how LTSI-like partnerships could be (or are being) leveraged during library professional degree programs like the MLIS.

Conclusion

This chapter provides a case study of how libraries can leverage existing faculty training programs and the expertise of colleagues to create library instruction-specific pedagogical development. Although every institution has unique teaching needs and responsibilities, we believe this study offers a useful precedent for other pedagogical collaborations between libraries and teaching and learning centers.

The collaboration was motivated by two factors: the distinct demands of one-shot instruction, which were not addressed in teacher training available to UVic librarians, and the need for a more evidence-based approach to teaching practices among librarians, who typically do not receive teacher training as part of their formal and on-the-job training. At UVic Libraries, we focused on building a pathway to pedagogical improvement by inviting librarians to engage in appreciative reflection and discussion of their teaching strengths and skills. This allowed us to then co-develop with librarians some evidence-based ideas for where their teaching could be enhanced.

We benefited greatly from the expertise of our LTSI colleagues to help us develop our understanding of core pedagogical principles, such as learning-centered design, backward design, active learning, ILOs, and assessment. Sharing these skills and concepts within the library helps us move toward a common understanding of effective pedagogical practices that we should all be using. Developing a library-specific pedagogical program helped us to address librarians' concerns about their specific instruction modes and to use library-specific teaching examples that resonated more effectively with their experiences.

Librarians who participated in the LLIP were asked to complete an assessment of it. Only a small number of librarians completed the survey. Responses indicated that participants found the LLIP most useful in helping them to understand and create effective ILOs. Several librarians offered suggestions for improving future versions of the LLIP, including rescheduling it to align more closely with the annual need for ATWP 135 instruction and inviting more librarians with pedagogical skills to lead LLIP sessions. There was interest in developing more LLIP sessions on topics such as Universal Design for Learning, culturally inclusive pedagogy, and creating effective ILOs.

Librarians who participated in LLIP were also offered the opportunity to participate in a follow-up study asking them to demonstrate how they put their learning into practice, but almost no participants responded to the invitation. We hypothesized this was due to two constraints: time and comfort. Most teaching librarians are very busy in fall semester, the term when we invited their participation, and they may not have had time to gather their materials, submit them for review, complete a survey, and participate in an interview. Some may also have felt uncomfortable being asked to complete these steps, as they may have felt the study was evaluating their own teaching rather than the success of the LLIP. Future efforts to evaluate the effects of this type of training on librarians' teaching will need to take such factors into account.

While we have not formally assessed the impact of the initiative at the individual librarian level, we believe that the LLIP has had a beneficial impact on participants' awareness of evidence-based teaching practices. Librarians now lead a task group that facilitates regular peer sharing sessions around topics including instruction and student engagement. In the context of that group, several librarians have shared their experiences with evidence-based teaching strategies, such as active learning and assessment.

We expect to return our attention to support for evidence-based teaching practices in the library, supported by several structural developments. A new head of Engagement and Learning position has recently been filled, which will increase our capacity to develop our instructional program. In addition, a new Learning and Teaching Working Group has been struck, with a charge that includes pedagogical professional development and the creation of guiding principles for library instruction. Finally, new language in the collective agreement for faculty and librarians requires peer review of classroom teaching as part of the professional evaluation process. Each of these developments offers opportunities for us to deepen our collective pedagogical knowledge and adopt more evidence-based teaching practices in line with the goals of the LLIP.

Notes

1. Barbara Smith, "Background Characteristics and Education Needs of a Group of Instruction Librarians in Pennsylvania," *College & Research Libraries* 43 (3) (1982): 205–06, https://doi.org/10.5860/crl_43_03_199.
2. Diana Shonrock and Craig Mulder, "Instruction Librarians: Acquiring the Proficiencies Critical to Their Work," *College & Research Libraries* 54 (2) (2017): 137–49, https://doi.org/10.5860/crl_54_02_137.
3. Theresa Westbrock and Sarah Fabian, "Proficiencies for Instruction Librarians: Is There Still a Disconnect Between Professional Education and Professional Responsibilities?," *College & Research Libraries* 71 (6) (2010): 585, https://doi.org/10.5860/crl-75r1.
4. Brady D. Lund, Michael Widdersheim, Brendan Fay, and Ting Wang, "Training and Practice of Instructional Librarians: Cross-Population and Longitudinal Perspectives," *The Reference Librarian* 62 (2) (2021): 126–43.
5. Claudene Sproles, Anna Marie Johnson, and Leslie Farison, "What the Teachers Are Teaching: How MLIS Programs Are Preparing Academic Librarians for Instructional Roles," *Journal of Education for Library and Information Science* 49 (3) (2008): 195–209.
6. Laura Bewick and Sheila Corrall, "Developing Librarians as Teachers: A Study of Their Pedagogical Knowledge," *Journal of Librarianship and Information Science* 42 (2) (2010): 97–110, https://doi.org/10.1177/0961000610361419.

7. Heidi Julien and Shelagh K. Genuis, "Librarians' Experiences of the Teaching Role: A National Survey of Librarians," *Library & Information Science Research* 33 (2) (2011): 103–11, https://doi.org/10.1016/j.lisr.2010.09.005.

8. Emily Wheeler and Pamela McKinney, "Are Librarians Teachers? Investigating Academic Librarians' Perceptions of Their Own Teaching Skills," *Journal of Information Literacy* 9 (2) (2015): 111–28, https://doi.org/10.11645/9.2.1985.

9. Evgenia Vassilakaki and Valentini Moniarou-Papaconstantinou, "A Systematic Literature Review Informing Library and Information Professionals' Emerging Roles," *New Library World* 116 (1/2) (2015): 37–66, https://doi.org/10.1108/NLW-05-2014-0060.

10. Rachel W. Gammons, Alexander J. Carroll, and Lindsay Inge Carpenter, "'I Never Knew I Could Be a Teacher': A Student-Centered MLIS Fellowship for Future Teacher-Librarians," *portal: Libraries and the Academy* 18 (2) (2018): 331–62, https://doi.org/10.1353/pla.2018.0019.

11. Ada Ducas, Nicole Michaud-Oystryk, and Marie Speare, "Reinventing Ourselves: New and Emerging Roles of Academic Librarians in Canadian Research-Intensive Universities," *College & Research Libraries* 81 (1) (2020): 43–65, https://doi.org/10.5860/crl.81.1.43.

12. Scott Walter, Lori Arp, and Beth S. Woodard, "Instructional Improvement: Building Capacity for the Professional Development of Librarians as Teachers," *Reference & User Services Quarterly* 45 (3) (2006): 214.

13. Trudi E. Jacobson, "Partnerships between Library Instruction Units and Campus Teaching Centers," *The Journal of Academic Librarianship* 27 (4) (2001): 311–16, https://doi.org/10.1016/S0099-1333(01)00217-8.

14. Emily Mazure, Nicole Scholtz, Maura Seale, and Joan Durrance, "An Outcome-Based Evaluation of the University of Michigan University Library Instructor College," ResearchGate, 2007, 7.

15. Mazure et al., "An Outcome-Based Evaluation," 8.

16. Idid., 9.

17. Joni E. Warner and Nancy H. Seamans, "Teaching Centers, Libraries, and Benefits to Both," *Resource Sharing & Information Networks* 17 (1–2) (2004): 33, https://doi.org/10.1300/J121v17n01_04.

18. John Bolan, Patricia Bellamy, Carol Rolheiser, Joanna Szurmak, and Rita Vine, "Realizing Partnership Potential: A Report on a Formal Collaboration Between a Teaching and Learning Centre and Libraries at the University of Toronto," *Collected Essays on Learning and Teaching* (June 2025): 191–200.

19. Bolan et al., "Realizing Partnership Potential," 192.

20. Ibid., 197.

21. Amy Hoseth, "Library Participation in a Campus-wide Teaching Program," *Reference Services Review* 37 (4) (2009): 371–85, https://doi.org/10.1108/00907320911006985.

22. Hoseth, "Library Participation," 380.

23. Grant Wiggins and Jay McTighe, "Backward Design," in *Understanding by Design, Expanded 2nd Edition*, 2nd ed. (Upper Saddle River, NJ: Pearson, 2005), 13–34.

24. John Biggs, "Constructive Alignment in University Teaching," *HERDSA Review of Higher Education* 1 (2014): 5–22.

25. "Universal Design for Learning Guidelines Version 2.2," CAST, 2018, http://udlguidelines.cast.org.

26. Nancy Van Note Chism, Thomas A. Angelo, and K. Patricia Cross, "Classroom Assessment Techniques: A Handbook for College Teachers," *The Journal of Higher Education (Columbus)* 66 (1) (1995): 108, https://doi.org/10.2307/2943957.

Bibliography

Bewick, Laura, and Sheila Corrall. "Developing Librarians as Teachers: A Study of Their Pedagogical Knowledge." *Journal of Librarianship and Information Science* 42 (2) (2010): 97–110. https://doi.org/10.1177/0961000610361419.

Biggs, John. "Constructive Alignment in University Teaching." *HERDSA Review of Higher Education* 1 (2014): 5–22.

Bolan, John, Patricia Bellamy, Carol Rolheiser, Joanna Szurmak, and Rita Vine. "Realizing Partnership Potential: A Report on a Formal Collaboration Between a Teaching and Learning Centre and

Libraries at the University of Toronto." *Collected Essays on Learning and Teaching* (June 2015): 191–200. https://doi.org/10.22329/celt.v8i0.4241.

CAST. "Universal Design for Learning Guidelines Version 2.2." 2018. http://udlguidelines.cast.org.

Chism, Nancy Van Note, Thomas A. Angelo, and K. Patricia Cross. "Classroom Assessment Techniques: A Handbook for College Teachers." *The Journal of Higher Education (Columbus)* 66 (1) (1995): 108. https://doi.org/10.2307/2943957.

Ducas, Ada, Nicole Michaud-Oystryk, and Marie Speare. "Reinventing Ourselves: New and Emerging Roles of Academic Librarians in Canadian Research-Intensive Universities." *College & Research Libraries* 81 (1) (2020): 43–65. https://doi.org/10.5860/crl.81.1.43.

Gammons, Rachel W., Alexander J. Carroll, and Lindsay Inge Carpenter. "'I Never Knew I Could Be a Teacher': A Student-Centered MLIS Fellowship for Future Teacher-Librarians." *portal: Libraries and the Academy* 18 (2) (2018): 331–62. https://doi.org/10.1353/pla.2018.0019.

Hoseth, Amy. "Library Participation in a Campus-wide Teaching Program." *Reference Services Review* 37 (4) (2009): 371–85. https://doi.org/10.1108/00907320911006985.

Jacobson, Trudi E. "Partnerships between Library Instruction Units and Campus Teaching Centers." *The Journal of Academic Librarianship* 27 (4) (2001): 311–16. https://doi.org/10.1016/S0099-1333(01)00217-8.

Julien, Heidi, and Shelagh K. Genuis. "Librarians' Experiences of the Teaching Role: A National Survey of Librarians." *Library & Information Science Research* 33 (2) (2011): 103–11. https://doi.org/10.1016/j.lisr.2010.09.005.

Lund, Brady D., Michael Widdersheim, Brendan Fay, and Ting Wang. "Training and Practice of Instructional Librarians: Cross-Population and Longitudinal Perspectives." *The Reference Librarian* 62 (2) (2021): 126–43. https://doi.org/10.1080/02763877.2021.1944450.

Mazure, Emily, Nicole Scholtz, Maura Seale, and Joan Durrance. "An Outcome-Based Evaluation Of the University of Michigan University Library Instructor College." ResearchGate. 2007. SI623.

Shonrock, Diana, and Craig Mulder. "Instruction Librarians: Acquiring the Proficiencies Critical to Their Work." *College & Research Libraries* 54 (2) (2017): 137–49. https://doi.org/10.5860/crl_54_02_137.

Smith, Barbara J. "Background Characteristics and Education Needs of a Group of Instruction Librarians in Pennsylvania." *College & Research Libraries* 43 (3) (1982): 199–207. https://doi.org/10.5860/crl_43_03_199.

Sproles, Claudene, Anna Marie Johnson, and Leslie Farison. "What the Teachers Are Teaching: How MLIS Programs Are Preparing Academic Librarians for Instructional Roles." *Journal of Education for Library and Information Science* 49 (3) (2008): 195–209.

Vassilakaki, Evgenia, and Valentini Moniarou-Papaconstantinou. "A Systematic Literature Review Informing Library and Information Professionals' Emerging Roles." *New Library World* 116 (1/2) (2015): 37–66. https://doi.org/10.1108/NLW-05-2014-0060.

Walter, Scott, Lori Arp, and Beth S. Woodard. "Instructional Improvement: Building Capacity for the Professional Development of Librarians as Teachers." *Reference & User Services Quarterly* 45 (3) (2006): 213–18.

Warner, Joni E., and Nancy H. Seamans. "Teaching Centers, Libraries, and Benefits to Both." *Resource Sharing & Information Networks* 17 (1–2) (2004): 29–42. https://doi.org/10.1300/J121v17n01_04.

Westbrock, Theresa, and Sarah Fabian. "Proficiencies for Instruction Librarians: Is There Still a Disconnect Between Professional Education and Professional Responsibilities?" *College & Research Libraries* 71 (6) (2010): 569–90. https://doi.org/10.5860/crl-75r1.

Wheeler, Emily, and Pamela McKinney. "Are Librarians Teachers? Investigating Academic Librarians' Perceptions of Their Own Teaching Skills." *Journal of Information Literacy* 9 (2) (2015): 111–28. https://doi.org/10.11645/9.2.1985.

Wiggins, Grant, and Jay McTighe. "Backward Design." In *Understanding by Design, Expanded 2nd Edition*, 2nd edition, 13–34. Upper Saddle River, NJ: Association for Supervision and Curriculum Development, Pearson, 2005.

CHAPTER 22

Best of Both Worlds:
Training for New and Experienced Library Instructors

David X. Lemmons, Ashley Blinstrub, Kayla M. Gourlay, Maoria J. Kirker, Janna Mattson, and Anna K. Murphy-Lang

LEARNING OUTCOMES

Readers will be able to
- articulate the importance of pedagogical training for library instructors;
- describe the process of developing the Library Teaching Institute (LTI); and
- identify strategies for bringing a series similar to LTI to their context.

Introduction

During the summer of 2021, the George Mason University (Mason) Libraries' Teaching & Learning Team piloted a new instructional training program, the Library Teaching Institute (LTI). This training program, which is open to all Mason Libraries employees, is designed to give both new and experienced instructors the tools and strategies they need to be successful in the classroom. Because it was created to include instructors with no prior teaching experience, the training covers a comprehensive range of topics and issues. By building a broad teaching community, the program aims to improve awareness of library instruction across the libraries, improve confidence and preparedness among library instructors, and foster interest in teaching.

This chapter engages with the existing literature on competencies for library instructors, current approaches to instructional professional development and training, approaches to project management in libraries, and instructional design in libraries. It also outlines the process of designing and implementing LTI, including the process for establishing core competencies and learning outcomes for participants. The chapter concludes with a section detailing lessons learned from each LTI iteration as well as related recommendations for other institutions hoping to adopt a new instructional training program or expand on an already-existing program.

Literature Review

Lack of Teacher Education in LIS Curriculum

It is well-documented in library science literature that teacher education is lacking in LIS curricula. Godsett and Koziura's research indicates that while practical experience is most lacking in LIS programs, right behind that are "courses in instruction."[1] This perception is echoed in Saunders' study on LIS syllabi:

> Despite the fact that LIS programs are offering courses on instruction, studies of practicing librarians indicate that most did not learn instruction or teaching skills in their master's program, and many feel underprepared to take on a teaching role. Although librarians largely agree that they would prefer to learn instruction competencies in their LIS programs, it appears that most learn their skills on the job. Learning opportunities on the job largely consist of observation and feedback from colleagues, and many librarians also pursue professional development opportunities.[2]

Further, the LIS courses that do exist in teacher education rarely include immersive teaching experiences such as apprenticeships or student teaching.[3] Bryan notes that librarians with non-library graduate degrees believe that required internships and teaching assistantships in these programs provided them with noteworthy teaching experience.[4]

In all these cases, hands-on experience is key, but what about foundational education knowledge?

Why Teacher Training and Education Matter

Brecher and Klipfel point out that "a background in pedagogy is particularly important for these librarians, who are increasingly expected to collaborate on equal terms with faculty in teaching information literacy and critical thinking skills."[5] Negotiations with faculty are key in determining learning outcomes and activities for library sessions. To take an even wider view, if academic librarians want a seat at the table when discussing new and revised curriculum changes, they must be able to speak the language. Hensley writes that "becoming well-versed in and practicing the elements of educational theory, curricular learning goals, and student learning assessment could significantly aid in advocating for and shaping institutional long-term goals of guiding students along the long road of information literacy."[6] Students, finally, are at the center of it all because it is "difficult to help students learn without a basic grounding in the theory and psychology of how students learn."[7] Creating on-the-job teacher training opportunities to fill any gaps in the LIS curriculum is key to a successful information literacy program.

Teaching Competencies and Roles for Librarians

In 2007, ACRL outlined a set of skills for effective teaching in information literacy programs through its "Standards for Proficiencies for Instruction Librarians and Coordinators."[8] The twelve categories outlined in this document read like a checklist for skills ranging from administrative and planning to instructional design and subject expertise. This approach aligned with the checklist style of the ACRL *Information Literacy Competency Standards for Higher Education*.[9] What followed in the years after the approval of these documents was institutional adaptations to translate these documents to local needs. One example of this comes from Oregon State University Libraries (OSUL), where they created internal teaching proficiencies for all librarians with teaching responsibilities.[10] In focusing on new and experienced teaching librarians, OSUL envisioned that their local adaptation could serve as a model for other institutions wishing to adapt the ACRL Proficiencies.

When the ACRL *Framework for Information Literacy for Higher Education*[11] replaced the Competency Standards, the Proficiencies also received an update. The ACRL *Roles and Strengths of Teaching Librarians*[12] shifted from proficiencies to roles, from skills to strengths, and from a checklist approach to a conceptual framework. In essence, it was "designed to act as a bridge between concept and practice"[13] with one of its objectives being to aid in goal-setting for professional development of teaching librarians. As with the Proficiencies, examples of combining the Framework and the Roles and Strengths documents emerged. Armstrong[14] suggested the role of lifelong learner could be integrated with the framework by substituting the word "research" with "teaching." With such amalgamations as "Teaching as inquiry" and "Teaching as strategic exploration," what resulted was a suggested list of dispositions and knowledge practices for teaching librarians.

Professional Development—From National to Local

Many national and association-level professional development programs have tried to meet the needs of teaching librarians. As new librarians enter the field with little to no pedagogical training or experience, professional development programs attempt to fill that gap. In the United States, one of the most notable examples is the ACRL Immersion program.[15] Immersion not only builds librarians' teaching skills but also provides a conceptual, theoretical, and social justice basis for teaching librarians. Other countries have also attempted national or multinational approaches to post-LIS training, focusing on their respective national information literacy standards with emphasis on community-building among peers and practical skill development.[16] Local solutions for training teaching librarians existed long before the ACRL Competency Standards and Proficiencies. Sare, Bales, and Neville called for academic libraries to begin identifying and tracking these informal learning experiences of librarians "in order to develop appropriate learning toolkits for new librarians."[17] Institutions begin creating internal competencies or skills lists as a necessity for training ill-prepared new teaching librarians.[18] As academic libraries developed local proficiencies, they also developed local professional development. Many focused on new teaching librarians, while some saw the need to reach both new and experienced teaching librarians.[19] This push to include experienced teaching librarians into regular professional development continues. In her study on librarians' teaching identities, Nichols Hess found that a librarian's time at their institution, opportunities for professional development, and relationship-building with colleagues all had an impact on teacher identity formation. These inputs can be fostered and shared with new teaching librarians through local professional development.

> And overall, library leaders invested in building teaching capacity should support both newer and more veteran instructional librarians in pursuing these targeted, meaningful influences over those inputs which perhaps have less resonance. While these types of support may mean more than a one-size-fits-all professional learning environment, it may help to foster teaching transformation across instructional units.[20]

Since the publication of ACRL's *Roles and Strengths of Teaching Librarians*,[21] local professional development programs have continued to fill the gaps where LIS education lacks.

Planning LTI
Historical Background

The Library Teaching Institute was created to supplement and expand an existing training program for library instructors, known as the Introduction to Instruction Training. This initial summer training program, developed in 2018, was primarily used as an onboarding tool for members of Mason's undergraduate-focused Teaching & Learning Team. The Introduction to Instruction training was modeled after the Association of College & Research Libraries' (ACRL) Immersion program, which provides extended training to give attendees the tools they need to gain skills and confidence in library instruction. Our program was designed to introduce library employees to basic instructional concepts, such as the ACRL Framework and Backward Design, as well as teaching logistics, such as booking a library classroom space, setting up teaching technology, negotiating with faculty members, public speaking, and classroom management.[22] The outcome for training participants was to create an activity with learning outcomes and lead a brief teaching demonstration.

When a new Instruction Coordinator began at Mason Libraries in 2020, they inherited the Introduction to Instruction training. Along with two instructional staff members, they began exploring the idea of expanding that training to be more formalized and inclusive of other library employees. Library employees across the Libraries taught information literacy sessions, but the Teaching & Learning Team was the only team that received any sort of training or onboarding with teaching. The vision, as established by this smaller team, was to create a training program to fill that gap.

Starting the Planning Process

After establishing that an internal training program in library instruction was needed at the Mason Libraries, the team established a planning process involving key stakeholders and experts in various aspects of library instruction. Each of these stakeholders convened a planning committee in January 2021 to establish the curriculum for the teaching institute, with the Instruction Coordinator taking the lead on this process. First, the committee established three guiding principles to frame the curriculum.

The first guiding principle is "to support those who are new to library instruction by providing clear direction for our library instruction efforts." This is important to the program because it establishes a baseline of support for new instructors and ensures that they know the direction of the instruction program at Mason Libraries.

The second guiding principle is "to have a set of core competencies that we can expect from library instructors that have participated in this program." This tenet of the program allows the Instruction Coordinator to have an established set of skills that LTI graduates need in order to teach the most common library and research skills in our context. It also allows for a wider pool of participants in library instruction, as more library employees have access to standardized training in teaching.

The third guiding principle is "to have something to point to that helps us define what library instruction at Mason looks like." This is an important tenet as the Mason Libraries had many new staff and faculty members and it was crucial to create a shared understanding of what is expected during library instruction. It helped the Instruction Coordinator create documentation on how to do different aspects of instruction, such as booking rooms and responding to instructors. Each of these principles was considered throughout the planning process, especially during the planning phases.

Creating Core Competencies

Once the planning committee established these guiding principles, they worked to create a list of core competencies that participants should have after participation in LTI. The idea of this institute is that everyone has room to grow, and this institute is designed to help library instructors continually improve their teaching skills. During this process, the planning committee consulted the ACRL *Roles and Strengths of Teaching Librarians* to create competencies for this program. The full list of core competencies for LTI is available in the chapter appendix.

One set of core competencies revolved around knowledge of important information literacy concepts and guiding frameworks. The planning group identified that familiarity with the ACRL Framework, Universal Design for Learning, the Teaching & Learning

Team's teaching philosophy, and major learning theories were necessary for effective library instruction.

Another set of core competencies revolved around the lesson planning process. Creating learning outcomes, conducting student learning assessment, principles of active learning, and other related concepts were all identified as necessary for library instructors. Being able to interpret lesson plans, modify them, and create their own were all covered in these competencies.

The final set of core competencies was attitudinal in nature. From negotiating with faculty to feeling confident in the classroom, we wanted to ensure that our library instructors felt prepared for the classroom. These attitudinal pieces were the most challenging to learn and the most likely to come with practice. Because LTI was designed to orient new instructors without needing to go through their personal experience, these were a focus of many of the sessions.

Two Tracks

During the planning processes for LTI, it became clear that there needed to be two tracks for the institute—one that heavily focused on someone delivering a lesson created by another person and another track focused on creating a new lesson. This development came about because we had a diverse set of teaching experiences and responsibilities within the Libraries. Additionally, because we have a repository of lesson plans for Mason Libraries, many newer instructors can rely on lesson plans others have created instead of creating their own.

Training Format

LTI takes place over the summer with a series of weekly ninety-minute sessions. These sessions are held online via Zoom. LTI began in 2021, so the first sessions were held on Zoom to limit the spread of the COVID-19 pandemic. Since then, LTI has continued on Zoom for those reasons and to allow colleagues at our distributed campuses to participate. Hosting sessions on Zoom allows the facilitators to record the sessions and post them after the fact, which enables asynchronous participation in the series as needed.

In addition to Zoom sessions, LTI includes an accompanying Blackboard course. This course contains content for participants to review and engage with, including recordings of all LTI sessions, homework assignments, and additional resources—e.g., important links, supplemental readings, and guiding library documents. The Blackboard course also remains open after the series concludes, which allows LTI participants to go back to the content and refresh their memories.

Requirements for Participants

Library faculty and staff were able to participate in LTI in a variety of ways. Full participation in LTI culminates in a certificate of completion. Criteria for full participation include attending all LTI sessions and completing all assigned homework outside of the sessions. Those who intended to receive a certificate but were not able to attend one or more sessions were given an option for an asynchronous attendance assignment, which involved watching a session recording and completing an assignment via Blackboard in place of live attendance. Examples of assigned homework include an introductory discussion board or a reflection journal asking participants to apply concepts learned in a particular session.

Alternatively, participants who did not wish (or were unable) to receive a certificate were offered an à la carte approach where they could attend any of the workshops. This à la carte option allowed returning LTI participants to attend sessions of interest in each training iteration without having to retake the training. It also opened sessions to those who could not complete the entire program due to summer commitments and vacation schedules but who still wanted to benefit from the sessions.

Inclusion of All Library Employees

One key feature of LTI is that all employees are invited, regardless of teaching responsibilities or employment classification. Because Mason Libraries is a large organization, one reason for this inclusivity was to ensure that everyone who taught, regardless of placement in the organization, was included. Additionally, the coordinators felt it was important to provide a professional development opportunity for all employees in case a current Mason employee was interested in learning more about instruction to expand their professional toolkit.

The Library Teaching Institute

List of Sessions

The table that follows outlines the sessions from both years of the Library Teaching Institute at George Mason University Libraries. The team adjusted the format between the two years, so the 2022 series does not include the same number of sessions as the 2021 series. The table identifies the three sessions that were cut between years as well as how the outcomes from those cut sessions were incorporated into the other sessions.

TABLE 22.1

An outline of the sessions from both years of the Library Teaching Institute at George Mason University Libraries.

Session Title	2021 Learning Outcomes Participants will:	2022 Learning Outcomes Participants will:
Introduction	• Define library instruction • Identify Mason Libraries' instruction initiatives • Review the logistical steps for in-class instruction • Review the logistical steps for workshops	• Define information literacy • Identify the infrastructure of library instruction at Mason • Discuss major learning theories used in adult learning • Apply the ACRL Framework to library instruction

TABLE 22.1

An outline of the sessions from both years of the Library Teaching Institute at George Mason University Libraries.

Session Title	2021 Learning Outcomes Participants will:	2022 Learning Outcomes Participants will:
Anatomy of a Lesson Plan	• Summarize the role and key features of a lesson plan • Describe learning outcomes • Identify the role of learning activities • Define learning assessment for our library instruction context(s)	This session was not a part of our 2022 series; outcomes from this session were covered in sessions on Learning Outcomes, Activities, and Student Learning Assessment.
Building Confidence	• Develop a checklist to prepare for class sessions • Apply best practices for classroom management • Identify steps to take after class to prepare for the next class	• Reflect on their role in the classroom and their relationship to instructional faculty • Develop a checklist to prepare for class sessions • Apply best practices for classroom management • Identify steps to take after the class to prepare for the next class
Conclusion (Delivering a Lesson)	• Synthesize their work during the Delivering a Lesson series • Reflect on the Delivering a Lesson series • Deliver a 5-minute portion of a lesson	This session was not a part of our 2022 series; outcomes from this session were moved into homework assignments for other sessions.
Learning Theory	• Define major learning theories used in adult learning • Determine the most effective learning theory for an instructional context • Apply learning theories to the ACRL Framework for Information Literacy for Higher Education	This session was not a part of our 2022 series; outcomes from this session were streamlined and redistributed to the Introduction session.
Learning Outcomes	• Develop measurable learning outcomes • Create learning outcomes specific to your instructional context • Articulate best practices for creating learning outcomes	• Describe the importance of learning outcomes • Write measurable learning outcomes for their instructional context • Articulate best practices for creating learning outcomes
Activities	• Describe activities' importance to the learning process • List commonly used activities in the library classroom • Connect a session's learning activities to its learning outcomes	• Describe activities' importance to the learning process • List commonly used activities in the library classroom • Connect a session's learning activities to its learning outcomes

TABLE 22.1

An outline of the sessions from both years of the Library Teaching Institute at George Mason University Libraries.

Session Title	2021 Learning Outcomes Participants will:	2022 Learning Outcomes Participants will:
Student Learning Assessment	• Discuss best practices for library instruction assessment techniques • Apply best practices to design an instructional assessment	• Describe the importance of student learning assessment in the library classroom • List commonly used assessment techniques • Identify Mason-specific resources for student learning assessment

Format

LTI 2021, the first year of the program, was comprised of two separate series. Delivering a Lesson, the first series, was aimed at the true beginner, with a goal of participants being able to confidently deliver a lesson that someone else had created. Sessions focused on learning the basic definition of library instruction, logistics for how to lead a session, the anatomy of a lesson plan, how to build confidence in the classroom, and concluded with participants delivering a short portion of a lesson for feedback.

The second series, called Designing a Lesson, was held after the first. This series targeted an intermediate audience and aimed for participants to be able to design their own lessons. Sessions focused on learning theory, writing learning outcomes, designing and leading activities, and student learning assessment.

Overall Impressions and Lessons Learned

LTI had a good turnout in its first year, especially for the Delivering a Lesson series. The Delivering a Lesson series had twelve to fifteen participants per session, with three eventually completing the certificate. The second series, Designing a Lesson, had a lower turnout with six to eight participants per session and no one completing the certificate. Feedback from these sessions was primarily positive, with participants indicating that their confidence and knowledge had grown as a result of participating in the program.

However, one major piece of feedback was that the division between the two series was confusing to the participants. Participants were unclear, for example, if they could participate in Designing a Lesson if they had not completed Delivering a Lesson. The distinction between the two series was another point of confusion. When beginning to plan for the second year of the program, the team decided to take this feedback and make some major adjustments.

LTI 2022

LTI's second year began in Summer 2022. The second version of LTI was based on the first: the list of core competencies, for example, was unchanged. However, one major change was the elimination of the two-track system in favor of a condensed single series. Feedback from the 2021 edition revealed that the division between the two tracks was confusing and led participants to not know how to participate. Additionally, upon reflecting on the process, the planning committee for the second year realized that newer instructors would benefit from, for example, writing their own learning outcomes. We condensed the series into the shorter one-series model, with one certificate of completion at the end. What follows is a short discussion of each of the five sessions in this new series.

Introduction

In the first session in 2022, participants were introduced to LTI and some of the major theories that underpin our work at Mason Libraries, including a section about learning theories and the ACRL Framework. One example of an activity we conducted during the session asked participants to do a deep dive on a specific frame and then report out to their colleagues about that frame and what it includes. For homework, participants wrote an opening reflective piece that set some intention for their participation in LTI.

Building Confidence

The second session focused on ways to build comfort and confidence in the classroom. We discussed how to interpret body language from students, for example, and participants built a toolkit of materials they'd bring to an in-person session to feel more comfortable. Reflective practice was also emphasized here as well as how our library instructors might relate to the teaching faculty as partners.

Learning Outcomes

In the third session, participants learned about learning outcomes. The homework for this week asked participants to think about their own setting—teaching in classes, workshops, or other contexts—and write some sample learning outcomes for that setting. Participants built on those learning outcomes for the remainder of the homework assignments.

Activities

This session modeled learning activities and problem-based learning by using these techniques to show participants how to facilitate activities and learn about other active learning techniques. For example, we provided participants with a list of activity types, then broke them into groups which were each assigned an activity. Then, we reshuffled the groups to include members of each original group; using this jigsaw format, each member of each original group was able to become an expert on a type of activity and introduce it to their fellow participants.

Student Learning Assessment

For the final session of LTI 2022, participants were introduced to student learning assessment. Grounded in the assessment program at Mason Libraries,[23] participants learned the many ways to assess student learning in a library instruction context. For homework, participants used the learning outcomes they wrote in a prior homework assignment and designed a student learning assessment technique to use to assess those outcomes.

Overall Impressions and Lessons Learned

In its second year, LTI had approximately fifteen participants per session from across the Libraries. Five of those participants completed the certificate. Some participants even returned to LTI for a second year in a row, citing its sense of community among instructors as a major reason to return.

As we move into planning for our 2023 session, we are making some improvements to the series. One major change we hope to make, in response to participant feedback, is to add more ways for participants to apply our content outside of a teaching context. Because we invite participation from across the Libraries, having a more explicit discussion of, for example, running effective meetings using teaching techniques will improve the ability of non-instructors to directly apply this content. We also plan to move some of the introductory content about the certificate into an asynchronous introduction session, allowing us more time in the first live session to focus on items like the ACRL Framework.

Recommendations
Dual Audience: Challenge and Opportunity

Designing a training program for both new and returning library instructors was a challenge. It necessitated creating multiple modes of participation, for example, and creating scaffolding for both those who attended the entire series and those who attended only one workshop. This, however, also created two important opportunities: repeat attendance and mixing of experience levels.

In the second year of LTI, some instructors who had participated in the first year returned for a couple of workshops. For example, if someone who earned the certificate in 2021 wanted to refresh their knowledge about student learning assessment, our flexible schedule allowed them to do so. This ability to attend in subsequent years also underlines that developing as a teacher is a consistent and recursive process: by attending after you have been teaching for a year, you will learn different things.

Additionally, allowing for flexible participation enabled experienced and new instructors to learn together. Both groups contribute something unique to the learning process, and this mixture has become a signature of the breakout rooms and other activities during LTI. Sharing knowledge and building community, especially during an era of web conferencing rather than in-person meetings, were both benefits gained by this mixture of experience levels across LTI.

Include, Rather Than Exclude

A major focus during the planning process for LTI was identifying the program's audience. Would LTI only include those people who currently teach or work within the department that focuses on teaching? What we ultimately decided, however, was to open LTI to all library employees at our institution, whether they currently taught for their job or not. This decision was made specifically with inclusivity in mind: as a professional development opportunity, keeping LTI as open as possible was important.

This decision led to participation from employees outside the Teaching & Learning Team during both iterations of LTI. Perspectives from employees in Access Services, Metadata Services, Interlibrary Loan, and other departments brought in diverse ideas of what teaching encompasses. These employees were then able to take what they learned during LTI and either document that they had some exposure to library instruction for future positions or apply it in other contexts, like training student staff or leading meetings.

Simplify When Possible

In the first year of LTI, it included two tracks: Delivering a Lesson and Designing a Lesson. The hope with the two-track model was that instructors would have an easier time identifying which sessions they would want to attend. After the 2021 iteration, however, we found that this distinction left the audience unclear about which sessions to attend. Additionally, because the Designing a Lesson series occurred later in the summer, its attendance was not as high as the first series.

By the second year of LTI, the planning committee condensed it into one series. While this did necessitate streamlining or cutting content altogether, the committee also found that the flow of the series was more natural and easier to understand. This also eliminated the need to run the series twice during the summer, so the committee could select a time during the summer when most people would be in the office.

Scaffolding and Final Product

Throughout LTI, participants interested in the certificate complete homework assignments. These short, asynchronous assignments reinforce the skills taught during a session. For example, after a session about learning outcomes, the homework assignment might be to create learning outcomes for a specific class session or workshop. These assignments are further scaffolded by asking participants to build on past work: taking the learning outcomes they wrote in a previous week, for example, and creating a student learning assessment to measure that learning outcome. Creating the homework assignments to build on each other in this way helped to build continuity between sessions for those who participated in the certificate.

Structuring homework like this also gave participants a tangible product at the end of LTI. Beyond obtaining a certificate of completion, for example, participants could also leave with a mostly complete lesson plan for a class or workshop in their context. Bringing skills into a practical and individual focus for participants was an important part of our design, as well, as LTI was designed to be useful and timely for each participant.

Collaborate When Planning

The planning process for LTI involved experts from across the Teaching & Learning Team. Because LTI was designed to provide a baseline level of knowledge for all library instructors, a big tent was necessary to ensure participants learned important knowledge across the many facets of instruction. Having a large group did mean that the process went slower than it otherwise would have, but the knowledge that each member of the team contributed was invaluable. Building in enough time at the beginning of the program to include these diverse perspectives was a crucial part of LTI's success.

Have a Point Person

LTI at Mason Libraries, while a collaborative process, also had either one point person or a small team of point people leading the charge, depending on the year. This point person made sure that the Blackboard course for LTI included all homework assignments and session recordings and that each homework assignment was read and evaluated. Having a small group ensured that everyone who participates receives feedback on their work and a certificate at the end. It also helps to have a leader when participants have questions or want to further discuss something they learned during a session.

Moving Forward

At the time of writing this chapter, the team behind LTI is in the beginning stages of planning for the 2023 edition of the program. Much of the program is currently planned to remain the same, including the option for a certificate or à la carte attendance and recruiting all library employees. Some questions to consider include whether the core competencies list needs to be revisited or revised as well as whether the 2022 LTI program adequately covered the teaching skills and concepts needed by library faculty and staff. Our goal with LTI as we plan for the future is for the program to be as dynamic and responsive to participants' needs as our teaching.

Conclusion

A local training program might be implemented for a variety of reasons. In our case at George Mason University, we had a large and distributed network of library instructors with a variety of experience levels. By creating a training program that could be flexibly applied, we were able to create a program that would be useful for many participants. The community we continue to build as a part of LTI is another crucial component of our success: by bringing participants together across the Libraries, we are able to build connections between employees who would not normally work together.

APPENDIX
List of LTI Core Competencies

1. Foundational Knowledge
   a. Know what lesson plans are and why they are important.
   b. Define learning outcome, learning activity, and student learning assessment.
   c. Define library instruction and information literacy.
   d. Familiar with the ACRL *Framework for Information Literacy for Higher Education*.
   e. Familiar at a basic level with major adult learning theories: Universal Design for Learning, Backward Design, anti-racist pedagogy, and feminist pedagogy.
2. Applied Knowledge
   a. Write learning outcomes based on their own instructional context.
   b. Design learning activities and student learning assessment to support their created learning outcomes.
   c. Negotiate with teaching faculty surrounding classroom expectations and the content of the library instruction lesson plan.
3. Attitudes and Values
   a. Facilitate activities and lead lessons comfortably and confidently.
   b. Committed to continued professional development.
   c. Understanding of reflective practice in teaching.
4. Logistics and Local Context
   a. Understand which teaching rooms are available, what technology they include, and how to reserve them.
   b. Understand how library instruction requests work and how to take a request that comes in via the form.
   c. Understand the local library instruction landscape, including what courses and workshops we frequently teach and which modalities we teach in.
   d. Familiar with Mason-specific library instruction support documents and resources.

Notes

1. Mandi Goodsett and Amanda Koziura, "Are Library Science Programs Preparing New Librarians? Creating a Sustainable and Vibrant Librarian Community," *Journal of Library Administration* 56, no. 6 (September 8, 2016): 707, https://doi.org/10.1080/01930826.2015.1134246.
2. Laura Saunders, "Education for Instruction: A Review of LIS Instruction Syllabi," *The Reference Librarian* 56, no. 1 (January 2, 2015): 5, https://doi.org/10.1080/02763877.2014.969392.
3. Merinda Kaye Hensley, "Improving LIS Education in Teaching Librarians to Teach," in *ACRL 2015 Proceedings* (Portland, OR: American Library Association, 2015), 318–19.

4. Jacalyn E. Bryan, "The Preparation of Academic Librarians Who Provide Instruction: A Comparison of First and Second Career Librarians," *The Journal of Academic Librarianship* 42, no. 4 (July 1, 2016): 348, https://doi.org/10.1016/j.acalib.2016.05.010.

5. Dani Brecher and Kevin Michael Klipfel, "Education Training for Instruction Librarians: A Shared Perspective," *Communications in Information Literacy* 8, no. 1 (March 2014): 44.

6. Hensley, "Improving LIS Education," 315.

7. Brecher and Klipfel, "Education Training for Instruction Librarians," 44.

8. "Standards for Proficiencies for Instruction Librarians and Coordinators," Association of College & Research Libraries, ACRL Instruction Section, 2007, https://acrl.ala.org/IS/instruction-tools-resources-2/professional-development/standards-for-proficiencies-for-instruction-librarians-and-coordinators/.

9. *Information Literacy Competency Standards for Higher Education*, Association of College & Research Libraries, January 18, 2000, http://www.ala.org/acrl/standards/informationliteracycompetency.

10. Uta Hussong-Christian, "Adapting and Using Instruction Proficiencies to Encourage Reflection, Goal Setting and Professional Development," *Communications in Information Literacy* 6, no. 2 (September 2012): 160–72.

11. *Framework for Information Literacy for Higher Education*, Association of College & Research Libraries, February 2, 2015, http://www.ala.org/acrl/standards/ilframework.

12. *Roles and Strengths of Teaching Librarians*, Association of College & Research Libraries (ACRL), May 15, 2017, https://www.ala.org/acrl/standards/teachinglibrarians.

13. *Roles and Strengths of Teaching Librarians*, ACRL.

14. Annie Armstrong, "New Models for Instruction: Fusing the ACRL Framework and Roles and Strengths of Teaching Librarians to Promote the Lifelong Learning of Teaching Librarians," *College & Research Libraries News* 80, no. 7 (August 7, 2019): 378–86, https://doi.org/10.5860/crln.80.7.378.

15. "Immersion Program," Association of College & Research Libraries (ACRL), 2020, https://www.ala.org/acrl/conferences/immersion.

16. Mary Delaney et al., "Library Staff Learning to Support Learners Learning: Reflections from a Two-Year Professional Development Project," *New Review of Academic Librarianship* 26, no. 1 (January 2020): 56–78, https://doi.org/10.1080/13614533.2019.1681483; Agnes Namaganda, "Continuing Professional Development as Transformational Learning: A Case Study," *The Journal of Academic Librarianship* 46, no. 3 (May 1, 2020): 102152, https://doi.org/10.1016/j.acalib.2020.102152.

17. Laura Sare, Stephen Bales, and Bruce Neville, "New Academic Librarians and Their Perceptions of the Profession," *portal: Libraries and the Academy* 12, no. 2 (April 2012): 200, https://doi.org/10.1353/pla.2012.0017.

18. Carroll Botts and Mark Emmons, "Developing Teaching Competencies for Instructors in the Academic Library: A Case Study," *Public Services Quarterly* 1, no. 3 (March 2002): 65–81, https://doi.org/10.1300/J295v01n03_07.

19. Botts and Emmons, "Developing Teaching Competencies"; Hussong-Christian, "Adapting and Using Instruction Proficiencies."

20. Amanda Nichols Hess, "Academic Librarians' Teaching Identities and Work Experiences: Exploring Relationships to Support Perspective Transformation in Information Literacy Instruction," *Journal of Library Administration* 60, no. 4 (June 5, 2020): 345–46, https://doi.org/10.1080/01930826.2020.1721939.

21. *Roles and Strengths of Teaching Librarians*, ACRL.

22. "Immersion Program," ACRL.

23. Maoria J. Kirker and Ashley Blinstrub, "Improving Information Literacy Instruction through Programmatic Student Learning Assessment," in *Leading Dynamic Information Literacy Programs*, ed. Anne C. Behler (London, UK: Routledge, 2023).

Bibliography

Armstrong, Annie. "New Models for Instruction: Fusing the ACRL Framework and Roles and Strengths of Teaching Librarians to Promote the Lifelong Learning of Teaching Librarians." *College & Research Libraries News* 80, no. 7 (August 7, 2019): 378–86. https://doi.org/10.5860/crln.80.7.378.

Association of College & Research Libraries. *Framework for Information Literacy for Higher Education*. February 2, 2015. http://www.ala.org/acrl/standards/ilframework.

———. "Immersion Program." Text. Association of College & Research Libraries (ACRL). 2020. https://www.ala.org/acrl/conferences/immersion.

———. *Information Literacy Competency Standards for Higher Education*. January 18, 2000. http://www.ala.org/acrl/standards/informationliteracycompetency.

———. *Roles and Strengths of Teaching Librarians*. Text. Association of College & Research Libraries (ACRL). May 15, 2017. https://www.ala.org/acrl/standards/teachinglibrarians.

———. "Standards for Proficiencies for Instruction Librarians and Coordinators." ACRL Instruction Section. 2007. https://acrl.ala.org/IS/instruction-tools-resources-2/professional-development/standards-for-proficiencies-for-instruction-librarians-and-coordinators/.

Botts, Carroll, and Mark Emmons. "Developing Teaching Competencies for Instructors in the Academic Library: A Case Study." *Public Services Quarterly* 1, no. 3 (March 2002): 65–81. https://doi.org/10.1300/J295v01n03_07.

Brecher, Dani, and Kevin Michael Klipfel. "Education Training for Instruction Librarians: A Shared Perspective." *Communications in Information Literacy* 8, no. 1 (March 2014): 43–49.

Bryan, Jacalyn E. "The Preparation of Academic Librarians Who Provide Instruction: A Comparison of First and Second Career Librarians." *The Journal of Academic Librarianship* 42, no. 4 (July 1, 2016): 340–54. https://doi.org/10.1016/j.acalib.2016.05.010.

Delaney, Mary, Ann Cleary, Philip Cohen, and Brendan Devlin. "Library Staff Learning to Support Learners Learning: Reflections from a Two-Year Professional Development Project." *New Review of Academic Librarianship* 26, no. 1 (January 2020): 56–78. https://doi.org/10.1080/13614533.2019.1681483.

Goodsett, Mandi, and Amanda Koziura. "Are Library Science Programs Preparing New Librarians? Creating a Sustainable and Vibrant Librarian Community." *Journal of Library Administration* 56, no. 6 (September 8, 2016): 697–721. https://doi.org/10.1080/01930826.2015.1134246.

Hensley, Merinda Kaye. "Improving LIS Education in Teaching Librarians to Teach." In *ACRL 2015 Proceedings*, 315–22. Portland, OR: American Library Association, 2015.

Hussong-Christian, Uta. "Adapting and Using Instruction Proficiencies to Encourage Reflection, Goal Setting and Professional Development." *Communications in Information Literacy* 6, no. 2 (September 2012): 160–72.

Kirker, Maoria J., and Ashley Blinstrub. "Improving Information Literacy Instruction through Programmatic Student Learning Assessment." In *Leading Dynamic Information Literacy Programs*, edited by Anne C. Behle. London, UK: Routledge, 2023.

Namaganda, Agnes. "Continuing Professional Development as Transformational Learning: A Case Study." *The Journal of Academic Librarianship* 46, no. 3 (May 1, 2020): 102152. https://doi.org/10.1016/j.acalib.2020.102152.

Nichols Hess, Amanda. "Academic Librarians' Teaching Identities and Work Experiences: Exploring Relationships to Support Perspective Transformation in Information Literacy Instruction." *Journal of Library Administration* 60, no. 4 (June 5, 2020): 331–53. https://doi.org/10.1080/01930826.2020.1721939.

Sare, Laura, Stephen Bales, and Bruce Neville. "New Academic Librarians and Their Perceptions of the Profession." *portal: Libraries and the Academy* 12, no. 2 (April 2012): 179–203. https://doi.org/10.1353/pla.2012.0017.

Saunders, Laura. "Education for Instruction: A Review of LIS Instruction Syllabi." *The Reference Librarian* 56, no. 1 (January 2, 2015): 1–21. https://doi.org/10.1080/02763877.2014.969392.

PART VIII:

REFLECTIONS

CHAPTER 23

The Introverted Instructor:
Tackling Library Instruction When It's Out of Your Comfort Zone

Ginelle Baskin

LEARNING OUTCOMES

Readers will be able to

- understand the challenges faced by introverted instructors in library settings;
- implement strategies to overcome nervousness associated with library instruction and build confidence as a library instructor; and
- acquire practical preparation techniques for library instruction.

Introduction

When you are an introvert like I am, library instruction duties can be challenging. Okay, they can be more than just challenging. They can be downright terrifying. Sometimes just the thought of standing up in front of a bunch of people can make me squeamish. In fact, when I first started as a library instructor, I would actually feel physically ill before teaching a class. My palms would sweat, my heart would race, my voice would shake, and my stomach would be doing somersaults. It was more than a case of the jitters for me. Being a library instructor was completely out of my comfort zone. However, with time and practice, it has gotten easier, and now, I dare say, I enjoy being a library instructor. Rather than dreading library instruction duties, I actually look forward to them. So, how did I make this transition from being a nervous wreck before a class to being calm, cool, and collected? And how does my introverted personality affect my overall approach to teaching? Let me share with you some of the challenges that I faced as an introverted instructor and explore what has helped me become more comfortable in the library instructor role. I'll talk about what training helped and what training didn't, and I'll offer practical tips and strategies for how you can prepare for teaching a library class yourself.

My Personality and Teaching Background

Let me start by sharing a little bit about myself and my teaching background. As for my personality, I have always considered myself to be an introvert. An introvert is a colloquial term often used for "people who are quiet, reserved, thoughtful, and self-reliant and who tend to prefer solitary work and leisure activities," and it is also normal for introverts "to mull things over before formulating a reaction, and their energy is replenished by time spent alone."[1] In general, I'd say this is a fairly accurate description of my personality. As for social interaction, it's not that I don't like being around people, because I do. In fact, interacting with patrons and helping them is one of the things I love the most about being a librarian. It's just that my first tendency in a social situation is to sit back, observe, and keep to myself. When I began thinking about possible careers, being a teacher was not at the top of my list. In fact, when I decided to pursue a career as a librarian, it never even occurred to me that teaching might be part of my job duties. I loved learning and loved being a student, but I never saw myself fitting into a "teacher" role. Too much interaction, too much public speaking, too much out of my comfort zone.

Nevertheless, despite my best efforts to run away from teaching, I found myself in two librarian positions with teaching duties. My first teaching experience came as a school librarian at a rural elementary school that served approximately 500 students in grades PreK through the fifth grade. I was responsible for managing the library while also teaching seven library classes each day. This was a trial-by-fire experience for me, especially since I was hired prior to completing my student teaching requirements. I quickly learned just how challenging and time-consuming it was to create weekly lesson plans from scratch and to customize them to six different grade levels. I also learned that being a teacher was exhausting! Physically, mentally, and emotionally. I struggled with classroom management, and the daily expectations of the job were overwhelming. I frequently experienced bouts of laryngitis because my voice was so worn out from talking all day, and I often felt unappreciated by and isolated from the other teachers in the school.

My second teaching experience came as a user services librarian at a large academic library. My main duties consisted of reference, instruction, and liaison work. The library classes I taught were primarily one-shot sessions taught to freshmen and sophomores. Due to the pandemic, most of the classes in my first year were taught remotely via Zoom. In my second and third years, most of my classes were back to being in-person. In general, I found the academic library setting to be a much better fit for me. During the busiest times of the semester, I would teach two to three library classes a week, which was much more manageable than what I had experienced as a school librarian. However, I still found myself grappling at times with how to approach library instruction as an introvert and how to overcome my uneasiness in the instructor role.

Challenges of Being an Introverted Instructor

As an introverted instructor, I faced three main challenges: nervousness, fear of making a mistake, and feeling like an impostor. The first and most obvious challenge was nervousness. This is something I still deal with occasionally, especially if it's been a while since teaching my last class. However, I've learned that the more I teach, the less nervous I am. It often just takes getting over that initial hump to feel comfortable in the instructor role again. Another thing that helped me immensely is realizing that the students are not judging me nearly as much as I think they are. Consider the perspective of Scott Berkun, a public speaker, who thinks that most people listening to presentations are simply hoping you will end soon and aren't really thinking about you at all.[2] Knowing this helps me focus more on the content of my class rather than worrying about what students might be thinking about me.

Another challenge I faced as an introverted instructor was being afraid of making a mistake. Berkun points out: "If you'd like to be good at something, the first thing to go out the window is the notion of perfection. Every time I get up to the front of the room, I know I will make mistakes."[3] For myself, I've learned that striving for perfection often leads to unnecessary anxiety. For instance, early on in my career, I would worry about trivial things like my appearance or if my Southern accent made me sound less intelligent. I eventually learned to relax and not stress about these things. I learned that mistakes are inevitable and that there is no such thing as a "perfect library instructor" or a "perfect library class." I still strive to do a good job and to improve, of course, but I've learned not to sweat the small stuff, like when a database crashes, or, gasp, when a student falls asleep in one of my classes. I've also learned that it is okay to say, "I'm not sure about that. Let me find out and get back to you." Besides taking the pressure off myself to be perfect, this attitude also models for students that we are all a community of learners. By admitting when I don't know something, I am demonstrating that I am willing to learn right along beside them.

Another challenge I've dealt with as a library instructor is my struggle with imposter syndrome. Although I'm not certain this necessarily has anything to do with being an introvert, it is something that can definitely affect your self-confidence as a teacher. Found in faculty and students alike, imposter syndrome is "a subjective experience of phoniness in people who believe that they are not intelligent, capable, or creative despite evidence of high achievement, and who are highly motivated to achieve but live in perpetual fear of being 'found out' or exposed as frauds."[4] These feelings of self-doubt can be crippling, and I've fought against them as both a teacher and a librarian. I've found myself playing the comparison game, assuming that other librarians must be smarter or more qualified than

I am. For me, the best way to overcome these negative thoughts is to shift my focus to my own successes. I remind myself of what I do well and think back on praise I've received from faculty, students, and other librarians. This helps validate my value and expertise and pumps me up to have a good class.

My Training

As for my training, I took one formal instruction course as part of my initial graduate program in information science, and I honestly don't remember much about it now. From what I recall, the class was mostly grounded in theory. I remember taking away more from my other classes, which focused on practical skills like how to search databases or were focused on a specific type of library. Maybe that's just because that's what I was interested in. When I later returned to graduate school to become certified for school librarianship, I took a few education courses. Again, these courses covered aspects of instruction, but I still don't feel like I received much practical, hands-on training. It felt more like an overview of topics related to instruction. Therefore, most of my "real" training came on the job.

The two main things that helped me the most as a new library instructor were observing other library instructors and having hands-on experience. Observing other librarians in the classroom helped me in so many ways. It helped me to see how other librarians organized class content, how they interacted with students and faculty, how they incorporated activities into the class, and what kinds of search examples they used. When I first started my job as a user services librarian, I was fortunate that my boss arranged for me to observe several different librarians in our department teach a variety of different classes. This was great because I was able to see how each one put their own unique spin on it. For example, one librarian began the class by explaining why it's better to start your research on the library web page rather than starting with Google, and another librarian started by telling a personal story. Some instructors liked to provide handouts, while others relied heavily on using the classroom whiteboard. I learned that you don't have to teach a class exactly the same way a co-worker does it, and it's okay to put your personality into it. It was also helpful to get an idea of how long I should talk and what questions students might ask. So, when you are starting, I highly recommend that you take a few weeks to observe other library instructors at your institution if you can.

How I Prepare for a Class

So, how do I prepare for teaching a library class? Here are a few tips and strategies that work for me. I hope they will be beneficial to you.

Make an Outline

I make an outline for each class I teach. This helps me to plan and organize the content I want to cover. These were very detailed outlines when I started (see appendix A) but are less detailed now (see appendix B). Do not write out what you plan to say word-for-word.

EXCERPT 1 FROM APPENDIX A: VERY DETAILED OUTLINE EXAMPLE

English 1020 Outline (Zoom)

Introduction

A. Introduce myself
B. Goal: <u>I am going to show you how to utilize library resources to gather sources that are credible and useful.</u>
C. Start at library homepage. Why???
    a. Why not start at Google/Wikipedia? They are great for getting background info, exploring topics, getting keywords. NOT something you want to cite as a source in a college paper.
    b. Library pays for a subscription for you to access these databases, so you need to access them through our website. On or off campus.
D. How to access Course Research Guide (put URL in chat)
E. Cover 3 main library tools (databases) In each database, I'll show you ways to keep your sources organized.
F. Evaluating sources tab: Questions to ask, scholarly vs. popular (scholarly is gold standard)
G. "Choosing a topic" tab:
    ▪ Resources to consult when looking for ideas
    ▪ I'd love for you to share your topics with me as we go along because I can use those in our search examples. (share link in chat and show how to post)

EXCERPT 2 FROM APPENDIX B: LESS DETAILED OUTLINE EXAMPLE

English 1020 Outline

Introduction

A. Mentimeter poll
B. *Goal*: Demonstrate 3 tools for finding sources for your assignments with time for hands-on practice
C. *Topics covered*:
    ▪ How to explore topics & search in library databases
    ▪ Evaluating sources
    ▪ Search strategies/choosing keywords

Start at Library Website

1. Research Guides>ENGL 1020 Guide
2. Evaluating Sources Tab
    ▪ Brief explanation of scholarly vs. popular sources

You will be tempted to read from your script instead of looking at your audience. Instead, bring it with you as a backup in case you need it.

Know Your Content

Familiarize yourself with the assignment your students will be working on and spend a good amount of time navigating the databases and web pages you will be showing. I've found that most faculty are happy to share assignments with me, and I generally reach out to them via email about a week before a class to touch base, ask for the assignment if I don't already have it, and see if they have any questions for me. I prepare search examples specific to each assignment, and I practice walking through them to see how they turn out. Also, try to anticipate what questions you might receive.

Practice, Practice, Practice

While I know this is not groundbreaking advice, I can't emphasize enough how important it is. For me, personally, I feel much more at ease when I come into a class knowing that I have practiced and that I am prepared. It calms my nerves and builds my confidence. I also recommend practicing in the actual space, if possible, to get comfortable and familiarize yourself with the technology, especially if it's your first time in that classroom. It can also be beneficial to routinely have a colleague observe one of your classes and give feedback. Although this is something I have only done once and it can be tricky to schedule during busy times of the semester, I wish I did this more often because I think it's a good practice.

Be Prepared for the Unexpected

No matter how prepared you are, there will be times when things do not go according to plan. So, be flexible and ready to change course if necessary. One thing I've learned from experience is to have handouts ready to go in case of technology issues. Also, be prepared to change your mode of delivery at the drop of a hat. There have been several times I've had to unexpectedly teach a class on Zoom when it was supposed to be in person. Another possibility I've experienced myself is a professor asking you to show a database that you had not planned to cover. Once I was asked to teach a freshman library orientation in a building across campus with only an hour's notice. We normally have our freshmen classes complete a scavenger hunt in the library on iPads, so I had to quickly come up with a different game plan. You'll learn to pivot and make adjustments on the fly. Although these circumstances are not always ideal, prepare yourself mentally for them the best you can.

Be Authentic

Each of us has our own unique teaching personality, and that's perfectly fine. Don't try to mimic someone else. If your personality is naturally quiet and subdued like I am, don't feel like you must reinvent yourself to be boisterous and outgoing in the classroom. If you do that, you'll probably come across as fake. Rather, put forth the effort to be friendly and engaging, but remain true to yourself. Students will connect with you more when you are authentic.

Develop a Teaching Mindset

I do this by taking advantage of professional development opportunities, both at my university and online. This helps me to grow as a teacher and to stay fresh and current. At my university, for example, I completed a faculty fellows program where I wrote a teaching philosophy statement and where I was observed by a colleague. Other things that have helped me develop a teaching mindset are attending library instruction workshops and participating in faculty book groups.

Conclusion

Even if you do all the things I suggest in this chapter, there is no guarantee that any of it can truly prepare you for being a library instructor. In my opinion, what truly helps the most is hands-on experience. To use the analogy of riding a bike, no matter how much I may try to explain to you how to do it, eventually, you just need to hop on the bike and give it a try for yourself. Yes, you'll probably fall a few times. Yes, you'll make mistakes, but you'll learn from those mistakes and you'll make adjustments. It is in these firsthand teaching experiences where true growth and learning will occur.

APPENDIX A:
Very Detailed Outline Example

English 1020 Outline (Zoom)

Introduction

    A.   Introduce myself

    B.   Goal: I am going to show you how to utilize library resources to gather sources that are credible and useful.

    C.   Start at library homepage. Why???

        a.   Why not start at Google/Wikipedia? They are great for getting background info, exploring topics, getting keywords. NOT something you want to cite as a source in a college paper.

        b.   Library pays for a subscription for you to access these databases, so you need to access them through our website. On or off campus.

    D.   How to access Course Research Guide (put URL in chat)

    E.   Cover 3 main library tools (databases) In each database, I'll show you ways to keep your sources organized.

    F.   Evaluating sources tab: Questions to ask, scholarly vs. popular (scholarly is gold standard)

    G.   "Choosing a topic" tab:

        ■   Resources to consult when looking for ideas

        ■   I'd love for you to share your topics with me as we go along because I can use those in our search examples. (share link in chat and show how to post)

First Tool—Opposing Viewpoints

Great place to explore topics, find multiple and diverse points of view on today's issues

    1.   How to browse topic—**Standardized Testing**

    2.   Point out Overview

    3.   Explain different source types. Pay attention to your assignment requirements here.

    4.   Look at Viewpoint articles

    5.   Open article → Tools at top: how to email, download, cite. Very important to cite your sources. Keep a running list of sources on a Word Doc or in citation manager like RefWorks. Citation styles—usually MLA for English classes

    6.   Look at a few examples of other source types

    7.   Can also search by keyword—(ask students to suggest topic via chat or use "air pollution and…")

    8.   Topic finder—discover subtopics—(ask for suggested topic via chat or use air pollution → mental health)

    9.   Questions so far????

Second Tool—JEWL Search (James E. Walker Library)
Great starting point when you know your topic. A JEWL search tells you what books we have, simultaneously searches about 150 article databases. Variety of source types (books, articles, videos, etc.)

Model a search.
1. Break your research topic/question into keywords
2. Enter **engineering and women and challenges**
3. Look over results then explain limiters
   - Limiters on Left → Source types (check assignment requirements) Look at few different source types.
4. Limit to scholarly. (Show examples)
5. Narrow by date, full text

Be flexible with your search terms
1. **AND**—Narrows your search to include records containing all of the words. Ex: nursing and men and challenges
2. However, if you want to **BROADEN** and get more results, then use **OR** to connect terms. Ex: men or males or man or male
3. Try different terms: nursing or nursing career and gender diversity
4. Research is a process! It evolves as you go. Your topic may change as you go.

Evaluate sources for relevance and appropriateness
5. Read the **abstract** before the article. Questions to ask: who is the audience? What is the scope? an overview or highly specific?
6. View Full Text of an Article—How to print, email, cite

Sidenote: Library catalog is best place to search for books.
7. Keyword search for climate change.
8. Accessing print/ebooks

Questions?

Third Tool—Statista
Use Statista to find graphs, charts, data to back up your writing.
1. Sample search on **climate change**
2. Point out types of statistics and reports available
3. View statistic from results list
4. Tools and download options
5. Source information
6. How to view full reports
7. Questions?

Conclusion
A. Briefly go over other Tabs on LibGuide
B. Ask Us feature & Get Help at top

Final Questions??

APPENDIX B
Less Detailed Outline Example

English 1020 Outline

Introduction

    A. Mentimeter poll

    B. *Goal*: Demonstrate 3 tools for finding sources for your assignments with time for hands-on practice

    C. *Topics covered*:

- How to explore topics & search in library databases
- Evaluating sources
- Search strategies/choosing keywords

Start at Library Website

    1. Research Guides>ENGL 1020 Guide

    2. Evaluating Sources Tab

- Brief explanation of scholarly vs. popular sources

First Tool—Opposing Viewpoints

Great place to explore topics

    1. How to browse topics—**plastic waste**

    2. Tools (how to email, download, cite)

    3. Can also search by keyword—human trafficking and…

    4. Topic finder—great place to discover subtopics—Search for Gaming

Student Task #1: **Look up a topic in the topic finder and explore what's available.**

Second Tool—JEWL Search

Great starting point when you know your topic.

Model a search.

    1. Broad topic like **artificial intelligence**, narrow results by adding more keywords (benefits, higher education)

    2. Use database limiters (source type, full text, scholarly, date).

    3. Evaluate the source (look at the abstract)

    4. How to view full text, email, cite, etc

Student Task #2: **Enter your search terms, limit to full text, and 2019-2024.**

Give 2nd Mentimeter poll to demonstrate the importance of keywords.

3rd Tool—Statista

Find graphs, charts, data to back up your writing.

    1. Sample search on **book banning**

    2.   Point out types of stats and reports

    3.   View statistic from results list

    4.   Tools and download options

    5.   Source information

Student Task #3: **Search for your topic in Statista and find a statistic.**

Wrap-Up

    A.   How to Get Research Help

    B.   Questions?

Notes

1.   "Introversion," in *The Gale Encyclopedia of Psychology*, 3rd ed., ed. Jacqueline L. Longe (Farmington Hills, MI: Gale, 2016), 608.

2.   Scott Berkun, *Confessions of a Public Speaker* (Beijing; Sebastopol, CA: O'Reilly, 2010), 4.

3.   Berkun, *Confessions of a Public Speaker*, 4.

4.   Andrew M. Colman, "Imposter Phenomenon," in *A Dictionary of Psychology* (Oxford, UK: Oxford University Press, 2008).

Bibliography

Berkun, Scott. *Confessions of a Public Speaker*. Beijing; Sebastopol, CA: O'Reilly, 2010.

Colman, Andrew M. "Imposter Phenomenon." In *A Dictionary of Psychology*. Oxford, UK: Oxford University Press, 2008.

"Introversion." In *The Gale Encyclopedia of Psychology*, 3rd ed., edited by Jacqueline L. Longe, 608. Vol. 1. Farmington Hills, MI: Gale, 2016.

CHAPTER 24

(Eventually) Learning to Look Before I Leap:
Discovering Instructional Design Mid-Career

Nicole Westerdahl

LEARNING OUTCOMES

Readers will be able to

- summarize the benefits of instructional training for both traditional instruction and library work not typically identified as instruction;
- recognize the importance of communities of practice and the input of others in their instructional development; and
- plan how to engage in instructional development in their professional setting.

Introduction

Until recently, I was one of the many academic librarians who had received no instructional training,[1] either in graduate school or on the job. I worked as a credentialed librarian in an academic library for eleven years before pursuing such training. Now that I've learned about instructional design, it is clear to me that this training is relevant for all librarians, regardless of our teaching responsibilities, as "instructional roles for librarians are found across library and librarian categories"[2] and job functions.

In this chapter, I reflect on the reasons for this gap, which range from the institutional to the personal, and explore the negative impact of the absence of instructional training on my early career work. In early 2022, I transitioned into a new academic librarian position with a new institution, and my instructional training was just beginning. I will share the ways in which I am pursuing this training within my new institutional context, its positive impact on my mid-career work, and how it will inform my work moving forward.

How It Started

The gap in my instructional training began with my library and information science (LIS) graduate education. I did not have any kind of background in teaching, and while my LIS program offered courses in instruction, these were not required for the MSLIS degree, and instructional training was not otherwise incorporated into the core curriculum. When I entered library school, I was not and had never been interested in teaching. I planned to enter technical services, preferably in special collections or archives, and saw no reason to use my limited elective credits on a topic I wasn't interested in and considered irrelevant to my career plans. Many electives were only offered once every two years, further limiting my options: in a two-year program, this meant I had only one chance to take several of the courses I was interested in. Additionally, I received no guidance from my advisor on how instructional training could help me with non-teaching functions, nor were these benefits mentioned in classes or in assigned readings, further minimizing the importance of these electives. Financial limitations further prevented me from pursuing instructional classes, even if I had been aware of the wider benefits across library roles. I could have taken extra credits beyond what was required, but I was already working three part-time jobs and reliant on student loans, and I never entertained the idea of spending extra money and time on credits I didn't need to graduate.

My career plans changed as I progressed through the MSLIS program and took on more part-time work in libraries. I began to focus more on pursuing public-facing roles in special collections or academic libraries, and that was when I realized that I might need to teach. I was nearing the end of my degree program, and the instructional electives that semester were more advanced than I was ready for, but I still needed to complete a required internship, so I started looking for internship opportunities that included teaching. Finding any such internship proved more difficult than I expected in my region: most of the internships were offered in public libraries and were not explicitly framed as including instructional opportunities, and at the time my graduate alma mater's libraries offered few internship opportunities to LIS students. I finally secured an internship at a different academic institution, but when I looked at my schedule, juggling full-time classes and multiple part-time jobs, I didn't see a way to accommodate the extra commuting time to the internship site. I very much needed the money from my part-time work for rent, utilities, and food, and while I needed an internship to graduate, I didn't need this particular internship—and so I accepted a different one, focusing on data management, which was more conveniently located and easier to schedule around my existing commitments.

After earning my MSLIS degree, I worked in public services for an academic library's special collections and archives department, first as a supervisor and then as a librarian. A combination of personal intention and structural omission contributed to a continued lack of engagement with instructional training during the eleven years I worked at this institution. While instruction was included in my job description and was part of my work, especially in the librarian role, my primary job duties were in public services, supervision, and management. Limited professional development funding required me to prioritize training opportunities, pursuing some and neglecting others. I was personally most interested in, and encouraged at a departmental level to pursue, professional development in these primary job areas, but not in instruction, even though instruction was relevant to these aspects of my work as well as my teaching. The absence of departmental and institutional prioritization of instructional training also contributed to my decision not to pursue these learning opportunities. Librarians at this institution were classified as staff, not faculty, and there was no explicit expectation of continuing improvement and education in teaching. Instructional skills were also not mentioned in my yearly performance evaluations, and my teaching was never observed by my peers or supervisors, nor was feedback about my teaching ever solicited from instructors or students. My library did offer monthly roundtables for instructors, but with limited work time and no encouragement to participate, I only rarely attended.

The Pitfalls of Diving Right In

While I didn't notice it at the time, this absence of instructional training negatively impacted my early career work. I was able to pick up some basic teaching skills on the job, but looking back, my instructional practices lacked the intentionality and clarity instructional design provides. I quickly learned that planning and preparation were necessary for successful instruction, but I wasn't familiar with lesson plans or learning objectives. Situated as I was in special collections and archives, I interpreted most of the act of preparation for a class to mean selecting appropriate collection materials to display during the session. Depending on the specific materials and the class subject, I might also review some particular component of the collection materials themselves or complete some brief readings in advance to brush up on a topic. I would also have a general idea of the broad topics I would cover and the rough order I would address them, but I rarely recorded that information and often didn't even bring notes to refer to while teaching. Unsurprisingly, my limited preparation affected my instructional delivery. Without a lesson plan to follow, I sometimes forgot to cover things or addressed them out of logical order, resulting in an inconsistent and sometimes confusing experience for the students. I also relied heavily on lecture, only inviting the students to review and interact with the materials after I had finished speaking. I didn't understand that more active, engaged learning activities would benefit the students, and I certainly didn't dedicate the necessary preparation time to plan any such activities. I also didn't complete any formal assessment of my instructional work. I might have a quick chat with the requesting instructor afterward, but that was the most substantial feedback I sought or received. I did notice whether or not students generally seemed to be paying attention during the session, but of course they were typically interested: most people are curious when presented with an illuminated manuscript or a cuneiform tablet for the first time! Since I didn't know how to assess my instruction, I also didn't really know how to improve it. All of these factors limited my ability to engage students in learning in the already intimidating special collections and archives setting.

As mentioned before, instruction wasn't a primary job duty for me at this institution, but my lack of instructional training also negatively impacted my primary duties in public services and supervision. Public services combined aspects of both reference and circulation roles, and, as Turner points out, librarians in these roles also teach as part of their day-to-day work, "[instructing] patrons on how to use resources on a one-to-one or one-to-many basis … [and teaching] visitors how to check out, renew, and return materials."[3] I regularly oriented researchers to what a special collections and archives department is; explained department and reading room policies; demonstrated how to search for, identify, and request materials; provided guidance on topic and research strategy development using primary sources; and showed visitors how to safely handle materials. In other words, I taught our researchers all of these things. As a supervisor, I often trained employees, whether onboarding new hires or teaching new skills and tools to existing employees. While I was successful in my public services and supervisory duties, instructional training could have improved my work. Incorporating informal formative assessment checkpoints into my public services work, such as confirming understanding and walking them through hands-on handling practice, would have allowed me to better respond to researchers' individual needs and to set them up for success working with primary source materials. Defining specific learning objectives would have streamlined and focused onboarding and supported new hires in identifying and retaining the most necessary information.

My lack of instructional training also substantially impacted my communication with my colleagues. I see now that I had unconsciously incorporated aspects of backward design and Universal Design for Learning into my reference work, but I lacked the vocabulary to articulate these practices. This limited my ability to discuss them within communities of practice and effectively transfer that knowledge, both when training employees and within the profession more broadly.

Learning to Look Before I Leap

After eleven years working in an academic library with no instructional training, I transitioned into a new role with a different institution in early 2022. Instruction was now a primary duty and even part of my job title, and I suddenly realized how little instructional preparation I'd received. Thankfully, instructional training and assessment are supported at the departmental and institutional levels in my new role. Librarians are classified as faculty, which means I have more flexibility to pursue professional development as I choose. Faculty also routinely receive information about, and are eligible to participate in, instruction-focused training opportunities and events on campus and online—offerings I was often excluded from in my previous staff role. Additionally, instruction is an explicitly shared librarian responsibility regardless of librarians' functional positions. This institution prioritizes instructional practice and training, and a program of both informal and formal observation and assessment of librarian teaching is in place. I was immediately welcomed into a "teaching triangle," small communities of practice among our librarians that provide informal observation of teaching and feedback in advance of the formal observation incorporated as part of our performance reviews. I was also invited to observe other librarians' class sessions outside of my teaching triangle, exposing me to a variety of instructional techniques and styles.

Based on her own positive experience, one of my new librarian colleagues suggested I consider participating in a small cohort at our institution who were about to complete CornellX's Teaching & Learning in the Diverse Classroom MOOC[4] together through our institution's Center for Excellence in Learning and Teaching (CELT). The course began just the week after I started, but CELT accepted my application to participate, and I joined the cohort right away. The MOOC course itself was valuable, especially as my introduction to instructional training, walking me through learning about my new institutional context and our students and introducing me to things like developing learning objectives and outcomes; representing students' interests, needs, and existing and prior knowledge in instructional content; active learning; and handling uncomfortable classroom discussions. Even more valuable was the opportunity to participate in the cohort, connecting and learning with faculty from different areas across the institution. The MOOC was designed with semester-long courses in mind and included many recommendations that were not obviously applicable to the one-shot instruction sessions I typically teach. The members of my cohort brainstormed with me on ways to incorporate course takeaways into my own practice. They also helped me understand concepts that were new to me and launched me into participating in an even broader community of instructional practice within my institution.

I could also pursue professional development opportunities soon after I arrived at my new institution. I had been introduced to instructional training and design through the MOOC, and now I understood just how big of an educational gap I had in that area. I wanted to pursue further training in library-specific instruction, so I turned to Library Juice Academy,[5] through which I had previously taken several courses on other subjects. I enrolled in Inclusive Instructional Design[6] and Crash Course in Assessing Library Instruction.[7] In Inclusive Instructional Design, I learned various instructional design models, Universal Design for Learning and backward design, active learning, accessible practices, community-building in the classroom, and the importance of reflective and critical assessment. I especially benefited from some of the handouts provided by my instructors, Kristina Clement and Samantha Peter: their handouts with Universal Design for Learning suggestions specifically for one-shot library instruction sessions helped me make connections to my own practice that I otherwise could not have, and the lesson plan template they provided in support of our final course assignment has guided my planning ever since. In Crash Course in Assessing Library Instruction, I learned about assessment types and purposes; about formative and summative assessments and various methods for conducting both, including how activities can double as both active learning opportunities and assessments; how to evaluate completed worksheets; how to interpret data gathered using those assessments; and how to use that understanding to inform decisions and iterate moving forward. In both Library Juice Academy courses, assignments helped me apply these concepts to relevant, concrete examples and practice new skills. I also benefited from the impromptu community of practice fostered by the students on the discussion boards in both courses. The diversity of experiences and viewpoints combined with the ability to ask each other questions and brainstorm solutions was hugely impactful.

How It's Going

I've just completed my first full semester at my new institution, and I have been regularly teaching one-shot library instruction sessions. Instructional design training has had a significant impact on my teaching practice. A year ago, I didn't know what a lesson plan was, and now I've written (and used) eight. Intentional lesson plan design based on an achievable number of reasonable, relevant learning objectives has significantly focused my instruction sessions and helps me maintain a logical order as I teach. While lectures and demonstrations are still a part of my instruction practice, they are no longer the only tool: I provide clarity on the learning objectives and general plan for the session at the beginning; I ask more questions and invite student input throughout my sessions; I've introduced Google Jamboard as an engagement option for students who would prefer to interact digitally or anonymously rather than speaking in class; I pause frequently to invite student questions and input; I explore multiple different ways to complete tasks; I explicitly relate lessons to students' lives, coursework, and careers; and I provide hands-on activities and practice—I've even developed two worksheet assignments myself! All of these practices have improved my ability to engage students and help them learn.

I also prioritize assessment as an essential component of my instructional practice. I use ACRL Project Outcome[8] surveys to conduct Kirkpatrick level one assessments, which measure "learner reaction"[9] to the instruction session and allow me to assess student confidence in completing library research via both quantitative and qualitative survey questions. While I have not regularly incorporated any formal Kirkpatrick level two assessments, which measure "the knowledge and skills learners have acquired as a result of [instruction],"[10] I typically informally assess learning by observing the class during hands-on activities: are students generally able to complete the activities? What kinds of questions are they asking while they work? Are they able to help each other and explain concepts? Where are they getting stuck? I also engage in critical reflective practice, "intentional and analytic" self-examination and self-evaluation in which instructors "apply what we learn from our reflection to inform our practice" and focus on "uncovering the assumptions and biases that influence our teaching and surfacing the politics and power dynamics of the classroom."[11] I write a summary of my observations and interactions and reflect on my own behaviors, documenting what I felt was successful and unsuccessful. I compile this information after each class session, review the data for patterns, and record specifics of concrete things I will continue doing and concrete things I will change, which I then incorporate into my instruction moving forward. Ongoing assessment makes my instruction more intentional, more inclusive, more equitable, and more responsive.

Instructional training has also improved my non-teaching work. I now integrate more flexibility into my reference transactions, inviting student input about how they prefer to learn. For example, if a student isn't sure how to locate a book in our stacks using Library of Congress call numbers, I ask them how they would prefer to learn: do they want me to explain it and then they try to locate the book on their own? Do they want me to accompany them to the stacks and lead them through the process? Do they want me to accompany them to the stacks while they take the lead? I also incorporate regular checkpoints into each transaction, where I pause to understand the student's confidence level and whether they are receiving the particular assistance they want and need. I also use lesson planning to prepare for scheduled research consultations and staff training sessions, and I share information about the learning objectives and general plan for the consultation or training when they start.

Conclusion

I am committed to continuing my instructional training. I will pursue more formal educational opportunities as they arise and, in the meantime, I continue to learn by reading books and journals and participating in listservs and ALA Connect[12] communities. I also regularly participate in communities of practice, both within my library/institution and externally through groups such as the State University of New York Librarians Association Information Literacy Committee.[13] Now that I've experienced how beneficial instructional training can be for all aspects of my work, I will definitely not neglect it again.

I encourage every librarian to participate in instructional professional development, even if you aren't interested in instruction or aren't aware of what you don't know. Librarians in all roles can benefit from instructional training: in addition to strengthening your teaching, you can also improve the effectiveness of your circulation and reference interactions, your research consultations, your handouts and digital learning objects, and your employee onboarding and training. If you aren't sure how to get started, I recommend talking to people: ask your library colleagues, peers in professional organizations, and faculty and instructors at your institution about how they learn teaching skills and what instructional design concepts they find most helpful. If you can, invite a colleague to observe your teaching and provide feedback; this is extremely useful for identifying challenges and gaps you cannot identify yourself. Surveying library users and colleagues (e.g., students attending classes, users at the circulation and reference desks, and training session participants) is another excellent way to help you find areas for improvement. Finally, remember that instructional training and development is an ongoing journey, so keep those conversations going!

Notes

1.   Andrea Baer, "Academic Librarians' Development as Teachers: A Survey on Changes in Pedagogical Roles, Approaches, and Perspectives," *Journal of Information Literacy* 15, no. 1 (2021): 27.
2.   Jennifer Turner, "Instructional Design: Skills to Benefit the Library Profession," *portal: Libraries and the Academy* 16, no. 3 (2016): 478.
3.   Turner, "Instructional Design," 478.

4.   CornellX, "Teaching & Learning in the Diverse Classroom," edX, https://www.edx.org/course/teaching-learning-in-the-diverse-classroom.
5.   Library Juice Academy, https://libraryjuiceacademy.com/.
6.   "Inclusive Instructional Design," Library Juice Academy, https://libraryjuiceacademy.com/shop/course/258-inclusive-instructional-design/.
7.   This course is not currently available.
8.   ACRL Project Outcome, https://acrl.projectoutcome.org/.
9.   Dominique Turnbow and Annie Zeidman-Karpinski, "Don't Use a Hammer When You Need a Screwdriver: How to Use the Right Tools to Create Assessment That Matters," *Communications in Information Literacy* 10, no. 2 (2016): 149.
10.   Turnbow and Zeidman-Karpinski, "Don't Use a Hammer," 151.
11.   Laura Saunders and Melissa A. Wong, "Practicing Reflective Teaching," in *Instruction in Libraries and Information Centers* (Urbana, IL: Windsor & Downs Press, 2020), https://iopn.library.illinois.edu/pressbooks/instructioninlibraries/chapter/practicing-reflective-teaching/.
12.   ALA Connect, https://connect.ala.org/. ALA membership and ALA Connect registration required.
13.   SUNYLA Information Literacy Committee, https://sunyla.org/informationliteracy/.

Bibliography

ALA Connect. https://connect.ala.org/.

Association of College and Research Libraries. ACRL Project Outcome. https://acrl.projectoutcome.org/.

Baer, Andrea. "Academic Librarians' Development as Teachers: A Survey on Changes in Pedagogical Roles, Approaches, and Perspectives." *Journal of Information Literacy* 15, no. 1 (2021): 26–53.

CornellX. "Teaching & Learning in the Diverse Classroom." edX. https://www.edx.org/course/teaching-learning-in-the-diverse-classroom.

Library Juice Academy. https://libraryjuiceacademy.com/.

———. "Inclusive Instructional Design." https://libraryjuiceacademy.com/shop/course/258-inclusive-instructional-design/.

Saunders, Laura, and Melissa A. Wong. "Practicing Reflective Teaching." In *Instruction in Libraries and Information Centers*. Urbana, IL: Windsor & Downs Press, 2020. https://iopn.library.illinois.edu/pressbooks/instructioninlibraries/chapter/practicing-reflective-teaching/.

SUNYLA Information Literacy Committee. https://sunyla.org/informationliteracy/.

Turnbow, Dominique, and Annie Zeidman-Karpinski. "Don't Use a Hammer When You Need a Screwdriver: How to Use the Right Tools to Create Assessment That Matters." *Communication in Information Literacy* 10, no. 2 (2016): 143–62.

Turner, Jennifer. "Instructional Design: Skills to Benefit the Library Profession." *portal: Libraries and the Academy* 16, no. 3 (2016): 477–89.

CHAPTER 25

Learning from Each Other:

Peer Observation for On-the-Job Library Instructor Development

Alexandra Mitchell

LEARNING OUTCOMES

Readers will be able to

- reflect on the different paths librarians take to become instructors;
- gain insight into the challenges of a transition between classroom teacher and information literacy instructor; and
- describe how instructors can be supported through communities of practice.

Sometimes when I'm standing at the front of a classroom, I wonder how I ended up there. You can find yourself in the right place, even though it might be somewhere other than where you intended. I went through student teaching and the teacher education program as an undergraduate, which was an intensive, multi-semester experience. Student teaching, and subsequently substitute teaching, were largely unpleasant experiences for me. I went to grad school to flee the world of K-12 and had no intention of teaching regularly again. I wanted to become an archivist, and my first job was doing cataloging and archives-related

345

work. I know I'm not the only one who has taken a long and winding road to information literacy instruction. I have found, through both experience and conversation, that not everyone who finds themselves in library instruction graduated from library school with the goal to teach. I did not take a single graduate-level course on information literacy, nor did I truly understand what teaching looks like in libraries. For many years, I wondered if I had wasted time by taking so many education classes and going through some occasionally painful student teaching experiences. Over a decade later, these experiences did prove to be beneficial.

While I understood the fundamentals of teaching and running a classroom, I did not really comprehend exactly what I was getting myself into with a shift to library instruction. I knew that I needed to see what an instruction environment with limited time and access to students looked like. I could create a lesson plan, understood Bloom's taxonomy and the basics of pedagogy and learning, and could structure lessons to reinforce learning and build on concepts over the course of the semester, but this was different. While the first two helped with the transition, since they are basically Education 101, librarians often only see students once. Navigating how to get students the information they needed in a short period of time in addition to having them practice their skills was the first challenge that I had to wrap my head around in order to be able to even start to create a successful lesson plan. The next was to understand the ACRL *Framework for Information Literacy for Higher Education* as this was new to me. I knew I needed the language to be able to talk about the information literacy skills our students need not just with other librarians but with faculty as well. An education background is helpful and gives you a good foundation, and I think it is ultimately a great tool if you have it, but when you transition to information literacy instruction there are still some knowledge and experience gaps to explore and solve regardless of where you are coming from.

Academic librarians find themselves teaching in many different contexts, whether or not they have any formal instruction training. There is no one-size-fits-all approach to training librarians to teach once they are out of school and working as librarians. Ideally, I think the first semester of a new library instructor's job would be spent observing, co-teaching, reading, and learning, but that is likely impractical for the immediate needs of most institutions. Even once you are no longer a brand-new instruction librarian, there are benefits to having time to learn about the institution and the services and resources offered. Time to explore would give the librarian time to adjust to their new role, but academic libraries do not always have the luxury of time when there are classes well into the double digits that need a librarian to teach them. If there are only a few teaching librarians, then you are more likely to find yourself thrown straight in, whereas if you are one of twenty or so people who have instruction responsibilities, you might find that you have the opportunity to ease into the classroom and learn the culture of the university and department, though that is not a guarantee. I've worked for both a campus of 2,000 and a campus of 70,000+, so I've seen a range of needs, resources, and approaches. I have a somewhat idealistic view of how training could or should work, so I acknowledge that my thoughts on this may not be achievable in every circumstance.

I do believe that teaching is most effectively learned by actually doing. You can read all the theory in the world, and theory is knowledge we all need, but applying it is a more difficult task. I'm grateful for the knowledge and theory I gained through my undergraduate coursework, but I think opportunities for observation and hands-on learning have had the greatest impact on me as a teacher and allowed me to see some of that theory applied by other instructors. As a student teacher, we did a lot of observing before we were allowed to teach a class ourselves. Observation allows you to explore other teaching styles, how different instructors approach situations, and how they engage students. What works for one instructor, while interesting and effective, may not be the best path for another due to their teaching style, preferences, or personality. There is a lot of room to borrow and learn from each other. You can take what you've learned from others and twist it to be your own. Observation is the technique that I have found most useful regardless of my level of experience.

When I transitioned from my cataloging and special collections role over to instruction, I had half of the spring semester and a full summer to figure out what I was doing. I had not heard of the ACRL Framework before this transition, so I spent a lot of time reading and participating in different webinars. While I could explain classroom management, engaging students, creating a lesson plan, and learning outcomes to anyone, I had no idea what it really meant to teach a one-shot. These were students I would see once, maybe twice if I was lucky. What does it mean to walk into a classroom as a guest and then walk out to likely never see them again? Teaching a one-shot is also different in that you're walking into the middle of the conversation. The students have an assignment they need to complete, so you have to figure out what they already know and where you need to start. That doesn't even begin to touch on understanding the ACRL Framework and how to adjust lessons and learning outcomes to fit into one fifty- to seventy-five-minute session. So yes, I understood some of the foundational knowledge when it comes to teaching, but I can't say I fully understood how to apply it to my current context.

During this transition period, I was able to observe one instructor a few times before the spring semester ended. This was a very informal arrangement. I just sat in the back of the class, watched, took notes, and asked questions later. I saw maybe two or three classes, but I feel like this did make a great difference in my comfort level when I started picking up instruction in the fall. I do not know that I would have had a solid idea of where to start a one-shot if I had not been able to observe another librarian. During that first semester, I largely used borrowed knowledge from my observations. As time went on, I developed my own lessons and added in activities I created. Our circle of available instructors was small, though. Two regular instructors, to be exact. We were a small institution with only a handful of librarians. I cannot say that I remember a whole lot about this semester. I know I taught a variety of subjects and at different times felt like I had no idea what I was doing, but the teaching from that first semester is truly a blur. I distinctly remember thinking in later semesters that it was much easier the second time around.

After almost five years at my first job, close to three of those in instruction, I ended up taking a job at the main campus of Texas A&M University. I went from a branch campus where I knew many of the students to a truly gigantic school. On a smaller campus, I would often see students again, either in another class or around campus and the library, so I did get to know some students over time. As a First Year Experience librarian, I saw first-year students in a variety of contexts. There are 12,000 first-year students alone. The change in resources and the sheer number of people was somewhat overwhelming. Teaching did not feel quite as scary this time. I had done this before. I had opportunities to observe but found myself in the classroom not long after starting. I clearly remember my first class at Texas A&M, though. It was an English Composition class I taught at eight a.m. about two and a half weeks after I started. While I had some familiarity with the subject and had taught some of the English Composition classes at my previous university, I also was still trying to figure out what databases we had and what our services were. I still had a lot to learn. I had been pretty confident when I left my last job, but walking into a new teaching environment managed to set off my nerves again, largely from fear that I would not be able to answer their questions about services. In the first-year experience classes, I could not pad the lesson with explanation and more detail because I didn't know all of it yet! I spent a lot of time hoping students would not ask questions and frantically doing some more research and asking questions in my free time, so I at least looked like I knew what I was talking about when I was teaching. I laugh at this a little bit now because I can more or less do these classes in my sleep at this point. I now run short on time rather than frantically trying to find additional things they need to know.

In my new job, I was given the option to join the Library Instruction Training Peers (LIT Peers) program that had been created in the libraries specifically for instruction librarians. LIT Peers was twofold. It involved optional gatherings a few times a semester where instruction librarians could discuss specific topics, such as educational technology they had experience with, which really helped create a community of practice in the library. Through LIT Peers, library instructors also had the option of being paired with another instructor to work together to improve our teaching through observation and discussion. The director of Learning and Outreach created these pairings. As a new instructor at the university, I was paired with someone with years of experience. In some pairs, both people had long-term experience while others were new/experienced librarian pairs. The partner would be someone from a different area and never someone that you directly reported to, to take out some of that feeling of being "observed" by your supervisor.

At the first kick-off meeting of the semester, everyone was given a framework for observation, constructive feedback, and discussion. The goal was to make this relationship beneficial to the instructors rather than making them feel judged. Constructive feedback was emphasized with instructors also voicing what areas they would like feedback in. This is also where we discussed emphasizing good things as well as suggestions that the instructor could try in areas where they wanted feedback. We were encouraged to meet before we observed each other to discuss what areas where we would like feedback and how we wanted to communicate. We also had a guiding document to follow during the observation where we noted what areas our partner was interested in receiving feedback, so we had notes to follow when it came time to observe. After both partners observed each other, they met to discuss. Part of why this felt so supportive is that we were both able to express our interests and communicate with each other rather than creating an odd, one-sided power dynamic that you so often get in formal observation environments. I will also give credit to my fantastic partner for welcoming me and supporting me when I expressed a bit of hesitation due to my previous student teaching observation experiences, both good and bad. I found value in the open discussion we were able to have. Neither of us was there to judge the other.

This experience did remind me a bit of my student teaching, but in a way not at all because it was a much more casual environment. Unlike some of my student teaching experiences where my grade was riding on not only my performance but also the opinion and preferences of the observer, we were just there to learn and help each other. I will admit to being hesitant to participate in this because of some of my student-teaching experiences. Some of my instructors and mentors were great at constructive feedback, but all it takes is one person who does not know how to give constructive advice to demoralize someone new to teaching. This was also a culture that felt, as the newcomer, like it had been deliberately built to be supportive. Building a culture is difficult, but having that understood set of values that everyone supports contributes to making new participants feel welcome. I had some concerns going into this experience but found the program well-designed.

I did end up truly enjoying the experience, including observing my partner and seeing their interactions with students and the success of their lesson. I liked having the opportunity to ask my partner questions about what they observed and being open about skills and areas I thought were struggles for me. What would they have changed about this specific activity? This execution didn't feel great to me. What did you see from the students? Sometimes the things that bother me the most about the lesson—the things that I dwell on later—go completely unnoticed by both the students and anyone observing. I think reflection on our teaching is important and is how we grow, whether that's through self-reflection or through discussion with others. Self-reflection is something I try to do, particularly when I'm experimenting with a new lesson. It is important to figure out what works well and what might need some tweaks to make a better and more impactful lesson for the students and what did or did not work for me as an instructor. While I was apprehensive about LIT Peers initially, I found it to be an experience that was thoughtfully created to foster a supportive environment for us to grow as instructors, and I think many of us can benefit from this type of casual observation relationship with our fellow library instructors. It has to be constructed well, though, with guidance in constructive criticism and productive conversation and with the opportunity for instructors to steer the conversation on where they would like feedback and help.

As a librarian, observation opened a lot of opportunities and gave me a different perspective. Sometimes, observation also came in a much less formal environment, such as co-teaching, where you are working together but also learning from each other. I have been able to see how different instructors interacted with students before and during class and built trust with them. We see students once, maybe twice. It is a very different type of relationship with students. Hearing others talk about our services was also the most efficient way for me to learn about them. Observation allowed me to watch people run different activities. Even instructors who did the same activities executed them differently, so it was interesting to see how one tweak to an activity engaged students differently. I had been running Citation Relay (an idea I borrowed from a presentation by the University of Northern Colorado) for a couple of semesters in an English Composition class but could not figure out how to fix the point where the students always got bogged down. I watched another instructor who also taught Citation Relay and how they had fixed the pinch point that I couldn't quite work out. I borrowed that change when I taught citations in the future and have tweaked it in other ways since then. The activity now works much better than the first time I tried to figure it out on my own. I've also had the chance to see instructors try different activities and lessons that I had not done myself but wanted to try, so it opened the possibilities I had to choose from when teaching. It makes a difference when you can see activities in person rather than just reading about them.

Conclusion

Observation and the opportunity to interact with other instructors, whether informally through asking to observe other librarians or co-teaching or formally through communities of practice like LIT Peers, has shaped my approach to teaching, and I think it can be beneficial to all of us regardless of years of experience and background. I know creating a program for observation, reflection, and feedback is not practical for everyone, sometimes based on numbers alone. I would encourage instruction programs, regardless of the size of the institution, to look for opportunities to share with their colleagues because there is so much that we can learn from each other. If you are a librarian at a small institution, are the lone instructor, or have other obstacles, this is more of a challenge. There may be opportunities to contact other librarians and libraries in the area to see if you can work together to offer workshops, observation, or teaching conversations. This could be a fantastic opportunity to learn from librarians of all types in your area and get a different perspective. If your campus has a Center for Teaching Excellence, or something similar, that provides additional training and workshops for instructors, ask if you can attend the workshops. Better yet, propose some yourself if you're looking for some of the educational theory and application side of things. If you have a limited number of people, you may have to think outside of your own institution, but there can still be opportunities to learn from the librarians in your community.

If you've suddenly and surprisingly found yourself in the classroom, you are not alone. Plenty of us have taken a circuitous route to instruction. Your background is not ultimately the thing that will make or break you. Was my teaching background incredibly helpful to me because I was able to jump into a shared understanding of the vocabulary and theories around teaching? Yes, and I will always appreciate and acknowledge that my background did make my transition into library instruction easier. If this is new to you, though, remember that there are fantastic library instructors out there who do not have an education degree. I would guess that most do not. If the first time (or semester/year) you teach feels difficult, that's because it is! Teaching is hard, but it does get easier and more intuitive as you go along. As you can, take the time to learn from others. Reflect on the gaps in your knowledge you may want to fill or where you would benefit from a refresher or new concepts even after years of teaching. And, most of all, learn from your peers. Ask to attend some of their instruction sessions to learn from them or create a community of practice at your own institution or with your community of librarians in the area. Librarians all come from a variety of backgrounds and experiences, and we each bring our unique perspective to the classroom. We have so much that we can learn from each other regardless of how experienced we are.

CHAPTER 26

Peer Observation and its Discontents:

Using Autotheory to Argue for Focused, Community-Centered Instruction Training

Russel Peterson

LEARNING OUTCOMES

Readers will be able to

- define the concept of autotheory and describe how it functions in academic scholarship;
- analyze the emergence and trajectory of LIS scholarship on peer observation of teaching; and
- evaluate the benefits and drawbacks of peer observation as a form of instructor training.

Introduction

We train librarians because we care. When a new librarian is in the classroom, we want them to succeed. Whether it is for that individual librarian's development or the instructional reputation of the library, all parties benefit from a program that harnesses a person's teaching abilities in order to meet specific learning objectives. How much guidance we provide, and the effort we put into that guidance, demonstrates what we prioritize.

I have often marveled at how little preparation is given to my friends who are teaching assistants in graduate school. One of these friends was completing a master's degree in biology, and he told me that his instruction training was more "baptism by fire" than thoughtful discussions on the application of pedagogy. Yet, he spent hours of class time with undergraduate students in large, lecture-driven classes, regardless of whether he knew the difference between constructivism and behaviorism. As long as these students were presented with the material, that is all that mattered. Whether they retained that information was a problem for the upper-level instructors to sort out.

Through these discussions with my friend, I concluded that effective teaching was not that high of a priority for this Biology department. The presence of care, or lack thereof, is the primary indicator of whether something receives time, attention, and consideration. The fact that we train new librarians in instruction, despite how little time most of us have with students, demonstrates our regard. The extent of that regard, however, depends on how we train new librarians and the guidelines we put in place.

This chapter is a personal reflection on my own instruction training and the level of regard afforded to me as I began my first job as an academic librarian. As I looked back on the first few months in that role, I realized that peer observation was the key method in which I was trained. As a necessary rite of passage for many fields, observation is a multi-step, collaborative learning process and, according to Graham Martin and Jeremy Double, a metacognitive practice. Martin and Double argue that "through analyzing and discussing the performance of others it is possible to attain otherwise largely inaccessible levels of self-awareness."[1] Observing my colleagues—studying them and taking cues from them—and discussing my observations afterward irrevocably shaped how I approached teaching during this initial phase of my career.

Nearly five years later, I cannot help but feel that I missed some core element during this training. I often felt like I was flailing around in those early days, overwhelmed by the sheer demand for instruction. Although I am far more confident in my abilities today, I often wonder if my training set me up for success. Did the peer observation actually help me? Or was the preparation not enough for the challenges I encountered in instruction? This emptiness, or persistent feeling of lack, is what drove me to incorporate theory and scholarship in my recollections. As bell hooks once said, "I came to theory because I was hurting."[2] As I looked back to recover what was missing, I turned to the literature on peer observation in libraries to make sense of that time. This fusion of reflection and scholarship is my own interpretation of autotheory, the space where "the location of healing"[3] is found and "no gap exists between theory and practice."[4]

What is Autotheory?

The term "autotheory" has exploded in popularity in academic circles in recent years, especially following the publication of Maggie Nelson's *The Argonauts*, a genre-bending work that blends autobiography with critical theory, queer theory, and art criticism.

Nelson attributed her own usage of the word "autotheory" to the experimental work of Paul Preciado's *Testo Junkie*. However, autotheory as a genre is notoriously difficult to circumscribe, as its definitional contours are more fluid than fixed. The scholar Robyn Wiegman underscores this fluidity when cautioning against using Nelson's work as a sole point of reference, stating that "other experiments in self-narration that now travel under the moniker of autotheory have significantly different aesthetic approaches and theoretical dimensions."[5] Other recent works that have been categorized under the autotheory genre include Christina Sharpe's *In the Wake: On Blackness and Being* and Emma Lieber's *The Writing Cure*. While autotheory has been a great source of analysis and debate among literature scholars and critics, it has not yet received the same level of engagement from LIS scholars.

I attempt to bridge this gap by weaving my experiences with peer observation as an instruction training method with LIS scholarship that views observations as a tool of formative and summative assessment. In this attempt, I eschew the autotheoretical convention of what Leila Nadir calls "trading in the stock market of names."[6] Instead of Rosseau, Foucault, or Butler directly influencing my reflections, it is the LIS scholars who have studied and analyzed peer observation in the context of library instruction. By adopting this posture, I inhabit "a space that is both analytic and personal"[7] when engaging with an aspect of library instruction training that I view as so foundational.

Taking Notes

When I started my first academic library job, I did not have much instruction experience, but my colleagues were nonetheless supportive. Rather than throwing me in front of a classroom right away, they invited me to attend their instruction sessions and observe. Sometimes my colleagues would share their lesson plan or learning objectives for the session ahead of time, but often the only information I was given was the course name and the room number. Each time I would sit in the back of the classroom and write down what I noticed: the hands-on activities, the databases that were covered, and the techniques or gestures that were used to grab and hold attention.

I remember one of my colleagues started her presentation for a first-year writing course by asking if anyone had used a public library or a school library before they came to college. She then explained what an academic librarian does in comparison and stressed to students that they should never feel like it is a burden to come to us for help if they need it, reassuring them that assisting students is "the best part of our jobs." I found this framing to be deeply affecting, as I saw library anxiety to be a key reason students might not reach out for assistance, so I wrote down this quote in my notes and I use this very framing when introducing myself to students to this day.

Other notes I wrote down were less useful, especially if they pertained to the content of the instruction session. I might have found it personally useful to record the bibliographic features that RefWorks provides at that given moment, but it does not give me much to say about the delivery of instruction. This jumbled notetaking, which sometimes provided insight for self-development or peer feedback, reflected a lack of purpose. What exactly was guiding my observation process? Looking to the LIS literature, it seems that most academic libraries that have implemented a peer review of teaching (PROT) program have provided some form of guidance for librarians tasked with observing other librarians. Cheryl Middleton, in describing a PROT program at Oregon State University Libraries, references a checklist that participants were asked to adhere to in the session. She notes, "Reviewers were asked to pay particular attention to the instructor's presentation skills, clarity of presentation, the class content, the instructor's relationship with the participants/students and, if appropriate, the instructor's relationship with the classroom instructor."[8]

By establishing areas of focus for an observer, Middleton is setting the parameters for the insight that the observer might retain and the feedback the observer might deliver. In their list of best practices for peer review of teaching, Jaena Alabi and William Weare, Jr. specifically mention having certain areas of teaching to focus on in order to give "targeted feedback."[9] Caroline Sinkinson stipulates that participants in a peer observation pilot program at the University of Colorado at Boulder determined their own areas of focus rather than an "[imposed] set of criteria for observation."[10]

Whether it is a formal list of criteria, or a pedagogical area of focus selected by the instructor, having a set of guidelines for notetaking is beneficial for both the observer and the observed. Had I been given an area of focus to pay attention to during my observations, I would have been able to gain more perspective on the dynamics of library instruction and develop an informed teaching mindset as a result. Furthermore, I would have been better suited to provide adequate and sensitive feedback.

Providing Feedback

In their seminal article on the matter, Lee-Allison Levene and Polly Frank describe a three-step process for what they call "peer coaching" in an academic library: the pre-observation conference, the observation, and the post-observation conference. The post-observation session has delineated roles and procedures for the observed instructor and the observer coach. The observed instructor first shares their "perceptions about their own teaching, focusing on self-selected targeted areas,"[11] which the observer coach addresses in a descriptive, non-evaluative way. It is the instructor's role to evaluate their own performance based on the coach's feedback.

This framework of roles and expectations that Levene and Frank outline was very influential in the literature, and subsequent authors highlighted the importance of guiding the post-observation process to ensure that relevant and specific feedback was delivered in an encouraging manner. One of my biggest regrets in my first few months as a librarian was not having this guidance when providing feedback. Not having a role or directive meant that I delivered a more freewheeling approach to assessing my colleagues. Sometimes this approach resulted in keen insight on how the instruction session played out, while other times my comments proved unproductive to the colleague I had observed.

I remember one exchange vividly. It was early October, the busiest time in the fall semester for library instruction. I observed a colleague who taught a film and media studies class how to search for journal articles in specific databases. For the most part, the students were not responsive to my colleague's attempts to ask them questions or otherwise engage in the session. During the post-observation conference, I led the discussion with a compliment sandwich, a predictable tactic for delivering bad news. I started by saying that my colleague did a great job explaining the differences between the databases that he covered, but I hesitated in delivering the critical comment. I was not sure how to phrase my next point; I had not written it down. In my hesitation, my colleague grew nervous and cried, "Oh God, just say it! What went wrong?" I was taken aback by this outburst, so I mumbled something about how the strategy of asking questions did not resonate with the unresponsive students. The rest of the post-observation conference focused singularly on what "went wrong" as opposed to a more productive conversation about the activities and learning objectives of the session.

Perhaps it was inappropriate for me to be in that situation to begin with. Although I might have been offering a fresh perspective, I was still a new librarian critiquing my more experienced colleagues. Addressing this dynamic is crucial to creating healthy dialogue about our teaching. In a study of their peers at a Swedish university library, Hultman Özek, Edgren, and Jandér describe what they call the "critical friend method" when observing instruction. To be a critical friend means building trust with your colleague in order to have meaningful and reflective discussions. They explain, "Once mutual trust and engagement have been established, the next step is to provide and receive structured feedback, and then use the benefits attained to develop teaching."[12] When engaging in peer observation as a form of library instruction training, there must be mechanisms in place that structure the dialogue and guarantee that they happen on solid ground. I believe having those safeguards in place would have benefitted me and my colleagues when I started.

Conclusion

When I look back at my library instruction training, I fondly remember my enthusiasm and optimism for my first position. The kindness and grace extended to me by my colleagues endeared me to the profession and all of the good work that comes from it. As I grew into being a professional in my field, I found myself looking back at this time and wondering if I actually missed something. By utilizing autotheory, integrating my recollections with the LIS literature, I realized that the priorities of this library were not community-building and quality instruction. The lack of structure and guidelines hampered those ideals, leading me to the painful realization that I could have been served better by my institution. If we train librarians because we care, we must offer support that sets up new librarians for success. If scholarship on peer observation has one consistent theme, it is that librarians felt less alone after engaging in a process of structured reflection and dialogue. A training method that cares is a training method that removes isolation and builds community.

Notes

1.   Graham A. Martin and Jeremy M. Double, "Developing Higher Education Teaching Skills Through Peer Observation and Collaborative Reflection," *Innovations in Education & Training International* 35, no. 2 (May 1998): 162, https://doi.org/10.1080/1355800980350210.

2. bell hooks, "Theory as Liberatory Practice," *Yale Journal of Law and Feminism* 4, no. 1 (Fall 1991): 1.
3. hooks, "Theory as Liberatory Practice," 1.
4. Ibid., 2.
5. Robyn Wiegman, "Introduction: Autotheory Theory," *Arizona Quarterly: A Journal of American Literature, Culture, and Theory* 76, no. 1 (2020): 1, https://doi.org/10.1353/arq.2020.0009.
6. Leila C. Nadir, "More Life After Ruins: Autotheory, the Politics of Citation, and the Limits of The Scholarly Gaze," *ASAP/Journal* 6, no. 3 (2021): 548, https://doi.org/10.1353/asa.2021.0053.
7. Max Cavitch, "Everybody's Autotheory," *Modern Language Quarterly* 83, no. 1 (March 1, 2022): 81, https://doi.org/10.1215/00267929-9475043.
8. Cheryl Middleton, "Evolution of Peer Evaluation of Library Instruction at Oregon State University Libraries," *portal: Libraries and the Academy* 2, no. 1 (2002): 73, https://doi.org/10.1353/pla.2002.0019.
9. Jaena Alabi and William Weare, Jr., "Peer Review of Teaching: Best Practices for a Non-Programmatic Approach," *Communications in Information Literacy* 8, no. 2 (2014): 187, https://doi.org/10.15760/comminfolit.2014.8.2.171.
10. Caroline Sinkinson, "An Assessment of Peer Coaching to Drive Professional Development and Reflective Teaching," *Communications in Information Literacy* 5, no. 1 (2011): 14, https://doi.org/10.15760/comminfolit.2011.5.1.99.
11. Lee-Allison Levene and Polly Frank, "Peer Coaching: Professional Growth and Development for Instruction Librarians," *Reference Services Review* 21, no. 3 (March 1, 1993): 39, https://doi.org/10.1108/eb049192.
12. Yvonne Hultman Özek, Gudrun Edgren, and Katarina Jandér, "Implementing the Critical Friend Method for Peer Feedback among Teaching Librarians in an Academic Setting," *Evidence Based Library and Information Practice* 7, no. 4 (December 11, 2012): 68, https://doi.org/10.18438/B81C8W.

Bibliography

Alabi, Jaena, and William Weare, Jr. "Peer Review of Teaching: Best Practices for a Non-Programmatic Approach." *Communications in Information Literacy* 8, no. 2 (2014): 180. https://doi.org/10.15760/comminfolit.2014.8.2.171.

Cavitch, Max. "Everybody's Autotheory." *Modern Language Quarterly* 83, no. 1 (March 1, 2022): 81–116. https://doi.org/10.1215/00267929-9475043.

hooks, bell. "Theory as Liberatory Practice." *Yale Journal of Law and Feminism* 4, no. 1 (1992 1991): 1–12.

Hultman Özek, Yvonne, Gudrun Edgren, and Katarina Jandér. "Implementing the Critical Friend Method for Peer Feedback among Teaching Librarians in an Academic Setting." *Evidence Based Library and Information Practice* 7, no. 4 (December 11, 2012): 68. https://doi.org/10.18438/B81C8W.

Levene, Lee-Allison, and Polly Frank. "Peer Coaching: Professional Growth and Development for Instruction Librarians." *Reference Services Review* 21, no. 3 (March 1, 1993): 35–42. https://doi.org/10.1108/eb049192.

Martin, Graham A., and Jeremy M Double. "Developing Higher Education Teaching Skills Through Peer Observation and Collaborative Reflection." *Innovations in Education & Training International* 35, no. 2 (May 1998): 161–70. https://doi.org/10.1080/1355800980350210.

Middleton, Cheryl. "Evolution of Peer Evaluation of Library Instruction at Oregon State University Libraries." *portal: Libraries and the Academy* 2, no. 1 (2002): 69–78. https://doi.org/10.1353/pla.2002.0019.

Nadir, Leila C. "More Life After Ruins: Autotheory, the Politics of Citation, and the Limits of The Scholarly Gaze." *ASAP/Journal* 6, no. 3 (2021): 547–50. https://doi.org/10.1353/asa.2021.0053.

Sinkinson, Caroline. "An Assessment of Peer Coaching to Drive Professional Development and Reflective Teaching." *Communications in Information Literacy* 5, no. 1 (2011): 9. https://doi.org/10.15760/comminfolit.2011.5.1.99.

Wiegman, Robyn. "Introduction: Autotheory Theory." *Arizona Quarterly: A Journal of American Literature, Culture, and Theory* 76, no. 1 (2020): 1–14. https://doi.org/10.1353/arq.2020.0009.

CHAPTER 27

It Takes a Village to Raise a Librarian:

Reflection on an Unconference Teaching Workshop

Sam Mandani and Fannie Ouyang

LEARNING OUTCOMES

Readers will be able to

- identify a process from the unconference-style workshop structure outlined in the chapter to support and engage novice librarians that fits their own needs and goals for them and their institutions;
- reproduce or replicate provided instructional examples with flexibility to remix, revise, or reuse any part of the presented structure; and
- reflect on their own teaching practice based on the provided reflections.

Introduction

It seems that no matter how many decades pass, these same topics of concern persist in librarianship: preparedness for library instruction and overcoming imposter syndrome.[1] Our intent in this reflection chapter is not to provide definitive solutions to existing issues within the field of librarianship but rather to bring attention to how early librarians can be supported in their teaching from the perspective of two early-career librarians. This chapter reflects on our experiences with teaching and our intention to provide an unconference-style workshop. We believe that the beauty of our workshop is that we are creating an accessible means for communities of practice to form where librarians of all levels can freely share their experiences around teaching.

When newly minted librarians enter the workforce, there is often an unspoken and implicit expectation of teaching, especially for candidates entering academic librarian positions.[2] This teaching responsibility can account for a large percentage of one's overall workload. It is not uncommon for a candidate to be asked to speak about their experiences with teaching and/or their pedagogical philosophies during job interviews. However, with a pervasive lack of instructional training in graduate school, a candidate may struggle to communicate their teaching methods during an interview.[3] If they are hired, those struggles can continue from a lack of overall support. For example, not all organizations may be equipped to sustainably mentor new hires as part of their onboarding process. Some smaller institutions may not have the staffing power to support the instructional demands of students and faculty, especially if there is only one or two librarians who do the bulk of the instruction. As a result, this can leave many new librarians at a disadvantage when starting out in their careers and their roles.

To address this lack or issue, we considered a space outside of the direct workplace that could help provide some support for new librarians, which is how the conferences came about. Having attended our own respective shares of conferences, we knew that conferences were professional development opportunities where librarians and library professionals shared their work and projects with others across the field. We also knew that professional development budgets varied greatly and that one or two conferences were all that a librarian could afford for the year. So, we wanted to ensure that the workshop we held would be readily useful to the participants who attended, to make the most of their time and resources.

Librarian Context and Background

Who Are We?

Prior to developing this workshop, we considered the points where we converged and diverged as librarians. We thought about our past work, our current roles, our educational backgrounds, and our approaches to instruction. From there, we found notable and interesting patterns and observations that helped to inform how we developed and built the workshop.

To start, our current positions are in academic libraries within private, predominantly white institutions (PWI): Colby College in Waterville, Maine, and New York University in New York, New York. Colby College is a small liberal arts school with fewer than 2,500 students while New York University is a large research university with more than 52,000 students.[4] The focus of our instructional work is also different. Fannie is a liaison librarian for the art department, whereas Sam works more generally with first- and second-year undergraduate students. In the end, we acknowledge that we are both fortunate enough to work in institutions that are not lacking in resources and that privilege us to certain working conditions.

We both attended the University of North Carolina at Chapel Hill for graduate school, going into the School of Information and Library Science (SILS) program. Fannie steered her focus toward library science and Sam toward information science. Despite focusing on different aspects in graduate school, we both ended up becoming instruction librarians. Although the curriculum was quite expansive in their course offerings, SILS did not offer any pedagogical courses at the time when we attended. As a result, neither of us received any formal pedagogical training on information literacy through the program.

What is Your Instructional Background and/or Experience?

Fannie: I gained experience with instruction through hands-on training during my time as a graduate research assistant in the art library. I shadowed my supervisor and after a few sessions, co-taught and then independently taught. The library research sessions all came in the form of one-shot instruction sessions that focused on research basics pertaining to the visual arts. They were fairly traditional in structure, first introducing students to the library, the library catalog, and then electronic resources, all elaborating on specific aspects of each. These sessions tended to be fairly short, lasting about fifteen to twenty minutes each. Due to my lack of formal training and exposure to research sessions (having never experienced one during my undergraduate education), I could only gauge my success through the responses to that single model. Eventually, I realized that a strong active learning component was missing from all of these sessions.

Sam: My experience with instruction stemmed from my previous career as a high school English teacher where I received formal pedagogical and instructional training. However, since there was no formal instructional training provided in SILS at the time of attending, I combined my previous teaching experience with library instruction from my work in the Undergraduate Library to inform how I approached library information literacy instruction. This seems to be the case for many second-career librarians who leaned into their past experience to help with their library instruction practice.[5] The combined experiences helped with lesson planning, how to manage time in the classroom, and how to be flexible and adaptable during the instruction sessions. However, I still had much to learn about how to use the ACRL *Framework for Information Literacy for Higher Education* as the basis of instructional standards for libraries. I also had to adjust my instruction for singular instances, like a one-shot session, and learn to collaborate with the instructor to make use of the limited time together.

How Does Your Instructional Background and/or Experience Influence Your Decision to Create This Workshop?

Fannie: After three positions and a three-year hiatus from consistently providing instruction, I found myself in my current liaison role where I teach regularly. Despite having previous exposure to instruction and models to work from, I still found it to be initially nerve-wracking to perform. Due to the lapse in regular teaching and because I was an early-career librarian, I felt a strong sense of imposter syndrome. This made it difficult for me to be vulnerable with new colleagues about an internally perceived weakness. In my initial year, I connected with other library colleagues to discuss their teaching practices but found that not all of those practices were transferable to the courses I provided instruction to. Some of the practices felt dated and traditional to me, but I wanted to hold sessions that would engage and empower the students so that when they left the classroom, they would have the knowledge and skills to conduct their own research. My want for better and more effective teaching practices pushed me to look outward.

How teaching practices are shared looks different in all institutional spaces, but for me, it felt like an isolating endeavor, one that required me to look to toolkits and conference sessions, both of which were extremely helpful. As a result of this experience, I saw a need for a community of practice—one that would bring together teaching professionals of all levels of experience to a neutral space to share their thoughts and ideas around pedagogy.

Sam: As a graduate student who got to teach, I was able to combine my previous teaching experiences with the instructional demands of library instruction sessions. However, I also noticed that without that experience and training, I would not have adjusted as quickly or as smoothly to do the same thing in the libraries, which is what happened to many of my peers who were teaching for the first time. They had little to no instructional training or background of any kind and relied on piecemeal guidance and practices of other librarians and graduate students doing the same thing. This brought a point of reflection for me about seeing my own peers who are leading these instruction sessions also burdened with the task of learning how to teach at the same time without getting full or adequate support, even though instruction is so closely tied with the library experience. The library department that I worked under was a small but supportive team of librarians and graduate assistants who held many instruction sessions. However, that was not always the case (and it continues to not be the case) for many others who are going into the field of librarianship.

Why Did We Do This Workshop?

Based on our regular conversations about our experiences in our new positions, what we realized was that there was a need within conferences to be able to have places to converse and work together about instruction and deal with imposter syndrome. Even though we are early-career librarians, we have had our fair share of attending conferences, and we have since experienced fatigue from conferences where we were talked *at* with information and content instead of something that's more group-oriented. We recognize that many conferences are about information sharing and it comes in the forms of lightning talks, presentations, and panels. But we thought that a workshop, especially an unconference style workshop, could be something different for no other reason than we thought it was valuable to do something *we* would have wanted to participate in as conference goers.

Transparently, we also wanted to address the need to try and participate in the field in some way, shape, or form that we thought would be most beneficial to us and the types of empathetic and supportive librarians we wanted to be.

Developing the Workshop

What is the Workshop?

The workshop description, as proposed to the SUNYLA Conference:

> When we first enter the library profession, we quickly become surrounded by the pressures of pretending to know more than we do—a breeding ground for imposter syndrome. Developing expertise is a good and fulfilling goal, but it can be punitive, intimidating, and limiting especially to early career librarians. To grow in the profession sustainably, it is important, and even necessary, to address those concerns early with experimentation and collaboration. In this unconference-style workshop, we will collectively build a temporal environment where we share strategies, activities, and approaches to meaningful one-shot library instruction. Using the workshop as an instruction template, we will collaboratively build a toolkit crowdsourced from participants of every level of expertise. In doing so, we learn various practices used by librarians from different fields and institutions. Participants will come away feeling empowered in their current level of expertise around library instruction.

We wanted to create a workshop for a professional conference that gave participants the opportunity to share and gather information and resources with other colleagues and peers from the field. We decided on an unconference-style workshop, which was semi-structured by pre-determined prompts but ultimately participant-driven and non-hierarchical. Our intentions were to foster and build a space where participants would feel comfortable sharing their knowledge or lack thereof. Though we do not assume that this is a unique idea by any real measure, the way we wanted to present it felt uncommon enough that it felt exciting to try and do. We also specifically tried to do something that we knew as current early-career librarians that we would have wanted to see in a conference workshop.

Who Was Our Target Audience?

Our intended target audience was everybody. We thought about the kind of representation we wanted for ourselves, so we wanted early-career librarians to participate. However, the resource and expertise sharing wouldn't be possible without the inclusion and participation of veteran and middle-career librarians. We hoped that even with librarians having been in the workforce for more than five years, they would be open to learning about new or modified strategies, lessons, and activities. Having a mix of individuals was important to us to garner multiple perspectives about the same topic.

When and Where Did This Workshop Take Place?

The workshop took place at the State University of New York Library Association (SUNYLA) Conference in East Farmingdale, NY, on June 8, 2022. It was one of two pre-conference workshops offered for the entire conference.

How Did the Workshop Go?

The workshop went fairly well. We had a total of nine participants (including us), ranging from pre-career to late-career librarians, which felt like a good number for our first experimental unconference-style workshop. The workshop ran for two hours, following this outline:

- Icebreaker
- Introduction
- Group norms
- Pre-activity
- Activity
- Reflection
- Closing

We wanted to encourage an environment where all participants could discuss their teaching practices without being judged, regardless of how long they had been teaching. We worked to ensure that the two hours were a productive use of time and that all participants would leave having learned something. We made it clear that we were not experts, but that alongside them, we wanted to facilitate discussion about our instructional experiences. Our focus was on creating a community of practice that could exist in the space and time provided to us as well as the potential to extend past the conference session.

We decided on a couple of group norms, to which the group was amenable:

- Chatham House Rules. When a meeting, or part thereof, is held under the Chatham House Rule, participants are free to use the information received, but neither the identity nor the affiliation of the speaker(s), nor that of any other participant, may be revealed.
- Take Space, Give Space. Take space to speak your mind and share. Give space to others to be able to do the same.

Then, we continued with the pre-activity where we asked participants to discuss with their groups any of the following questions:

- What do you want to get out of the workshop?
- What are your concerns about teaching?
- What are your interests in teaching?
- What is your current comfort level with teaching?

Following that, we went into the activity where we asked the participants to draft a sample lesson outline of something they had done or would imagine doing before coming together as a group and then building a group outline of a sample lesson. Our intention for this was to have them think about their current practice before joining forces with the other members of their group to consider how to combine or iterate on each other's experiences, lessons, and strategies. Eventually, we wanted to make sure that everyone had time to share and discuss their outlines and continue to reflect on their instructional practice.

After the workshop, we gathered immediate verbal feedback. We collected the outlines created during the session, transcribed them into a single document, and distributed them back to the participants for future reference. The materials exist on a Google Drive that was shared with all participants.

Workshop Context and Outcomes
What Did We Learn from Doing the Workshop?

We learned plenty from this workshop! For example, we learned additional methods of engagement, such as students being given a sticky note at the beginning of a session to write their response to a question. We used Instagram hashtags as a method to explain keywords. Again, as early-career librarians, the breadth and depth of our knowledge could only extend so far. We leaned into that, wanting to grow our expertise. We believe that doing that helped empower everyone in the group to share but also took the pressure off of us to "perform" as experts (thus eliminating another possible place from which imposter syndrome could come).

One point of reflection that we both wished we had done was to physically document our reflections after the conference. We hadn't anticipated reflecting on that experience and writing about it more formally, such as in this chapter. It was a case of we didn't know what we didn't know. In the future, we hope to be more organized and vigilant about documenting the process in order to fully iterate on the workshop.

We also learned quite a bit from the feedback we received from the group. One participant suggested that in the future we hold a three-hour workshop. Another suggested more participants. We recognized that this semi-guided workshop was completely reliant on the participation of the individuals. Since the attendees were so open and honest about their experiences with teaching, the workshop felt extremely fruitful.

Our goal of developing a community of practice after the session was good-intentioned but also suffered the fate of busy schedules beyond the conference and lack of formal organization. It made us reflect on the kinds of communities of practice we wanted to be a part of, what we wanted to foster, and what our own capacities were in helping to grow and maintain it.

Conclusion: Future Plans and Considerations

We want to continue bringing this unconference-style workshop into other conferences and adapt it as appropriate. We would like to continue doing something active and participatory in conferences because it is a matter of networking with peers and colleagues in the field and diversifying the experience that mostly happens in conferences. As stated previously, we'd like to ideally build a community of practice surrounding this workshop outside the scope of our existing community and workplace while considering the realities of how feasible this may be for us and the participants. Something that we are mindful of is the fact that conferences and workshop events are sometimes just glimpses into what people are able to avail themselves of with regard to time, energy, and resources.

Some of the prevailing questions that we've since thought about include, how can a community of practice sustain itself into the future post-conference? And what does it mean to have a community of practice *for us*? Blogs on information literacy such as https://infomational.com, http://pumpedlibrarian.blogspot.com and https://rulenumberoneblog.

com have been created, maintained, and ended. These continue to exist as records, but the robust communities that once existed within these digital spaces have moved. Additionally, there are already avenues in which communities of practice already exist, such as in local groups, library associations, and forums, so we are also trying to be mindful of not repeating or duplicating the work that is happening in these spaces.

At the time of writing, this workshop has been submitted and accepted into another conference, so we will be attempting to revise the workshop based on our reflections and documenting the process and the outcomes.

APPENDIX

This short list of activities is a combination of some of the activities we have used in our instruction sessions over time, especially as emerging librarians.

Keyword Exercises

Exercise 1.1

Title: What Do You Know About Your Research Topic?

Description: Take about 5 minutes to work with a partner to discuss your individually chosen topics. The existing knowledge does not have to be overly detailed or extensive; just say what you know. While one person is speaking, the other person will be writing down keywords based on the partner's descriptions. Switch and repeat the exercise with the other person's topic. Afterwards, you will exchange the keywords.

Explanation: It is very easy to become overly narrow in focus, so verbalizing the topic to another individual, such as a classmate, leads to an exchange of ideas and an extensively larger list of keywords.

Exercise 1.2

Title: Ask and You Shall Perceive

Description: Students spend 5 minutes writing down as many questions as they have about their topic, keeping in mind questions that address who is involved, what time frame they may want to focus on, where this topic takes place, etc. Quantifying the questions pushes students to avoid focusing on a highly polished research question but rather to develop prodding questions that could lead to a direction from their exploration.

Students then switch papers with a partner or partners where they will underline or circle words they consider important within the list of questions. After they finish, the original owner receives their paper and compiles a list of the underlined or circled words as a starting point of keywords.

Explanation: Similar to Exercise 1.1, by having the students explicitly write down their questions, they can focus on parts of their topic that they may want to find out or learn more about but do not yet know how to connect or synthesize. It also gives them a working list to use that does not add to the cognitive load of the search process. Having their peers check on their behalf helps with having "fresh eyes" take a look at their list and identify what their questions are focusing on which can be used to provide a direction for the research.

Exercise 1.3

Title: Expand Your Keywords!

Description: Create a mind map or a keyword chart to expand your list of keywords. Determine which form will be most effective for you. If you are a more visual person, a mind map might be better. This exercise is a free-form way for you to think of associated words, ideas, themes, and concepts.

Note to instructor: If your institution has access to the Credo Reference, this can be a great tool that can aid in explaining mind maps. See some examples below:

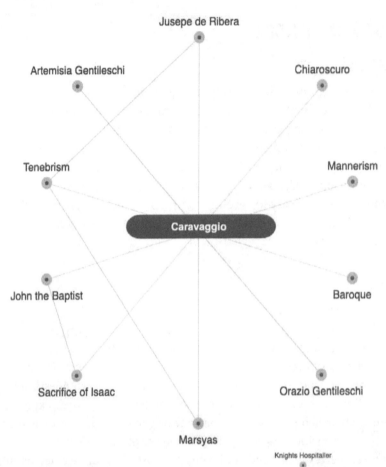

This image is an example of the interactive tool. When one clicks on a keyword, the map will change to reveal other keywords. For example, when we click on "John the Baptist," the diagram changes to reveal the following:

Database and Source Selection Exercises

Exercise 2.1

Title: Database Speed Dating

Note: We have both adapted this activity from library instruction activities taught at UNC-Chapel Hill due to our time as former library graduate assistants.

Description: Using a selection and combination of your keywords, enter them into each of the following databases. Assess each database and determine what you like or dislike about each. Share.

	Artstor	Oxford Art Online	Arts (Proquest)
What do you like about the database?			
What do you dislike?			
Was it helpful for the assignment? Why or why not?			
Did you find an artist and/or artwork that connects to your research?			

Note to instructor: Although each database has its differences, this exercise is meant to show that despite the variations, each database functions similarly. Each has its own set of facets. This means that if a user can learn the basics of using one database, they can transfer their skills to another.

If helpful to the students, this time can be spent on exploration. Have students find at least one usable book or article. You will find that some students may have difficulty scoping their searches. They will either be overly specific or general.

Exercise 2.2

Title: Is It Scholarly?

Social Media	Wikipedia	Newspaper	Academic Journal

Note to instructor: The categories can be changed to best fit what you'd like to explain. Using a real-time collaborative application like Padlet, go through each category one at a time and have students anonymously respond to why they think that each of these is scholarly or not scholarly. You might be surprised by the answers. After seeing the responses, explain. Is the category scholarly or not scholarly? If not scholarly, can the source still be used? How? In what ways?

Social Media	Wikipedia	Newspaper	Academic Journal
• No editorial standards or oversight • Vary widely in quality and reliability • High potential for bias • Informal • General audience	• Editorial standards set by community • Pages not frequently edited • Non-experts can edit pages • General audience • Reference list is great for finding other sources	• Reporters often aren't experts • Articles not peer-reviewed • Shorter articles, less detail • Contains fact-based reporting and editorial content	• Written by experts for experts in the field • Peer-reviewed • Includes citations • Written for scholars, researchers, professionals, and university students

After this exercise, you can use extra time to further discuss peer review and speak on why the peer-review process is important but can also have its own issues. It is important to be critical of sources and their authority.

Source Evaluation Exercises

3.1 Your Chosen Sources

Source:	Source Evaluation Criteria: (Choose 1 from the list)	Method for Checking: (What is your process for evaluating the source?)
Book, article, or some kind of text	• Author authority • Audience and purpose • Perspective and bias • Footnotes and documentation • Accuracy and completeness	

Description: This activity uses a book, article, or some kind of text that was found through a database search. Students are then asked to check one of the options of source evaluation criteria before writing down their process of determining if the source is a suitable or relevant item for their research.

Explanation: This aims to engage students from being a passive learner to an active participant in their research process by explicitly identifying the steps, if any, that they take to determine if their chosen sources are credible and relevant. By identifying the steps that they take, there's an opportunity to offer tips or redirections for them to identify if a source they're looking at is appropriate.

Notes

1. A. Click and C. Walker, Help Us Help Them: Instruction Training for LIS Students and New Librarians, LOEX Conference Proceedings 2009 (2011); Jessica Martinez and Meredith Forrey, "Overcoming Imposter Syndrome: The Adventures of Two New Instruction Librarians," *Reference Services Review* 47 (3) (2019): 331–42.
2. Margaret Dodson, "On Target Or Missing the Mark? Instruction Courses in LIS Graduate Programs," *Public Services Quarterly* 16 (2) (2020): 83–94.
3. Dani Brecher, Kevin Michael Klipfel, and The Claremont Colleges Library. "Education Training for Instruction Librarians: A Shared Perspective," *Communications in Information Literacy* 8 (1) (2014): 43–49.
4. "At a Glance," Colby College, https://www.colby.edu/academics/course-catalogue/admission-fees-about-colby/about-colby/; "NYU at a Glance," New York University, https://www.nyu.edu/about/news-publications/nyu-at-a-glance.html.
5. Jacalyn E. Bryan, "The Preparation of Academic Librarians Who Provide Instruction: A Comparison of First and Second Career Librarians," *The Journal of Academic Librarianship* 42 (4) (2016): 340–54.

Bibliography

Brecher, Dani, Kevin Michael Klipfel, and The Claremont Colleges Library. "Education Training for Instruction Librarians: A Shared Perspective." *Communications in Information Literacy* 8 (1) (2014): 43–49.

Bryan, Jacalyn E. "The Preparation of Academic Librarians Who Provide Instruction: A Comparison of First and Second Career Librarians." *The Journal of Academic Librarianship* 42 (4) (2016): 340–54.

Click, A., and C. Walker. Help Us Help Them: Instruction Training for LIS Students and New Librarians. LOEX Conference Proceedings 2009. 2011.

Colby College. "Colby at a Glance." https://www.colby.edu/academics/course-catalogue/admission-fees-about-colby/about-colby/.

Dodson, Margaret. "On Target Or Missing the Mark? Instruction Courses in LIS Graduate Programs." *Public Services Quarterly* 16 (2) (2020): 83–94.

Martinez, Jessica, and Meredith Forrey. "Overcoming Imposter Syndrome: The Adventures of Two New Instruction Librarians." *Reference Services Review* 47 (3) (2019): 331–42.

New York University. "NYU at a Glance." https://www.nyu.edu/about/news-publications/nyu-at-a-glance.html.

CHAPTER 28

Go and Get What You Need!:

Seeking Out Mentorship

Jamia Williams

LEARNING OUTCOMES

Readers will be able to

- distinguish between different types of mentorship in the context of academic library instruction, including formal, informal, and peer models;

- assess and analyze the role of mentorship in shaping instructional strategies within academic libraries; this involves understanding how mentorship influences teaching methodologies, information delivery, and student engagement; and

- apply the principles discussed in the chapter to real-world scenarios within academic library environments. This includes recognizing opportunities for mentorship, establishing effective mentor-mentee relationships, and utilizing mentorship for professional development.

Introduction

When I received my master of library science degree from North Carolina Central University, my concentration was in academic librarianship. I wanted to be an academic librarian, so I was glad to gain the necessary skills to thrive. However, we did not cover teaching pedagogy or andragogy. As a tenure-track faculty, I was supposed to be given a formal mentor, but this did not occur. As a result of the lack of formal mentorship within the academic library, it led me to explore outside mentorship opportunities. Two organizations were vital to my academic instruction journey. As a tenure-track librarian, I have to teach, so I knew I wanted to be successful and had to advocate for my success. Another tenet of librarianship is professional development, which I embrace fully. So, I had to learn some techniques by attending workshops and sessions that discussed library instruction. I also pulled from my previous teaching experiences.

The reflective narrative in this chapter provides some key takeaways on how to succeed when you're not given the necessary tools or support to thrive. As information professionals, we should continue to learn how to be better teachers. Professional development and mentorship are integral tools for achieving this learning and growth. Hopefully, the reflections and the key takeaways I share will inform and inspire you to improve your craft.

Seeking Out What You Need: Instruction Mentorship for Librarians

The academic libraries where we work frequently do not provide us with the necessary tools and support to succeed.[1] Therefore, we pivot to seek help outside of our workplaces. I could not stay stuck in the feeling that I was not set up for success; instead, I had to pivot to go after what I needed. Pivoting was necessary for my success with teaching at the university level. My career coach told me this pivoting is a sign of a good leader, which I never considered. Also, that is a sign of my resilience when not given what I need to be successful. I pushed through anyway, which I do not think anyone should have to do. Some of my colleagues engaged in what my career coach called "information hoarding." They were unwilling to share information with others because they wanted to be the only person with that knowledge. Davis Kendrick and Damasco cited Hathcock's scholarship, who wrote that whiteness appears when people engage in exclusionary practices in academic librarianship.[2] Pivoting can be necessary when working in toxic and/or low-morale work environments.[3] One of the things that I was able to seek out was mentorship around library instruction. This happened formally and informally.

So, what is mentorship? Hicks stated, "Mentoring relationships are often thought of as a way to pass along vital skills to new librarians that traditional LIS education LIS Professional Mentoring Culture cannot offer."[4] I think that mentorship is a helpful instructional strategy. Mentorship is cultivating a mutually respectful and beneficial relationship with an individual through consistent nurturing with being vulnerable and honest about various topics. One of those topics can be library instruction. Mentorship can be helpful if this is your first time doing instruction or even your first time with this frequency of leading instruction sessions. I think mentorship is a strategy that can improve and help your teaching techniques.

Formal Mentorship and Library Instruction

Formal mentorship is usually structured and coordinated by an institution or organization. Many institutions see how essential this relationship is for incoming librarians. The mentor can help the mentee with the unwritten rules of the library. Also, they can serve as the point person for important questions that might come up. Lastly, the mentor can introduce the mentee to critical people who can help ensure their mentee's success.

The Association of Research and College Libraries' Instruction Section has a mentoring program committee that created an opportunity for librarians who would like the benefits of instruction mentorship. The committee paired me with a mentor, and we were told that the mentor and I could schedule the meetings' frequency. I decided to meet my mentor every two weeks; then, I changed it to monthly due to my busy schedule. Each month, my mentor and I were emailed prompts from the Instruction Section mentoring program leadership to cover in our discussions.

During this time, I was mentored by a fantastic librarian. She guided me through my thoughts and ideas and discussed two articles. I decided to start an instruction journal to note tips during our meeting. This is also where I write my ideas to discuss with her and write down my webinars and article notes. This journal has been helpful to me because I can refer back to it when I need guidance on how to plan an instruction session. I could compile a list of resources my mentor and I spoke about and some I explored on my own (see appendix).

Informal Mentorship and Library Instruction

Informal mentorship happens when two people decide to have a mentorship relationship. This can be structured, unstructured, or semi-structured. This type of relationship can happen when the mentor or mentee seeks this type of relationship or when a mutual person connects these two people. The variety of this relationship can be for a season or a lifetime, depending on the goals of each party.

At the beginning of 2020, the Medical Library Association's (MLA) African American Medical Librarians Alliance (AAMLA) Caucus would have a weekly virtual "chat and chew" to support each other during the beginning of the COVID-19 global pandemic. During one of these weekly virtual chats, it was suggested that I reach out to two health sciences librarians to get support around instruction since they both supported nursing departments.[5] My connection with this caucus was essential, so this is another informal way to get your support. As a result of connecting with these two health sciences librarians, I shadowed one of them several times during their virtual instruction sessions. Also, these relationships became informal mentorships for me, which led to me getting resources to help me with supporting health sciences departments, particularly nursing departments. And the resources that were shared helped me to become a better teacher. It was great to have a safe space to speak my ideas and get advice on what I wanted to do regarding liaison work.

Peer-to-peer Mentorship

Peer-to-peer mentorship is a relationship between two people at the same career stage. This can be structured, unstructured, or semi-structured. In my experience, this type of mentorship has led to successful collaborations. In addition, this relationship is a way to celebrate and acknowledge the strengths of a peer. Lastly, this is a way to create a safe space to discuss or understand current trends in librarianship.

During the weekly AAMLA virtual chat and chew, another peer told me to contact her to shadow her and talk to her about library instruction. I was able to shadow her and was given instruction resources. This peer-to-peer mentorship helped me navigate the academic library space since I was used to working in health sciences libraries, so this was helpful in learning some tips and tricks for navigating databases like Google Scholar.

Having different types of mentorship relationships at one time, I think, adds to the success of a librarian. This variety can add to the level of expertise that is shared with a mentee. As a mentor and a mentee, I suggest reflecting on what you are looking for in the mentorship. Also, take the time to understand your strengths and areas for improvement. For instance, if you know that scheduling the next time you meet with your mentee will keep you on track, then do this.

Navigating Unsuccessful Mentorships

Establishing clear goals and priorities is fundamental to cultivating successful mentorship relationships. Before entering into a mentorship, it's crucial to reflect on your professional and personal objectives. Define what you aim to achieve through mentorship, whether it be acquiring specific skills, gaining industry insights, or enhancing leadership abilities. By setting these goals in advance, you provide a roadmap for the mentorship journey, ensuring a focused and purposeful engagement.

Moreover, prioritizing the mentoring relationship from the outset enables you to recognize when it isn't aligning with your goals. Regular self-reflection and evaluation of the mentorship's effectiveness are essential. If you find that the relationship isn't contributing to your growth or is hindering your progress, it's crucial to address these concerns proactively. Open communication with your mentor can help navigate challenges or reassess the mentorship's direction. Recognizing when a mentorship isn't serving your goals allows for timely adjustments or, in some cases, the possibility of seeking a new mentorship opportunity that better aligns with your evolving aspirations. Ultimately, the success of a mentorship hinges on the clarity of goals and the continuous commitment to prioritize the relationship's relevance to your professional journey.

Conclusion

My LIS master's programs did not prepare me to teach, and the lack of formal mentorship led me to explore outside mentorship opportunities. Two organizations were vital to my academic instruction journey. I truly benefitted from formal, informal, and peer mentorship. As a tenure-track librarian, I had to teach, so I knew I wanted to be successful despite having no support from some of my tenured colleagues. Sometimes mentorships do not work out and people are not appropriately paired. When this happens, regroup and try again with someone who can give you what you want in a mentorship relationship. Mentorships are important relationships that take time and energy. When done correctly, it is truly worth it. Consider contacting your peers or local and/or national organizations to help you connect to a mentor. This connection could lead you on a journey to explore the various pedagogies and andragogy frameworks that can guide you.

There are many frameworks that I would like to continue to understand and apply. For instance, care ethics and relational-cultural theory are new concepts that I want to explore and apply to my teaching. The critical librarianship framework has many elements like anti-racist, intersectionality, and feminist pedagogies, which I use in my teaching; however, I know that I can go even deeper into the framework's application. Teaching and instruction are an integral part of many of our job responsibilities. As professionals, we must be open to lifelong learning to grow our expertise. Consider being mentored to take your instruction sessions to another level.

Additional Resources

- hooks, bell. *Teaching to Transgress: Education as the Practice of Freedom*. Oxfordshire, UK: Routledge, 2015
- Stöpel, Michael, Livia Piotto, Xan Goodman, and Samantha Godbey. *Faculty-Librarian Collaborations: Integrating the Information Literacy Framework into Disciplinary Courses*. Chicago: ACRL, 2020.
- Thompson, Phyllis, and Janice Carello. *Trauma-Informed Pedagogies: A Guide for Responding to Crisis and Inequality in Higher Education*. London, UK: Palgrave Macmillan, 2022.
- Heinbach, Chelsea, Rosan Mitola, and Erin Rinto. *Dismantling Deficit Thinking in Academic Libraries: Theory, Reflection, and Action*. Sacramento: Library Juice Press, 2021.

APPENDIX
Resources That Guided Me

- Dr. Nicole A. Cooke's article, "Becoming an Andragogical Librarian: Using Library Instruction as a Tool to Combat Library Anxiety and Empower Adult Learners," discussed the five tenets of andragogy and the importance of keeping these tenets in mind when providing library instruction. Understanding adult learners is important for an academic librarian who does instruction.
- Chelsea Heinbach et al.'s article, "Dismantling Deficit Thinking: A Strengths-Based Inquiry into the Experiences of Transfer Students In and Out of Academic Libraries," helped me reframe how transfer students are perceived and that we should be leveraging their strengths rather than fixating on their shortcomings.
- Jeremiah Paschke-Wood et al.'s article, "Creating A Student-Centered Alternative To Research Guides: Developing The Infrastructure To Support Novice Learners," discussed that most research guides are used as resource lists instead of as a way to guide researchers. This article was helpful when creating and updating LibGuides to get to the reason and purpose of a guide.
- The book *The One-Shot Library Instruction Survival Guide*, 3rd ed., by Heidi E. Buchanan and Beth A. McDonough, was helpful when planning my instruction sessions because most were one-shot sessions.

Notes

1. Kaetrena Davis Kendrick and Ione T. Damasco, "Low Morale in Ethnic and Racial Minority Academic Librarians: An Experiential Study," *Library Trends* 68 (2) (Fall, 2019): 177, https://doi.org/10.1353/lib.2019.0036.
2. Kendrick and Damasco, "Low Morale."
3. Puneet Sandhu, "9 Signs You're in a Toxic Work Environment—and What to Do About It," the muse, January 24, 2023, https://www.themuse.com/advice/toxic-work-environment; Kaetrena Davis Kendrick, "The Low Morale Experience of Academic Librarians: A Phenomenological Study," *Journal of Library Administration* 57:8 (2017): 846–78, https://doi.org/10.1080/01930826.2017.1368325.
4. Lisa K. Hussey and Jennifer Campbell-Meier, "Is There a Mentoring Culture Within the LIS Profession?," *Journal of Library Administration* 57.5 (2017): 502–03.
5. Shannon D. Jones et al., "Virtual Chat and Chew: Radical Self-Care for BIPOC Information Professionals," in *Leadership Wellness and Mental Health Concerns in Higher Education*, ed. Cynthia J. Alexander and Amy Tureen (Hershey, PA: IGI Global, 2022), 257–71, https://doi.org/10.4018/978-1-7998-7693-9.ch013.

Bibliography

Buchanan, E. Heidi, and Beth A. McDonough. *The One-Shot Library Instruction Survival Guide*. 3rd ed. Chicago: ALA Editions, 2021.

Cooke, A. Nicole. "Becoming an Andragogical Librarian: Using Library Instruction as a Tool to Combat Library Anxiety and Empower Adult Learners." *New Review of Academic Librarianship* 16, no.2 (October 2010): 208–27. https://doi.org/10.1080/13614533.2010.507388.

Davis Kendrick, Kaetrena. "The Low Morale Experience of Academic Librarians: A Phenomenological Study." *Journal of Library Administration* 57 no.8 (September 2017): 846–78. https://doi.org/10.1080/0 1930826.2017.1368325.

Davis Kendrick, Kaetrena, and Ione T. Damasco. "Low Morale in Ethnic and Racial Minority Academic Librarians: An Experiential Study." *Library Trends* 68, no. 2 (Fall, 2019): 174–212. https://doi. org/10.1353/lib.2019.0036.

Heinbach, Chelsea, Brittany Paloma Fiedler, Rosan Mitola, and Emily Pattni. "Dismantling Deficit Thinking: A Strengths-Based Inquiry into the Experiences of Transfer Students In and Out of Academic Libraries." *In the Library with the Lead Pipe* (February 2019). https://www.inthelibrarywiththelead-pipe.org/2019/dismantling-deficit-thinking/.

Hussey, Lisa K., and Jennifer Campbell-Meier. "Is There a Mentoring Culture Within the LIS Profession?" *Journal of Library Administration* 57.5 (2017): 502–03.

Jones, Shannon D., et al. "Virtual Chat and Chew: Radical Self-Care for BIPOC Information Professionals." In *Leadership Wellness and Mental Health Concerns in Higher Education*, edited by Cynthia J. Alexander and Amy Tureen, 257–71. Hershey, PA: IGI Global, 2022. https://doi.org/10.4018/978-1-7998-7693-9.ch013.

Lorenzetti, Diane L., and Susan E. Powelson. "A Scoping Review of Mentoring Programs for Academic Librarians." *The Journal of Academic Librarianship* 41, no. 2 (2015): 186–96. Accessed February 15, 2023. https://doi.org/10.1016/j.acalib.2014.12.001.

Paschke-Wood, Jeremiah, Ellen Dubinsky, and Leslie Sult. "Creating A Student-Centered Alternative To Research Guides: Developing The Infrastructure To Support Novice Learners." *In the Library with the Lead Pipe* (October 21, 2020). https://www.inthelibrarywiththeleadpipe.org/2020/student-centered-alternative-research-guides/.

Sandhu, Puneet. "9 Signs You're in a Toxic Work Environment—And What to Do About It." the muse. January 24, 2023. https://www.themuse.com/advice/toxic-work-environment.

Conclusion
Moving Instruction Training Forward in Academic Libraries

Matthew Weirick Johnson

Each case provides all the pieces readers need to run with the ideas at their own institutions, and the reflections provide feedback from current librarians about what works. If our colleagues aren't prepared to teach, I hope this book prepares us to teach them and each other.

Victoria Caplan and colleagues point to the value of working together to provide better training, ignoring institutional and geographical boundaries: "A single library may have difficulty sourcing and paying for expert trainers from outside their home city or region. By combining budgets, skills, and staffing, a group can achieve higher-level training and economies of scale than a single library could have done." There's more that we can do together than we can do alone.

Kirstie Preest and Claire Sewell recognize the value of a common language and common experience for informing continued growth and learning together: "Having library staff take part in their own tailored program, covering similar topics, results in a common experience between the different types of staff, helps to raise the profile of librarians and allows their teaching to be taken more seriously by non-library colleagues. The program has helped to raise the profile of the teaching offered by libraries and demonstrate that it is based on sound pedagogical knowledge and reflection, further helping to enhance the reputation of the library as an educator."

Melissa A. Wong and Laura Saunders demonstrate the utility of the community of practice model for developing such a shared space: "Communities of practice offer a participant-led approach to professional development. By emphasizing shared expertise and mutual learning as well as sustained interactions between participants, they can be a supportive space for instruction librarians to build pedagogical knowledge; identify classroom practices that foster inclusive teaching; and find support and encouragement for both innovation and the affective aspects of teaching."

David X. Lemmons and colleagues remind us of the difficulty of catering to disparate levels of experiences but the value of bringing those varied experiences together in the community we create for learning about teaching: "Designing a training program for both new and returning library instructors was a challenge. It necessitated creating multiple modes of participation, for example, and creating scaffolding for both those who attended the entire series and those who attended only one workshop. This, however, also created two important opportunities: repeat attendance and mixing of experience levels."

Additionally, we see the value of on-the-job training, and Livia Piotto reminds us that many librarians only receive training to be library instructors once they start doing the work: "On-the-job training is what most instruction librarians get, and we need to try and create the most meaningful opportunity for providing guidance in a job that constantly change." She also reminds us that the work doesn't end after a finite length of training. In training library instructors, we're learning to be lifelong learners fascinated by the work of teaching and learning.

Ginelle Baskin echoes other authors' calls for practical and hands-on experience while reminding us that there's no one-size-fits-all solution to training library instructors: "Even if you do all the things I suggest in this chapter, there is no guarantee that any of it can truly prepare you for being a library instructor. In my opinion, what truly helps the most is hands-on experience." Many of the authors in this book discuss the need to create bespoke, reactive, and sometimes individualized programming to support the needs of specific learners.

While many of the cases presented demonstrate the value of librarians working together and sharing knowledge from different institutions, places, and experiences, Karen Munro and colleagues demonstrate the value of working together with other teaching and learning experts on our campuses: "We benefited greatly from the expertise of our LTSI colleagues to help us develop our understanding of core pedagogical principles, such as learning-centered design, backward design, active learning, ILOs, and assessment. Sharing these skills and concepts within the library helps us move toward a common understanding of effective pedagogical practices that we should all be using." We have a united mission and shared knowledge, and these collaborations work to cement academic libraries as centers for teaching and learning in their own right on our campuses. As with Preest and Sewell's case, improving our instruction and demonstrating our investment in the work of teaching shows our colleagues across our campuses that we are partners and collaborators in the teaching mission of the university.

Russel Peterson reminds us of one of the most important aspects of teaching: caring about learners and caring about learning. "The lack of structure and guidelines hampered those ideals, leading me to the painful realization that I could have been served better by my institution. If we train librarians because we care, we must offer support that sets up new librarians for success. If scholarship on peer observation has one consistent theme, it is that librarians felt less alone after engaging in a process of structured reflection and dialogue. A training method that cares is a training method that removes isolation and builds community."

If nothing else, this book makes clear that many of us are working to improve the way that we train library instructors. Academic librarians are listening to calls from colleagues for more training about teaching and are working together to address that need. These cases and reflections demonstrate the work that is already being done and collect those examples so that they can be used to inform the work that we have yet to do.

About the Editor

Matthew Weirick Johnson is the director of Research & Instruction at the University of South Florida (USF) Libraries on the Tampa campus. Prior to joining USF, Johnson was the librarian for English, History & Comparative Literature and lead for Teaching & Learning at UCLA Library. As lead for Teaching & Learning, Johnson led the development and delivery of UCLA Library's inaugural library instruction training for library student research assistants. Johnson serves on the editorial boards of *College & Research Libraries*, *Public Services Quarterly*, and ACRL's *CHOICE*, and has published in *The Journal of Academic Librarianship*, *College & Research Libraries*, *Journal of Library Administration*, *Library Trends*, *Reference Services Review* and others on various topics including academic librarian burnout, library instruction, and information literacy.

About the Authors

Breeann Austin (she/her) is the instruction and assessment librarian at California State University Channel Islands. She was part of the 2019 Information Literacy Scholar cohort at Syracuse University. Her research interests include the flipped classroom model, instructional design, and promoting marginalized voices in primary source instruction.

Ginelle Baskin is the student success and open education librarian at the James E. Walker Library at Middle Tennessee State University. She leads Walker Library's student success initiatives, including the development and oversight of the campus' open educational resources program.

Brie Baumert (she/her) is a library clerk at the Ramsey County Public Libraries in Minnesota. She was part of the 2020 Information Literacy Scholar cohort at Syracuse University.

Randi Beem (she/her) is the instruction librarian/archivist at the University of North Carolina at Charlotte. She earned her master of library science from Indiana University

Bloomington with a specialization in archives and records management and holds a bachelor's in history from Saint Mary's College, Notre Dame, Indiana. Her research interests include critical pedagogy, labor history, and getting students to guess how old the oldest book in the Reading Room is.

Marc Bess (he/him) is the first-year and online learning librarian and an associate professor at the University of North Carolina at Charlotte. He earned his master of library science from North Carolina Central University and master of education in learning, design, and technology from the University of North Carolina at Charlotte.

Ashley Blinstrub (she/her) is the student success and inclusion librarian at George Mason University Libraries. She has a master of science in information from University of Michigan. Her research interests include accessibility of information, inclusive teaching practices, and assessment of student learning.

Colin Braun is a library assistant at the Redwood Library and Athenaeum in Newport, Rhode Island. He earned his master of library science and information studies from the University of Rhode Island in 2022.

Victoria F. Caplan is the head of Research & Learning Support at the Hong Kong University of Science & Technology Library. In this role, she oversees the library's information and data literacy and research support services to HKUST students, faculty, and staff. She is particularly interested in working to mentor library staff members and develop their skills and knowledge. She received her BA in East Asian Studies from Yale College, her MSc from the University of Illinois (Urbana-Champaign), and an MPhil (Cultural Anthropology) from the University of Hong Kong.

Christopher Chan is the university librarian at Hong Kong Baptist University. In this role, he oversees the development and implementation of strategic initiatives to enhance library services and collections in support of the university's mission and vision. He holds a bachelor's degree in politics and history from the University of Durham, a master of library science from Charles Sturt University, and a master of education from the University of Hong Kong.

Erin Cunningham is a Youth Services librarian at South Kingstown Public Library. She earned her bachelor's degree in history with a focus on Medieval Europe and anthropology in 2021 and earned her master of library science in 2022, both from the University of Rhode Island.

Kelly Delevan (she/her) is the information literacy librarian at Syracuse University Libraries. She developed the Information Literacy Scholars program in 2019.

Tonya D. Dority is the cataloging and metadata librarian at Reese Library, Augusta University. She has a BA in history from Clark Atlanta University and an MS in library and information science from Simmons University (formerly Simmons College). Her research interests are inclusive cataloging and collection development.

Mark W. Duncan is the instruction and outreach librarian at Christian Brothers University in Memphis, TN. He received his MS in library and information science from Syracuse University in 2021 and BA in political science and religious studies from Grinnell College in 2019. His research interests include instructional assessment, information literacy, and instructional design.

Kala Dunn (she/her) received her MSIS from the University of Tennessee. She currently is the research and instruction librarian at Columbia College in Columbia, SC. She teaches the majority of the information literacy sessions for the college. In her time at Columbia College, she has developed a strong Instruction Program centered on active learning and engagement in the classroom. Her research interests include Universal Design for Learning and the flipped classroom model.

Ella Gibson is the online learning and instruction librarian at the University of Colorado Colorado Springs. She teaches information literacy sessions to students in the First Year Writing and Rhetoric program and collaborates with her liaison area faculty to provide library instruction appropriate for undergraduate and graduate research needs. Her research interests include instructional design and distance and online learning.

Kayla M. Gourlay (she/her) is the business and economics librarian at George Mason University. In this role, she supports over 6,000 students, faculty, and entrepreneurs via business reference services, outreach, and information literacy instruction. In addition to her MSLS from Clarion University, she holds a bachelor's degree in English and a bachelor's degree in Philosophy from Mount St. Mary's University in Maryland.

Ryan Harris (he/him) is the associate dean for Public Services at the University of North Carolina, Charlotte. In this role, he provides leadership and strategy to a wide range of public services, including research and instruction, collections maintenance, and circulation. He actively collaborates with the Education and Health Sciences faculty on systematic reviews research.

Lisa Janicke Hinchliffe is professor/coordinator for Research and Teaching Professional Development in the University Library at the University of Illinois at Urbana-Champaign. She is also an affiliate faculty member in the university's School of Information Sciences, European Union Center, and Center for Global Studies. At Illinois, she has also served as the coordinator for Information Literacy Services and Instruction, acting head of the University High School Library, head of the Undergraduate Library, acting coordinator for Staff Development and Training, and coordinator for Strategic Planning in the University Library. Lisa received her master of education in educational psychology and master of library and information science degrees from the University of Illinois at Urbana-Champaign and earned her bachelor of arts degree in philosophy from the University of St. Thomas in Minnesota.

Matt Huculak, PhD, MLIS, is head of Advanced Research Services at the University of Victoria Libraries. His research interests include book and print history, pedagogy through material culture, and trauma-informed archiving practices. He is the founding managing editor and codesigner of the *Modernism/modernity* Print + platform, winner of the 2018 Innovation in Publishing Award from the Association of American Publishers.

Amanda Izenstark (she/her) is professor, reference and instructional design librarian, University of Rhode Island. She teaches information literacy sessions and credit-bearing courses and has taught for URI's Graduate School of Library and Information Studies. Her research interests include information literacy, educational technology, and academic librarianship.

Reina Kirkendall (she/her) is an Information Services librarian at Providence Public Library. She earned her MLIS from University of Rhode Island in 2022.

Maoria J. Kirker (she/her) is the Teaching and Learning Team lead for George Mason University Libraries. Her research focuses on teacher-librarian identity, the influence of social and cultural capital on academic library usage, and person-centered management in academic libraries. She is a co-founder of the Conference on Academic Library Management (CALM).

Cynthia Korpan (she/her) is an adjunct professor in Educational Psychology and Leadership Studies at the University of Victoria (UVic), director on the Board of the Society of Teaching and Learning in Higher Education (STLHE), and facilitator for the Institute of New Educational Developers (INED) (a program of the Professional and Organizational Development Network). Cynthia held the position of director of Teaching Excellence at UVic with, to date, over eighteen years of experience as an educational developer. Cynthia earned her PhD at UVic, and her ongoing research focuses on the teaching development of early career academics.

Josette M. Kubicki was most recently a reference and instruction librarian at Augusta University in Augusta, GA. She served as the liaison librarian to the Department of Teaching and Leading and the Department of Psychological Sciences. She provided library instruction to first-year and second-year general education courses, and to upper-division and graduate-level courses in her liaison areas. She grew up in Sydney, Australia, where she earned her MA in information and knowledge management from the University of Technology, Sydney. Later she earned her MA in library and information science from the University of South Florida. Her research interests include information literacy, online learning, and mental health and well-being in the library and information profession.

David X. Lemmons (they/he) is the instruction coordinator for George Mason University Libraries and a PhD student in education, also at George Mason. Their research interests include the Scholarship of Teaching and Learning (SoTL), the relationship between teaching faculty and library instructors, teaching self-efficacy for library instructors, and anti-racist information literacy. They earned their master in library science from the University of North Carolina at Chapel Hill and their MA in political science from Appalachian State.

Michael Lines is a humanities and social sciences librarian at the University of Victoria and has taken the university's teacher training course. He studied classics at Concordia University and completed an MA in medieval studies and an MLS at the University of Toronto. He has experience in a number of academic and professional libraries, writes for academic and popular publications, contributes to professional associations, is active in climate change initiatives, and delivers talks and bookbinding workshops in the community.

Rachel Makarowski is the Special Collections librarian at Miami University. In her position, she is responsible for many of the functions for special collections, including instruction, outreach, reference, cataloging, curation, and collection management. She graduated from Indiana University Bloomington with an MLS, specializing in rare book and manuscript librarianship, and worked in numerous positions at the Lilly Library. She previously worked at the Rare Book School during her time as an undergraduate at the University of Virginia. Her research interests focus on teaching with primary sources. She has actively volunteered in a number of professional organizations, including the Rare Book and Manuscripts Section (RBMS) of the Association for College and Research Libraries (ACRL), and the Teaching with Primary Sources (TPS) Collective.

Sam Mandani is the online instruction librarian at New York University. She holds an MS in information science from University of North Carolina at Chapel Hill. Prior to librarianship, she used to work in a non-traditional high school where she was introduced to educational technology and digital learning. Currently, she is pursuing an MA in learning technology and experience design program at NYU Steinhardt. Her current research interests include digital accessibility, development of equitable online learning, and technology stewardship.

Laura Marasco earned her MLIS from the University of Rhode Island in 2022.

Maureen Maryanski (she/her) is the head of Teaching and Research at the Lilly Library, the rare books and manuscripts library at Indiana University. Previously, she was the Lilly Library's education and outreach librarian overseeing the library's extensive instruction program. She has been actively involved in the Instruction and Outreach Committee of the Rare Books and Manuscripts Section (RBMS) of the Association for College and Research Libraries (ACRL) and the Teaching with Primary Sources (TPS) Collective.

Janna Mattson is the online learning coordinator and instruction librarian at George Mason University Libraries. She is also an adjunct professor for Mason's Honors College. She holds a master of education with an emphasis in curriculum and instruction from George Mason University, a master of library science from Queens College – CUNY, and a bachelor of art in music from Virginia Commonwealth University. She is the co-editor of the book *Framing Information Literacy: Teaching Grounded in Theory, Pedagogy, and Practice*. Her research interests include instructional design, online learning, and librarian-teacher identity.

Rebecca McCall (she/they) is a member of the 2022 Information Literacy Scholar cohort at Syracuse University, graduating in May 2024. She will join Lafayette College as a reference and instruction librarian after graduation.

Jeremiah R. Mercurio is head of Humanities & History at the Columbia University Libraries. He previously served as a senior reference librarian, instruction coordinator, and adjunct English professor at Fairfield University, as well as a research librarian and visiting professor of writing at Haverford College. He holds a PhD in English literature from the University of St Andrews, Scotland, an MS in library and information science from Simmons University, and an MA in English/creative writing from Temple University. His research and teaching interests include Victorian fin-de-siècle literature and illustration, book and textual studies, literary doodling, and critical information literacy.

Alexandra Mitchell is the Learning and Curricular Services coordinator at Texas A&M University Libraries. At this point, she has taught a little bit of everything from K-12 to credit-bearing college courses and more one-shots than she can count. After earning her MS in library science from the University of North Carolina at Chapel Hill in 2014 she fell into library instruction somewhat by accident, but she enjoys the opportunity to help students develop their information literacy skills.

Abby Moore is an associate professor and the Education, Honors, and Global Engagement librarian at UNC Charlotte. She graduated from Lehigh University and in 2003 began teaching English in the Bronx after being accepted into the New York City Teaching Fellows program. She earned her master's in education in 2006. She transitioned to academic librarianship in 2011 after earning her master's in library science from Queens College. Her research interests include global librarianship, digital media literacy instruction, and instructional design and training.

Emma Kate Morgan (she/hers), formerly the Access Services librarian at Augusta University's Reese Library, is now the data governance coordinator at Augusta University (GA). Originally from Mississippi, she earned a BA in English studies, minoring in Spanish, from Mississippi State University, and her MLIS from the University of Southern Mississippi. Her current area of focus is on data literacy and access across her institution.

Karen Munro is director, Engagement and Learning at the University of Victoria Libraries. Previously she served as associate dean of Research and Learning at Simon Fraser University Library and head of the University of Oregon Portland Library and Learning Commons. She's interested in instruction program management and student engagement in public research university libraries.

Anna K. Murphy-Lang (she, hers) is the teaching and outreach specialist for the Teaching and Learning Team at George Mason University. She has her master of library science from Queens College – City University of New York and a bachelor of fine arts from The College of Santa Fe, New Mexico. Anna is passionate about creating events, workshops, and teaching materials that promote student engagement and academic success.

Chrissy O'Grady (she/her) is a research and education librarian and Library Instruction Program coordinator at the State University of New York at New Paltz. She holds an MSLIS from the University of Illinois at Urbana-Champaign. Chrissy values learning outside of the classroom and has mentored undergraduate students through independent research projects and internships. She is an advocate for higher education in prisons and regularly works with the Prison Library Support Network.

Natalie Ornat Bitting is the Humanities librarian and an associate professor at the University of North Carolina at Charlotte. Natalie holds an MSLS from the University of North Carolina-Chapel Hill and a BA in history from the University of Wisconsin-Madison.

Fannie Ouyang (she/her) was previously the Visual & Interdisciplinary Arts librarian at Colby College (until August 2023). She is now the community and student engagement Librarian and access services team lead at Barnard College. She holds an MSLS and an MA in art history, both from the University of North Carolina at Chapel Hill.

Amber Owrey, formerly Wessies, is the instruction librarian at Union University in Jackson, TN. In this role, she is responsible for conducting one-shot instruction sessions and individual reference interviews as well as overseeing assessment of the library. Previously, Amber worked as an elementary school teacher in Texas. She earned a master of library science with a School Library Certification from Texas Woman's University and a master of educational psychology from Texas A&M University. Her research interests include library instruction, teaching and learning strategies, and universal design.

Russel Peterson (he/him) is the head of Instruction and Engagement at Emory University Libraries. He was part of the 2020–2021 class of ALA Emerging Leaders, in which he co-wrote a white paper on how the University Libraries Section of ACRL could better support the needs of early-career librarians. Russel received his master of science in information from the University of Michigan. He also holds a bachelor of arts in history with a concentration in Latin American studies from Carleton College.

Livia Piotto (she/her) is currently the head librarian at John Cabot University (Rome, Italy), where she started working in 2006 as reference and instruction librarian. She holds an MLS from the University of Rome "La Sapienza." In her role, she oversees all library operations and coordinates all instruction and faculty liaison activities.

Kirstie Preest (she/her) is librarian, tutor, and fellow at Murray Edwards College, Cambridge. She is a Fellow of CILIP with twenty-five years of experience in academic and health libraries within a variety of subject areas, including student support, delivering information literacy classes, reader services, user experience, and archives and records management. She has a PG Dip in information and library management from Liverpool John Moores University, an MA from the University of Cambridge, and is a Senior Fellow of the Higher Education Academy. She is passionate about developing the next generation of teaching librarians and co-created the Teaching and Learning for Librarians course at the University of Cambridge. She also presents on inclusive practices within teaching.

Lauren Quackenbush (she/her) is a librarian-in-residence at the Library of Congress. She was part of the 2021 Information Literacy Scholar cohort at Syracuse University.

Logan Rath (he/him) is a research and instruction librarian at SUNY Brockport and a lecturer in the Information Science program at the University at Albany. He has a PhD in education and master of library science from the University at Buffalo. He is a recipient of the Chancellor's Award for Excellence in Librarianship.

Amanda Roth (she/her) is an instruction librarian with specific expertise as an instructional technologist. She ties computer or web-based technology to learning to use it effectively according to instructional best practices. She has co-taught classes for the American Library Association on designing instruction for virtual environments and presented at several conferences. Publications include the co-authored book *Demystifying Online Instruction in Libraries: People, Process and Tools* and the open-access article "Equitable but not Diverse: Universal Design for Learning is Not Enough." Amanda received her MLIS from San Jose State University in 2013 and has since worked in academic libraries providing instruction services to undergraduate students. She is the reference coordinator and subject specialist for Writing Programs and Psychology for the University of California San Diego Library.

Olivia Russo (she/her) is the outreach librarian at Le Moyne College. She is a member of the 2022 Information Literacy Scholar cohort at Syracuse University, graduating in May 2024.

Laura Saunders is a professor at Simmons University School of Library and Information Science who focuses on information literacy including mis- and disinformation, user services, and academic libraries. She also teaches a course on intellectual freedom and censorship. Her most recent books include *Reference and Information Services: An Introduction, 7th edition*, co-edited with Melissa Wong, and the open access textbook

Instruction in Libraries and Information Settings: An Introduction, co-authored with Melissa Wong. She co-founded LIS Pedagogy Chat, an online community of practice focused on instruction in library and information science, with Melissa Wong in 2020. Laura has a PhD and a master of library and information science, both from Simmons College (now Simmons University), and is the 2019 recipient of Simmons University's Provost Award for Excellence in Graduate Teaching.

Claire Sewell (she/her) is head of the Research Information Service at the House of Commons Library in the UK. In this role, she oversees a team of research support librarians who work to ensure that information plays a central role in the Parliamentary community. Prior to this, she worked in academic libraries for over twenty years including roles supporting students, researchers, academics, and librarians from a range of backgrounds. She holds an MSc in library and information studies from the University of Aberystwyth (Wales), a PGCert in teaching and learning in higher education from the University of Cambridge, and chartered librarian status with CILIP. She is a past president of SLA Europe, part of the editorial board of the international journal *The New Review of Academic Librarianship*, and the author of *The No-Nonsense Guide to Research Support and Scholarly Communication* from Facet Publishing.

Catherine Tingelstad is the head of Instruction & Curriculum Engagement and an associate professor at J. Murrey Atkins Library at the University of North Carolina at Charlotte. She earned her master of library science from North Carolina Central University, a master of healthcare administration from Virginia Commonwealth University, and a BA in English from Duke University. Her research interests include critical reading, media literacy, and curriculum development and integration.

Angel Truesdale (she/her) is the social sciences and business librarian at the University of North Carolina at Charlotte (UNC Charlotte) and a graduate of San Jose State University School of Information with a master of library and information science degree and the University of North Carolina at Charlotte with a bachelor's in political science and history. Previously, she worked at a public library and developed programming focused on digital literacy, nonprofit/small business reference, and the Black experience as told through film. As the business librarian, Angel is engaged in student-centered research, instruction, and programming that advocates for business information literacy and social awareness. She also enjoys learning about cinematic storytelling as a narrative tool, the documentary practice, and undervalued voices in cinema. Her other interests include diversity, equity, inclusion, and accessibility (DEIA), entrepreneurship in marginalized communities, facilitation, critical librarianship, international law, transformative justice, and housing equity.

Dominique Turnbow (she/her) is an instruction librarian with expertise in instructional design and design thinking approaches with nearly two decades of experience delivering online information literacy instruction to create diverse and inclusive learning opportunities. Published works about instructional design practices in academic library environments include the co-authored book *Demystifying Online Instruction in Libraries: People, Process and Tools* and co-authored open-access article "Equitable but not Diverse: Universal Design for Learning is Not Enough." She has co-taught classes for the American Library Association about designing instruction for virtual environments and has presented information literacy instruction topics at a number of conferences. Dominique received her MLIS from UCLA in 2002 and her master's in educational technologies from San Diego State University in 2013. She is the subject specialist for Education Studies, Human Developmental Sciences, and the Writing Programs at the University of California, San Diego.

Alayna L. Vander Veer (she/her) is a reference and instruction librarian at SUNY Oneonta in Oneonta, NY. She was part of the 2020 Information Literacy Scholar cohort at Syracuse University.

Alicia G. Vaandering (she/her) is the student success librarian at the University of Rhode Island where she supports the learning and research of students, with an emphasis on undergraduate first-year, international, first-generation, and transfer students. Her research interests include LGBTQIA+ representation in children's literature, information literacy, and ungrading.

B. Austin Waters (she/they) is the Student Services librarian at the University at Buffalo School of Law Library in Buffalo, NY. Austin was part of the 2019 Information Literacy Scholar cohort at Syracuse University.

Thomas C. Weeks (he/him) is a reference and instruction librarian at Augusta University, GA. He has a BA in English, an MLIS, and an MS in instructional design and technology. He is currently writing a dissertation for an EdD in cultural curriculum studies. Most recently, he co-edited a book about pop culture and libraries. His research interests include critical information literacy and cultural studies of education.

Nicole Westerdahl (she/any) is a research, instruction, and outreach librarian at the State University of New York at Oswego, where she serves as the open educational resources lead and as liaison librarian to the School of Business, the Communication Studies department, and the Triandiflou Institute for Equity, Diversity, Inclusion, and Transformative Practice. Nicole is a peer reviewer for several open access journals and loves all things sheep.

Jamia Williams (she/her) is the Consumer Health Program specialist with the Network of the National Library of Medicine (NNLM) Training Office. She earned her bachelor of science in history from the State University of New York (SUNY) at Brockport and earned her master of library science from North Carolina Central University. Williams is the co-creator and co-host of the podcast *LibVoices,* which amplifies the voices of Black, Indigenous, and People of Color who work in archives and libraries. Jamia founded *The Diversity Fellow's blog* to document her journey as a Black librarian. Her research interests are diversity, inclusion, equity, social justice, and health equity in and outside librarianship.

Kaci Wilson (she/her) is the reference and resource librarian at Nebraska Methodist College and previously served as STEM librarian at Louisiana State University Shreveport. She earned an MLIS with a specialization in academic librarianship at Louisiana State University and a BS in psychology at the University of Alabama. As a new professional with interests in pedagogy and student success, she enjoys finding creative ways to engage patrons and incorporating novel strategies and tools into her teaching. Her primary research interests focus on graphic novels, gamification, data literacy, and the relationship between psychological factors and information literacy.

Eunice S. P. Wong is the manager of Learning Support at the Hong Kong University of Science and Technology Library. She plans and administers the library's information literacy teaching, learning, and assessment. She has strong interest in promoting user engagement with library resources and services through outreach, social media, and general education activities. She set up the HKUST Library Facebook page and Instagram account and has been co-chair of the Library User Engagement Committee since 2021. She received her bachelor of optometry from UNSW Australia, master of information management-librarianship from UNSW Australia, and master of science in computing from City University of Hong Kong.

Melissa A. Wong is an adjunct instructor in the School of Information Sciences at the University of Illinois at Urbana-Champaign where she teaches courses in instruction, e-learning, higher education, and reference. She is the author of *Instructional Design for LIS Professionals* (Libraries Unlimited, 2019), a book on teaching LIS graduate students; co-editor with Laura Saunders of *Reference and Information Services, 7th edition* (Libraries Unlimited, 2024), a widely used textbook on reference; and co-author, also with Saunders, of the open access textbook *Instruction in Libraries and Information Centers: An Introduction* (Windsor and Downs, 2020). She co-founded LIS Pedagogy Chat, an online community of practice focused on instruction in library and information science, with Laura Saunders in 2020. Her work has been recognized with a Campus Award for Excellence in Online and Distance Teaching and the Reference and User Services Association's Isadore Gilbert Mudge Award.